D1476944

Introducing Management in a Global Context

凡治众如治寡
分数是也

Management of many is the same as management of few.
It is a matter of organization.

孫子 Sūn Zǐ; *The Art of War*
(c. 6th century BC)
Chinese General and Military Strategist.

THE GLOBAL MANAGEMENT SERIES

Introducing Management in a Global Context

Robert MacIntosh and Kevin O'Gorman

 Goodfellow Publishers Ltd

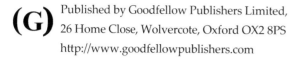 Published by Goodfellow Publishers Limited,
26 Home Close, Wolvercote, Oxford OX2 8PS
http://www.goodfellowpublishers.com

British Library Cataloguing in Publication Data: a catalogue record for this
title is available from the British Library.
Library of Congress Catalog Card Number: on file.

ISBN: 978-1-910158-48-7

 Design and typesetting by P.K. McBride, www.macbride.org.uk

Cover design by Cylinder

Printed by Baker & Taylor, www.baker-taylor.com

Contents

Dedications

To my beautiful wife Anne and our children Euan, Eilidh and Eva. There is nothing better in life than to spend time with you. Thank you.

RMacI

To my mother for the constant and continued support, and Diana and Keith for the never ending dinners, and Claire and her team for patience and printing; I could not have done it without you.

KDO

Acknowledgments

The genesis of this project can be traced to the decision to have the professoriate of the School of Management and Languages at Heriot-Watt University teach the first year undergraduate management course. The authoring teams responsible for each chapter have helped produce a book which offers a diverse set of perspectives on the main challenges facing those responsible for running global organizations. We are grateful to all those who helped shape the text and, alongside our authoring teams, there are a few individuals who deserve special mention. To our colleagues at Goodfellow Publishers, we remain indebted. Sally, Tim and Mac each showed a willingness to help bring a complex project to market in an unrealistically short time scale. Their calm and stoic acceptance of the production schedule were much appreciated and the professionalism of their work was exceptional. Thomas Farrington played a key role in checking and polishing the manuscript and we are also indebted to him for the speed and accuracy of his work.

RMacI & KDO

Biographies

Kyle Andrews is a Ph.D. student in Business and Management at Heriot-Watt University with research interests primarily in the commercialization process relating to university intellectual property. His work focuses on technology transfer offices and the ability of those working in such units to establish credibility when communicating between academics and industrial or commercial partners. Kyle has received both an MSc in International Business and Entrepreneurship (2012) and MSc in Media Management (2011) from the University of Glasgow. Kyle's BA in Mass Communication from the University of Tampa (2007) helped him establish a radio broadcasting career in both Tampa, Florida and Los Angeles, California where he worked as a producer, sound engineer and on air-personality.

Jiju Antony is recognised worldwide as a leader in Lean Six Sigma methodology for achieving and sustaining process excellence. He is a Professor of Quality Management in the School of Management and Languages at Heriot-Watt University, Edinburgh, Scotland. He is a Fellow of the Royal Statistical Society (UK), Fellow of the Institute for Operations Management (UK), Fellow of the Chartered Quality Institute (CQI) and a Fellow of the Institute of the Six Sigma Professionals. He has recently been elected to the International Academy of Quality and is the first one to be elected from Scotland and the fourth from the UK. He is a Certified Master Black Belt and has demonstrated savings of over £10 million pounds to the bottom-line of several organisations around Europe. He is currently serving as the Editor of the *International Journal of Lean Six Sigma* launched in 2010 by Emerald Publishers.

Praveen Balakrishnan Nair is an Assistant Professor in the School of Management and Languages at Heriot-Watt University, Malaysia Campus. He holds three post graduate qualifications in different functional areas of management and has earned his PhD in the area of environmental marketing. Prior to joining Heriot-Watt, he was attached to Curtin University of Technology and Swinburne University of Technology. His research interests lies in the area of corporate social responsibility, specifically environmental responsibility, and has written and presented papers in the area. Apart from these core research areas, Praveen is interested in 'greening' the business school curriculum, which he believes is an essential step towards moulding socially and environmentally responsible managers.

Dudley Peter Barrett (BSc. Economics and Accounting; Certified Financial Manager; ACCA; Senior Professional in Human Resources; Certified Supply Chain Professional; Operational Risk Manager) is a management consultant and school administrator based in Jamaica. His work focuses on the review and design of financial and operational management systems; the diagnosis and remedy of organizational efficiency and effectiveness issues; and the development, implementation and analysis of strategic change initiatives. He has over twenty years of experience in a wide variety of organisations in the Caribbean and a wide variety of management functions including strategic management, financial management, operations management, auditing, human resources management, information technology and marketing. He is been an Approved Tutor in the Heriot-Watt University programmes in Jamaica for over eight years, specialising in Strategic Planning, Marketing and Operations Management.

Umit Bititci is Professor of Business Performance at Heriot-Watt University, School of Management and Languages, Edinburgh, UK. Until December 2013 he was the Director of Strathclyde Institute for Operations Management and the Professor of Technology and Enterprise Management at the University of Strathclyde. In the past he served as: the Chairman of IFIP's Working Group on Advanced Production Management Systems and the Vice Chairman of the Institute of Operations Management. Currently he is a member of the Scottish Manufacturing Advisory Board. He has a blend of industrial and academic experience that spans across 35 years, and dedicated his career to understanding what makes high-performing companies different. He has worked with an international portfolio of companies and public sector organisations and has led several international research and development projects. He has published over 200 papers and regularly appears at international conferences and workshops as guest speaker.

Elaine Collinson is an Associate Professor in the Department of Management in the School of Management and Languages at Heriot-Watt University. With over 25 years of experience in the Higher Education sector, she has held a series of roles, primarily in an academic and research capacity but also in developing transnational education and industry links across the globe. Developing innovative approaches to high quality learning has always been a key focus of her activities for both the executive education participant as well as the full time student. Her extensive experience in international assurance of learning practices working with EFMD, AACSB and international partners across the globe, ensures that her teaching in the area of Marketing is global in outlook and practical in application. Core areas of both teaching and research interests include Strategic Marketing Management, Marketing for Small Businesses, Entrepreneurial Marketing, Inter-cultural Business Relationships and Customer Relationship Marketing.

Mike Danson is Professor of Enterprise Policy, Heriot-Watt University, Director of Doctoral Programmes in SML and Treasurer of the Academy of Social Sciences, and has published more than 200 papers, and edited academic journals and 13 books with over 15 different disciplines. He has a long experience of teaching economics, research methods and business studies at all levels within higher education. Mike has supervised many PhD students to successful completion. He has a wide range of academic and policy interests, including regional economic development, poverty, older people and early onset dementia, renewable energies, microbreweries and islands. He has advised national and local governments, development agencies, trades unions, the OECD, WHO and community groups. He is a frequent commentator on radio, TV, newspapers and on social media. You can follow him on twitter on @MikeDanson1.

Thomas Farrington is a Post-Doctoral Research Associate in Management and Organisation at Heriot-Watt University. His research examines contemporary issues in business and management, with particular emphasis on marketing and cultural authenticity; management practice and business ethics; consumer identity and tourism; colonial histories and intercultural studies. Thomas has taught at South East European University in Tetovo and at the University of Edinburgh, from which he received his doctorate, and where he was Co-Director of the Scottish Universities' International Summer School. His work has most recently appeared in the *Journal of American Studies*, *Research in Hospitality Management*, and the *Journal of Marketing Management*.

Laura Galloway is Professor of Business and Enterprise at Heriot-Watt University and Dean of the University for Arts, Humanities and Social Science. Based in the School of Management and Languages, her teaching focuses on leadership and entrepreneurship and her research interests are in these broad themes too. In particular, Professor Galloway's research involves studying theory and practice relating to entrepreneurship amongst different groups, leadership, and the effects of entrepreneurship education on skills and business outcomes. Examples of her recent work include exploring the experiences of being a leader or an entrepreneur. Professor Galloway is also involved in an ongoing international comparative study on small business engagement with ICT.

Steven Glasgow is a PhD student in the School of Management and Languages at Heriot-Watt University. His research primarily focuses on how gender inequalities within the workplace are produced, maintained and disrupted. He has published in journals such as *Feminism & Psychology* and will guest edit a special issue for the journal *Interdisciplinary Perspectives on Equality and Diversity* (IPED). Steven received his MA (Hons) in Business Management from Heriot-Watt University in 2014. His teaching commitments include Research Methods and Employee Relations.

Keith Gori is a doctoral researcher in the School of Management and Languages at Heriot-Watt University. His doctoral research engages with Consumer Culture Theory, identity and consumer narratives in the context of the British Home Front during World War Two. More widely his research interests lie in consumer and marketing history, the development of notions of responsible business and CSR, and experiential marketing. He has presented both historical and contemporary research outputs at international marketing conferences and has published work in the Journal of Marketing Management. He teaches on global management and marketing courses in the Department of Business Management.

Colin Gregor is a PhD student at Heriot-Watt University, Edinburgh. His PhD thesis involves a longitudinal study of a high performance sports team to investigate the process of conflict and its effects on the team. Further research will explore the impact of conflict on performance, the relationship between conflict and cohesion, and how conflict is rationalised within a team dynamic. Colin is former captain of Scotland's 7 a-side rugby team and the third highest points scorer of all time. He teaches on the Management in a Global Context course.

Ros Haniffa is currently Professor of Accounting and Editor of *Journal of Islamic Accounting and Business Research* (JIABR). She received her BSc Finance from Northern Illinois University, MSc Accounting & Finance from University of Stirling and PhD in Accounting and Finance from University of Exeter. She has taught in various countries in Asia, Middle-East and Europe especially at postgraduate levels. Professor Haniffa has published widely in the areas of accounting, auditing, corporate governance, corporate social responsibility and Islamic accounting and finance and her papers are highly cited. She was included in the Muslim Women Power List by the UK Human Rights Commission.

Gillian Hogg is Pro-Vice Chancellor of Heriot-Watt University and Professor of Marketing in the School of Management and Languages. Her research interests are consumer behaviour, in particular consumers' use of the internet as an information source and use of that information in non-internet situations. With colleagues in Loughborough and Manchester Universities she was part of the ESRC *Cultures of Consumption* programme looking at professional services and the internet and she is currently extending this research into the area of language.

Gordon Jack is a Ph.D. student in the department of Business and Management at Heriot-Watt University, with his current research interests focussing on management in highly autonomous environments. Gordon's work analyses whether or not people can in fact be managed in setting of quasi low-authority, including the judicial, medical and academic systems. Gordon received an MSc in Strategic Project Management from Heriot-Watt University in 2013 having gained a BSc (Hons) in Building Surveying from the same institution. His teaching commitments have included undergraduate Business Management and Business Entrepreneurship at 1st and 3rd year level respectively, with publications including *Who'd be a Dean* from the Association of Business Schools.

Julian D C Jones is Vice-Principal at Heriot-Watt University, Edinburgh, UK. He studied at the University of Wales, Aberystwyth before becoming a lecturer at the University of Kent at Canterbury. Since 1988, he has been at Heriot-Watt University, Edinburgh, establishing a research group in optical fibre sensors, optical instrumentation and laser-material interactions. In 2007, he became Deputy Principal for Strategy and Resources, in 2010 Vice-Principal, and additionally in 2013, Deputy Vice-Chancellor. He has over 500 publications. He is a Fellow of the Institute of Physics in the UK and is its Treasurer. He is also a fellow of the Royal Society of Edinburgh and the Optical Society of America. He received the UK honour of an OBE in 2002 for services to science and engineering.

Ihssan Jwijati is a Syrian academic who has gained an engineering degree from Nigeria, an Engineering Masters from the Imperial College in London and an MBA from Kuwait. He worked as a teacher during his degree years, and then assumed different management roles in retail and manufacturing. Currently he is preparing for his academia appointment after finishing his PhD in Heriot-Watt University. He is interested in understanding factors leading to successful performance management systems, and the impact of contextual factors such as national and organizational culture, leadership, and other factors such as organization structure, and governance.

Christopher Kerry is a PhD student in the School of Management and Languages at Heriot-Watt University. His thesis is centred on the theory of Open Innovation in the context of UK CATAPULT centres. It also addresses a variety of other concepts, most notably those of innovation systems and innovation policy, using a comparative case-study approach. He has taught on a variety of courses, including International Business, Enterprise and the Business Environment, Critical Approaches to Management and Operations Management. He has also delivered lectures on 'Sources of Innovation' and 'Innovation Networks' for the Innovation Management module. Christopher holds an MA (Hons) in Management having been awarded the W L Sleigh Prize and the Oxford University Press Crane and Matten Business Ethics Prize. He also holds an MRes in Research Methods for Business and Management.

Kevin Krebs is a PhD student within the School of Management and Languages at Heriot-Watt University, Edinburgh. His research in Business Strategy focuses on the utilisation of today's information technology by the informed customer, and the way it alters the purchase experience and customer-salesperson relationship in the high prestige automotive sector. Prior to this Kevin started his university career in one of Germany's elite Business schools, progressing to complete his Bachelor of Honours degree in Management, performing as one of the top 1% of his class at University of Strathclyde, testament to which is his nomination by the Google Undergraduate Awards in 2014. Kevin's academic interests have been rooted in his interest in corporate strategy and management consulting.

Dr. Min-Hsiu Liao is a lecturer at School of Management and Languages, Heriot-Watt University. Her research interests lie in discourse-based translation analysis and text producer-receiver interaction in communication. Her research addresses the issues of the spread of culture, and specifically on how the discourse from one culture influences that of another. She has studied the genre of popular science and multimodal communication in museum exhibitions. She has widely published in journals such as *Tourism Management*, *East Asian Journal of Popular Culture*, *The Translator*, and *The Journal of Specialised Translation*. She is currently involved in an interdisciplinary collaborative project on the internal and international narratives of dark heritage.

Robert MacIntosh is Professor of Strategy and Head of the School of Management and Languages at Heriot-Watt University. He trained as an engineer and has worked at the Universities of Glasgow and Strathclyde.

His research on the ways in which top teams develop strategy and on organizational change has been published in a wide range of outlets. He has a long-standing interest in research methods for business and management studies and has published on the relevance of management research using methods that include ethnography and action research. His blog doctoralstudy.blogspot.co.uk and his spin-out company stridesite.com both offer innovative ways of reaching new audiences. He has consulted extensively with public and private sector organizations and sits on the board of the charity Turning Point Scotland. His status as a dedicated fan of Aberdeen Football Club and the Scottish national team are part of an ethnographic study on persistent optimism.

Gavin Maclean is a PhD Student in the School of Management and Languages at Heriot-Watt University. His PhD thesis examines the work of professional musicians in terms of labour process theory and Pierre Bourdieu's theory of practice. More widely he is interested in sociological study of work and employment and 'symbolic' forms of work, particularly cultural production, public sector work and multilingualism in the workplace. He teaches on Human Resource and Critical Approaches to Management courses.

Abigail Marks is a Professor of Work and Employment Studies and Director of the Centre for Research on Work and Wellbeing at Heriot-Watt University. She has worked at Heriot-Watt since 2002. Previously she was employed at Edinburgh and Strathclyde Universities. Abigail's areas of research focus on Wellbeing, Social Class, the ICT sector, Identity at Work, Teamwork and Employability. She has published in many of the leading journals in her field including, *Work, Employment and Society, Sociology, Human Relations* and the *British Journal of Industrial Relations*. Abigail has had a number of editorial responsibilities and is currently on the editorial boards of *Work, Employment and Society*, the *Journal of Management Studies, New Technology, Work and Employment* and *Team Performance Management*.

Geraldine McKay is a Chartered Marketer with a special interest in the impact of branding across stakeholder groups. Following a career in marketing (financial services, publishing, industrial branding and small business enterprise) she became a University lecturer and has developed and led a number of post graduate, undergraduate and professional programmes. She moved to New Zealand where she managed an International project between a consortium of New Zealand Universities and the Ministry of Higher Education in Oman. On returning to the UK she became Academic Head for the globally delivered Heriot-Watt Management Programmes.

She is an Associate Professor in Marketing and is currently undertaking a PhD in Education investigating transnational education and the student experience.

Josh McLeod is a PhD student in the School of Management and Languages at Heriot-Watt University, where he teaches in Business Law and Global Management. His research focuses on the corporate governance practices of professional football clubs in Scotland. Further to this, his research interests include organisational change in the football sector, the feasibility of the supporter ownership model and football finance in a broader context.

Marlene Muller's career is firmly entrenched in the fields of education and empowerment. Having worked in highly disadvantaged South African communities, her commitment to service delivery and improved community leadership inspired her to divert to the areas of Local Governance and Leadership. She was the Academic Director of the Kwa-Zulu Natal Institute for Local Government and Traditional Leadership, successfully operationalising public-private partnerships by training traditional leaders and elected public officials. Marlene has furthermore assisted local government practitioners in matters of local governance, organizational development, effective leadership and policy making. Academically, Marlene received awards in Research and Teaching, and published in the fields of sustainable service delivery, poverty alleviation, effective leadership and municipal governance. Marlene is currently the Under-graduate Programme Director on the Dubai Campus, lecturing in the fields of Business Management and Human Resource Management. Her teaching focuses on management theories, entrepreneurial start-ups, diversity management in the workplace, as well as organisational culture.

Kevin O'Gorman is Professor of Management and Business History and Head of Business Management in the School of Languages and Management in Heriot-Watt University, Edinburgh. He trained in Glasgow, Salamanca and Rome as a philosopher, theologian and historian. His research interests have a dual focus: Origins, history and cultural practices of hospitality, and philosophical, ethical and cultural underpinnings of contemporary management practices. Using a wide range of methodological approaches he has published over 100 journal articles, books, chapters, and conference papers in business and management.

Jaydeep Pancholi is a PhD student within the School of Management and Languages at Heriot-Watt University, Edinburgh. His PhD thesis is investigating business strategy within the context of conflict zones, reviewing stakeholder influences on strategic decision and conflict resolution. Prior to this Jaydeep had gained a BA (Hons) in International Business and Marketing at the University of Strathclyde, Glasgow, including an exchange at Nanyang Technological University, Singapore, studying courses in management and culture. This was followed with working at a leading automotive manufacture in corporate fleet. Jaydeep's academic interests have been inspired by his extensive voluntary work in personal development and corporate sustainability, and being a trainer for a global NGO and an active member in the organisation of business ethics conferences.

Jane Queenan is an Associate Professor and Deputy Head of the Department of Business Management in the School of Management and Languages at Heriot-Watt University. She lectures in Entrepreneurship and Business Ethics. Jane has many years of experience in the field of business development and founded and managed two successful consultancy practices prior to entering academia.

Rebecca Stirzaker is a PhD student in the School of Management and Languages at Heriot-Watt University. Her research contributes to the field of entrepreneurship by advancing our understanding of entrepreneurial intentions in the third age. During her time at Heriot-Watt she has taught a variety of courses, including: Enterprise and the Business Environment, Enterprise Concepts and Issues, Human Resource Management and Research Philosophy and Practice. Rebecca received an MSc in International Business Management with Distinction from Heriot-Watt University in 2013 and holds an MA (Hons) in Management and Hispanic Studies from the University of Aberdeen. She has previous industry experience in both the banking and publishing sectors.

Helen Verhoeven holds an MBA, a Master in Managing Human Resources and a PhD (specialising in Internet recruitment). She is currently a lecturer in Management at Heriot-Watt University (Dubai Campus). She has been lecturing on courses such as introduction to management, competitive strategy, business ethics, organisational behaviour, professional HRM skills, HRM in practice and employee resourcing for over 10 years. Helen frequently presents papers at international conferences, is involved in the supervision of undergraduate and postgraduate dissertation projects and has published articles in international journals. Her research areas encompass Emiratisation, electronic HRM, expatriatism, Islamic leadership & Islamic entrepreneurship. Prior to obtaining her PhD in the UK, Helen was based in The Netherlands where she held positions in HRM departments in both the profit and not-for-profit sector.

Preface

Most of you reading this book will interact with global organizations on a regular basis. As we step off another plane, train, boat or bus in a new land it is highly likely that we will discover that some of the world's best known brands have already arrived. Hidden from view as we buy our coffee, consume the news or connect our technology, the inner workings of global organizations have been busy ensuring continuity of service, consumption and commerce. In monetary terms, many global organizations are larger than all but a few nation state economies. When disaster strikes, it is often the inter-governmental and charitable global organizations that are first on the scene. This book addresses the challenges of managing a global organization from a variety of perspectives, but it is worth noting that a little temporal perspective can go a long way.

In our estimation, global management should not be studied in a temporal vacuum; history, the historical context and the evolution of business, organisations and management thought are needed to develop our contemporary understanding whilst dispelling some of the snappy sounding myths found in the very airport-style self-help books which form the backdrop to our international travels.

The provision of management is nearly as old as recorded human history. The span of written history is roughly 5,000 years, with Sumerian cuneiform being the oldest form of writing discovered so far. Since this writing tends to be used as the beginning of history, the period before writing might be referred to as prehistory. The oldest collection of texts that refer to management practice would be from a literary genre known as 'Ancient Near East Texts'. These texts belong to a large family of Eastern Mediterranean traditions from Mesopotamia, Asia Minor, Syria-Palestine, and Egypt; certain works date back to around 3500 BC. This then is a global literature as old as the history of writing itself.

Construction management was at work during the building of Great Pyramid of Giza (2560 B.C.) and services management to the hostels and inns in Mesopotamia (at least 2000 BC). In Egypt some characteristics of tourism, travel for curiosity or pleasure, can be found from about 1500 BC. By 1500 BC the Sphinx and the three great pyramids were over a thousand years old, and on the wall of one of the chapels connected to the pyramids there is 3500-year-old graffiti written by students on an educational trip.

There is also a large diorite stela in the Louvre Museum containing inscriptions commonly known as the Code of Hammurabi (1800 BC). Although the original purpose of the stela is somewhat enigmatic, within the inscription there are laws governing commercial hospitality management from at least 1800 BC. The punishment for watering-down beer was death by drowning. There was also a requirement that tavern keepers, on pain of death, report all customers who were felons.

Time itself is an illusive concept. Cleopatra, Pharaoh of Egypt, lived closer to the time of mass manufacture and the Model T Ford than to the building of the Great Pyramid of Giza. Take a few moments to consider other forms of management, and their place in history:

Education Management: The University of Salamanca, Spain, predates the Aztec Civilization. The University of Salamanca was officially established by Papal Bull in 1218, over 100 year before Tenochtitlán was built in 1325, marking the accepted beginning of the Aztec civilization.

Technology Management: Warner Bros. was founded while The Ottoman Empire still existed. The first Warner Bros. theatre opened in 1903 and in 1918 the Warner Bros. studio on Sunset Boulevard in Hollywood was opened, while The Ottoman Empire was dissolved in 1923 after over 700 years of existence.

Innovation Management: The gap between harnessing the power of flight and landing on the moon was just 66 years. The Wright Brothers managed to stay in the air for just 59 seconds in 1903 and within decades, Apollo 11 landed on the moon before journeying safely home again.

France was still using the guillotine when Star Wars was released. Star Wars first aired in cinemas in May 1977, four months before the last guillotine execution in France in September 1977.

Any such juxtaposition is of course, intended to make a point. Our point is to make you stop and think about the many wondrous developments of our modern, deeply organizational and seemingly interconnected work and to place them in their proper chronological place. Global management is a phenomenon that, if better understood, will serve to strengthen our understanding of the development of civilization as a whole; indeed, learning from the past practice will also continue to help to inform the future.

Robert MacIntosh & Kevin O'Gorman

1 Introducing Management: Art or science?

Kevin O'Gorman, Thomas Farrington and Colin Gregor

Question, question and question once again. Take nothing at face value, and come to your own evidenced, considered, and reflected upon conclusions. Push at boundaries when you encounter them, and don't worry about leaving your comfort zones. Reflect upon the story of the traveller, who when walking past some elephants in a park suddenly stopped. He had noticed that these huge and beautiful animals were being held by only a small rope tied to their front leg. No chains, no cages, only a rope no thicker than a finger. It was obvious that the elephants could, at any time, break away and escape, but for some reason, they did not. The traveller asked why they simply stood there and made no attempt to get away. "Well," their keeper said, "when they are very young and much smaller we use the same size rope to tie them and, at that age, it's enough to hold them. As they grow up, they are conditioned to believe they cannot break away. They believe the rope can still hold them, so they never try to break free." Amazing. These animals could at any time break free from their bonds but because they believed they couldn't, they were stuck right where they were. Like the elephants, many of us go through life hanging onto a belief that we cannot do something, simply because we failed at it once before.

In the Social Sciences (management is probably a Social Science but more about that later) we are intrinsically more concerned with the intangible, soft and fuzzy aspects of life. There is a paradox in Social Sciences. Given the apparent fluidity between intangible concepts, you might expect interdisciplinary work to flourish. However, that is not the case. The reality is that in order to protect identity, many disciplines enter into a form of rhetorical and theoretical protectionism. Fields of study erect imaginary boundaries around their areas of enquiry, attempting to quarantine other research areas in case they reveal that, god forbid, they are all actually talking about the same thing!

and honestly, and merchants were expected to contribute to charitable causes such as schools and hospitals. The growth of trade required improvements in accounting and further developments in management.

Provision for travellers

The Roman Empire was the consummate management system and Hadrian was Emperor at its height (117 AD). Rome then dominated Western Eurasia and northern Africa, and encompassed the majority of the region's population; at this time the Roman Empire controlled approximately 6 million km² of land. The Roman citizen could travel throughout the Empire and be protected by one legal system, speak one administrative language and require only one currency. An extensive industry existed for travellers, merchants, and sailors who came to trade and sell, or those who were stopping overnight along the way to other destinations; these businesses are summarised in Table 1.2.

Latin name	Description and facilities	Modern equivalent
Hospitium	Larger establishments that offered rooms for rent, and often food and drink to overnight guests; often specifically built for business.	Hotel
Stabula	Buildings with open courtyard surrounded by a kitchen, a latrine, and bedrooms with stables at the rear. Often found just outside the city, close to the city gates; offered food, drink and accommodation.	Coaching inn
Taberna	Sold a variety of simple foods and drink. They usually contained a simple L-shaped marble counter, about six to eight feet long	Bar
Popina caupona	Served food and drink, offered sit down meals; often used to describe public eating-houses and sometimes included a few rooms	Restaurant

Table 1.2: Commercial hospitality establishments in Classical Rome

There were two basic types of establishment, one that dealt with accommodation, and one with food and drink. *Stabulae* were *hospitiae* with facilities to shelter animals; often found just outside the city, close to the city gates, and at 30km intervals along major roads. The Roman equivalent of coaching inns, stabulae had an open courtyard surrounded by a kitchen, a latrine, and bedrooms with stables at the rear for horses. Businesses within city gates were smaller than those in the countryside, due to spatial constraints. As O'Gorman (2010) observes, for any analysis of Roman commercial tourism and hospitality, the site of Pompeii in Italy near modern day Naples offers a unique perspective. This is based on the circumstances surrounding the almost instantaneous destruction of the city in history by the eruption of Mount Vesuvius in 79 AD, and its literal fossilisation as an archaeological site; at the time of its destruction the city of Pompeii had a population of approximately 10,000 people and 200 commercial hospitality establishments. Pompeii is of importance to the examination of tourism in the Roman Empire as it was a major destination resort, centre of commerce and entertainment in the Roman world, and managed in a highly organised fashion.

■ Organisational principles

St. Benedict of Nursia's Rule (c. 530 A.D.) was written in the period immediately following the decline of Rome and the fall of a universal controlling power in Europe. It is considered by O'Gorman (2010) as to be one of the foundational documents of contemporary management practice. St. Benedict's Rule shows that it is possible to construct and order a taxonomy of organisational principles that would be recognisable to the modern manager, as relevant today as they were 1500 years ago; these are presented in Table 1.3.

Business principles
- Customers are central to the purpose of the business
- When providing service, management and staff are separate from the society to which they are providing service
- The level of service offered is determined by the type of the business
- Businesses have a responsibility for the health, safety and security of the guests
- Management and staff should display personal integrity and be practically competent
- The business, its management and staff must maintain a professional relationship at all times

Staffing principles
- The person providing the service is seen by the customer as representing the business as a whole
- Personal characteristics of staff must be genuinely disposed to providing service
- There is a need for specialised staff as well as multi-skilled staff
- Roles should be clearly defined to show which staff interact with customers and how they do so
- The level of staffing needs to match the business demand
- Staff should maintain their dignity in providing service: service not servility
- Staff must not cause the guests unnecessary disturbance

Management principles
- Managers must be professional and competent
- Managers have a responsibility to balance the provision of service with the requirements of the business
- As well as having responsibility to manage the business, managers also have to be seen by the customers as the host and business personified
- Both expected demand and unexpected demand need to be prepared for
- Staff and customer areas should be separate and access controlled
- Staff must be fully resourced and supported by the management team
- Management is to blame if staff do not have the skills or equipment to carry out their duties
- Teamwork is important for efficient service

Table 1.3: Organisational principles derived from St Benedict's Rule

These organisational principles from the sixth century were to under-pin management practice in Europe for at least the next 900 years, until the Protestant reformation. They also influenced the approaches to caring for the sick (hospitals), the poor (hospices and charities) and the provision of education (the establishment of the first universities).

■ Banking and security

Under their founder, Hugues de Payens (*c.* 1070-1136) a French knight from the Champagne region, the Knights Templar revolutionised financial management, providing the equivalent of a European-wide banking system, and supplying security and protection to pilgrims travelling across Europe and the Near East. Like any good banker, the Templars were considered to be disciplined, honest and independent, and were trusted in medieval society (O'Gorman and Beverage, 2010). There was, of course, the recognised and established medi-eval practice of securing valuables within consecrated grounds to ensure their safety, so entrusting them to the Templars, who were running an international medieval safe-deposit system, was the next logical step.

There was no social stratification regarding the use of the Order's banking facility, and the Templars allowed borrowing too. For example, King John of England borrowed at the time of the Magna Carta in 1215; the last Latin Emperor of Constantinople, Baldwin II borrowed huge sums against supposed relics of the 'True Cross,' and Louis VII of France also borrowed to join the Second Crusade alongside the Templar Order. Their establishment as sound financial managers was not only indicative of their trustworthy status in medieval society but conveyed their progressive thinking towards the task they had taken on in defending pilgrims. They allowed the traveller to deposit their belongings for which they received a receipt bearing the Templar seal. In return they could carry this to any other Templar bank and withdraw the amount denoted on the receipt.

The Templars' existence was tied closely to the Crusades; when the Holy Land was lost, support for the Order faded, and King Philip IV of France (who was deeply in debt to the Order) took particular advantage of the situation. In June 1308 there was a papal inquiry into the Templars, and under interrogation, most probably including torture, 72 knights confessed to heresy (*Inquisitiones contra Templarios in Romana Curia*, 1308a, 1308b, 1308c). Many of the Order's members in France were arrested, tortured, and burned at the stake. The abrupt disappearance of the Order has, unsurprisingly, caused great speculation and the development of legends, which have kept the 'Templar' name alive. There is clear evidence in the Vatican Secret Archives, contained in a document known as the 'Chinon Parchment'(1308) dated 17–20 August 1308 (wrongly filed in 1628 and rediscovered 2001), that Pope Clement V absolved the Templars of all heresies in 1308 before formally disbanding the Order in 1312. With the publishing of the documents pertaining to the trial of the Templars (*Archivum Secretum Vaticanum*, 2007) the Catholic Church holds that the medieval persecution of the Knights Templar was unjust. Unlike those involved with some of the more recent banking crises, the Templars' reputation remains intact!

■ Trade routes

Shāh ʿAbbās I of Persia (1571–1629) established a comprehensive system of *caravanserais* all across his empire and throughout the Islamic world, providing hospitality and care for travellers both pilgrims and strangers. Caravanserais are hostels for travellers, where in the countryside accommodation was often given for free for the traditional three days, i.e. a day, a night and a day; although, in reality, most travellers wished to continue their journey after just one night. Caravanserais offered security for travellers and merchants and in contrast to the mediaeval western monasteries, caravanserais were also used as commercial centres for merchants, with a sales tax of 2% imposed by the caravanserai manager. Establishing a system of carefully managed caravanserais to provide hospitality for travellers is often reflected among the traditions and writings. For example, the historian al-Tabarī (c 910 AD) records how the governor of Samarqand (now called Samarkand, Uzbekistan) in 719 AD was ordered to:

> "establish inns in your lands so that whenever a Muslim passes by, you
> will put him up for a day, and a night and take care of his animals; if he
> is sick, provide him with hospitality for two days and two nights; and
> if he has used up all of his provisions and is unable to continue, supply
> him with whatever he needs to reach his hometown." (al-Tabarī, 1989)

Samarqand was located on one of the most important trading routes in the region, and no doubt had a regular supply of traders and travellers. This ancient route is one of the best known of the world's historical trading routes, running from Xian in northern China through Iran and on to Istanbul. There is other evidence from the seventh and eighth centuries: ibn Abd al-Hakam (1922), who died in 860 AD, makes mention of caravanserais built by the governor of Egypt; and there is evidence from 710AD when the ruler of Damascus was roundly criticised for funding the construction of a mosque rather than maintaining the roads and building caravanserais (al-Muqaddasī, 1877). In the ninth and tenth centuries there was a well-established record of hospitable works for travellers in Bukhara, Uzbekistan (al-Muqaddasī, 1877) and in the eleventh century a governor in Western Iran had "built in his territories three thousand mosques and caravanserais for strangers." (ibn Abd al-Hakam, 1922, p. 113). Provided for religious reasons, hospitality, like the building of caravanserais, would make the ruler "renowned for ever; he [the ruler] will gather the fruit of his good works in the next world and blessings will be showered upon him" (al-Mulk & Darke, 1994, p. 64).

Typically, each caravanserai is approximately 30-50 km from the next. One example is at Dayr-i Gachin, about two hours south of Tehran. A detailed archaeological and historical survey suggests that this caravanserai dates back to the 3rd Century A.D. It was originally established by the Sasanian Emperor Ardashir I (A.D. 224-41), and has had many uses over the last millennium and a half, including a Zoroastrian sanctuary. Its current form dates from Shāh ʿAbbās, and provides extensive accommodation for travellers. From the plan (Figure 1.4) the full extent of the caravanserai can be seen, including stratified accommodation, bathhouse, a mosque and a large, open central courtyard which would function as a market.

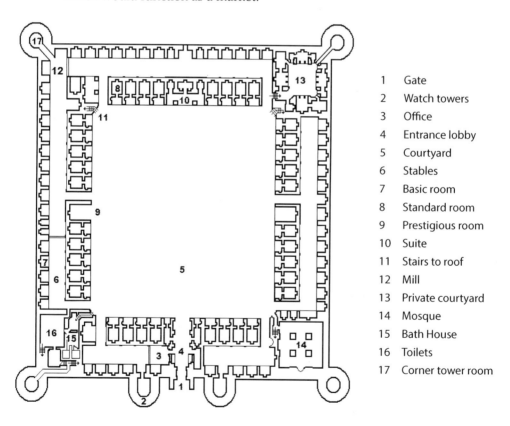

1	Gate
2	Watch towers
3	Office
4	Entrance lobby
5	Courtyard
6	Stables
7	Basic room
8	Standard room
9	Prestigious room
10	Suite
11	Stairs to roof
12	Mill
13	Private courtyard
14	Mosque
15	Bath House
16	Toilets
17	Corner tower room

Figure 1.4: Caravanserai at Dayr-I Gachin, Iran

As Bryce et al. (2013) note, in contrast to the monasteries of Western Christendom, caravanserai could also be used as commercial centres for merchants. As well as being located on trade and pilgrimage routes, caravanserai were also commonly found associated with the grand bazaars of Iranian cities and formed a backbone for trade. In an environment where the underpinning religious injunction is to provide hospitality for free, making a living from running a caravanserai had to be facilitated by accruing rent in other ways; thus, rather crucially, we see the development of the internalisation of markets within caravanserai. Indeed, despite the financial necessity of doing this in the period discussed, this is a true touchstone for contemporary commercial management. Accommodation provision became part of an integrated package for facilitating trade and the movement of traders encouraged caravanserai owners to expand.

■ The Age of Enlightenment and the Industrial Revolution

By the sixteenth century the world was a very different place, with the discovery of the New World, and advances in mapping that forged trade routes with India and the rest of Asia. Such changes saw management evolve from a focus on leadership, strategy and organisation to include technology, knowledge and trade (Witzel, 2012). Europe became the centre of industrial and technological advancement, and therefore was the hub of management development. Crucial to this were the contrasting economic policies of the mercantilists and the physiocrats. Mercantilism can be defined as an effort to achieve economic unity and political control through economic regulation primarily by ensuring a favourable balance of trade (Woodward, 2005). Private business was important as the success of mercantilism was measured on the quantity of precious metal held by your nation, arguably an early form of capitalism (Hooker, 1966). Colonialism was a direct consequence of such a policy, as mercantilist nations needed an outlet for their considerable volume of exported goods. Another important facet of mercantilism was the desire to keep workers poor and ill-educated, an issue that we will see caused problems as the Industrial Revolution gathered momentum. This policy was prominent in the UK and Spain, while the physiocrats held precedence in France, with their opinion that agriculture should be the sole industry, as governing the land was the key to a successful economy. Although this is a somewhat backward attitude, the physiocrats did develop *laissez-faire* economies, with their desire for open markets.

Europe and the United States became the fulcrum for the evolution of management during the Industrial Revolution. Previously, the United States had experienced an uneasy relationship between business and society, as there was a general reluctance to create a banking system, primarily because Jefferson wanted to keep business at a family level (Bodenhorn, 2002). Witzel (2012) cites three reasons that instigated change: a need to feed and arm the Northern Army during the Civil War; the growth of cities through mass immigration; and European influences. From small scale business, the Unites States went to the opposite extreme as big business became widespread. The government had no central institution to control economic activity so big businesses did it themselves. Those at the top happily encouraged monopolies to further fill their pockets. Although this was highly inefficient and did not develop management thinking, the government were reluctant to intervene in a system that kept socialism at bay. The situation drew attention to the shortage of capable managers and subsequent issues with the managing of people, and created the conditions for management to really develop.

The work of Adam Smith, on the division and concentration of labour in particular, had a major influence on the pace of the Industrial Revolution in the UK. Described as a political economist, Smith argued forcefully against the regulation of commerce and trade, and wrote that if people were set free to better themselves, then this would lead to economic prosperity for all. Another Scot, Andrew Ure, being an enthusiast for the new manufacturing systems introduced into factories during the Industrial Revolution, and an advocate for free trade, influenced the scientific management movement (Chodes, 1998). Ure used principles of chemistry and concepts from biology to make manufacturing more efficient but he also argued workers did not require a break and were merely cogs in the machine (Chodes, 2012).

Managers required training if they were to be effective and utilise the new thoughts around management. This was not always a given. Mill owners, for example, wanted to suppress workers to keep them focused on working. Even when Robert Owen showed in his own mill that productivity improved when hours were cut and breaks were given, nobody took much notice. Instead he was hounded out of his own mill for such a statement (Evans, 2013). Formal recognition of the working classes' desire for greater equality came with the Reform Act of 1867. The ensuing evolution of the trade unions and the threat from the United States to the trading supremacy of the UK created the conditions for Britain to develop ideas around management.

20th Century management thought

■   The turn of the century: science, progress, efficiency

Waves of strike action and increasingly violent revolt against the appalling working conditions, aggressive industrialism, and the widespread socio-economic injustices of the 1800s spurred a growing political consciousness amongst fin-de-siècle workers on both sides of the Atlantic. At the turn of the twentieth century, the unscrupulous practices and inefficient processes of managing these increasingly knowledgeable and politicised labour forces were deemed to be in dire need of revision and formalisation. In the United States, activists and politicians of the Progressive Era (1890-1920) drove the reformation of government, education, science, finance, industry, and infrastructure, with aims to reduce waste, corruption, and inefficiency by applying the principles of science and engineering to these often wilfully convoluted systems. At the same time, and by the same principle, the Progressives transformed intellectual pursuits such as history and politics into academic disciplines, thereby creating the social sciences.

This emphasis on science should not imply the passivity or irrelevance of the arts, with the investigative works of so-called 'muckraking' authors and journalists leading directly to policy-making and consequent shifts in industrial practice. The publication of *The Jungle* (1906), Upton Sinclair's infamous novelistic exposé of both the poor treatment of immigrants in the US and the unsanitary practices of Chicago's meatpacking industry, led to the Pure Food and Drug Act (1906) and the Federal Meat Inspection Act (1906). Herbert N. Casson's (1908, 1910, 1911) writings on advertising, business, and technology led him into intellectual partnerships with two of the first management consultants, Frederick W. Taylor and Harrington Emerson, as part of the Efficiency Movement. Following his emigration to Britain in 1914, Casson's (1935) prolific literary output helped establish the foundations of twentieth century management theory in the UK, affirming the role of manager as one of action, balancing the routine, day-to-day actions of the business with the creative actions required to move that business forward.

Early twentieth-century management thought responded to the notoriety of industrial deficiencies through a scientific emphasis upon efficiency and professionalism. This is embodied in the United States by Taylor's *The Principles of Scientific Management* (1911). Following Towne (1886), Taylor (1911), an engineer-turned-management theorist, demanded and devised principles of managerial organisation, so stimulating an associated body of literature through which to exchange such ideas. The aforementioned Efficiency Movement worked towards the systematisation of management practices, the most important of which for Taylor (1911) was strict enforcement of the highest standards. Although associated with the Efficiency Movement, Taylor's contemporary (and rival consultant) Emerson (1912) found this rhetoric of absolute managerial power over the physically capable but intellectually inferior labourer deeply troubling, offering no solution to the societal unrest arising inevitably from the treatment of human beings as factory components. As an alternative to Taylor's (1911) mechanistic perspective, Emerson's (1912) *The Twelve Principles of Efficiency* describes organisations as organisms, beginning with the ideals of the business and working back towards individual tasks. Witzel (2002) argues that Emerson's (1911, 1912) publications describing efficiency as organic and embodied rather than imposed, and standards as dynamic and achievable, are in fact early precursors of total quality management. Indeed, Emerson's (1911, 1912) awareness of an organisation's relationship with society, fair treatment and rewarding of employees, and its duty to evolve with technology arguably prefigure the human relations movement of the 1930s (discussed below), and the decidedly modern concepts of corporate social responsibility and globalisation.

Similar calls and responses could be found in industrial settings across Europe, with engineers such as Karel Adamiecki (Marsh, 1975), Ernest Solvay (1900), and Francis Burton (1899) again proposing solutions of efficiency to confrontations between workers and business owners. While the purposes were broadly similar to US scientific management, managerial thought in Europe had more in common with Emerson than Taylor, situating the needs of the business relative to those of individual workers and society (Witzel, 2012). Although influenced by the principles of scientific management, Edward Cadbury (1914) criticised Taylor's lack of humanity, and redressed this imbalance in his business by rewarding workers and valuing their opinions, championing gender equality in the workplace, and providing employees with housing and benefits. This humanistic management philosophy continued to develop during the First World War (1914–1918), with publications by Edward Elbourne (1914) and Sidney Webb (1917) tempering the organisational principles of scientific management with realistic understandings of workers' needs and rights.

■ Post-war management philosophy in Europe

During the First World War, Benjamin Seebohm Rowntree (1921) worked as the head of industrial welfare at the Ministry of Munitions, after which he organised management conferences featuring the leaders of British industry (Cassis et al., 1995). Child (2012) notes the influence of wartime munitions factory organisation and military leadership on management philosophy. The social responsibilities of business continued to drive managerial thought in the UK, with Rowntree asserting in *The Human Factor in Business* (1921, p. 156) that "industry should pay the greatest possible regard to the general welfare of the community, and should pursue no policy detrimental to it." In *The Philosophy of Management*, Oliver Sheldon (1923, p. 27) proposes that "the fundamental problem of industry [concerns how to] achieve and maintain a balance between the things of production...and the humanity of production." In offering an historical understanding of management, and asserting the tendency towards organisation throughout human history, Sheldon (1923) describes management as an art, which utilises and adapts certain scientific principles. Again, this human-centred approach to management was successfully implemented by some now very well-known companies in their relative infancy. Alongside the aforementioned Cadbury's and Rowntree's, the transformation of the decidedly autocratic John Lewis & Co. to the employee-owned John Lewis Partnership between 1928 and 1929 granted every employee equal shares in the business.

Britain's first management consultancy, Urwick Orr and Partners, was set up in 1934 by Lyndall Urwick (Kennedy, 2002). Inspired by Taylor's *Shop Management* (1911), Urwick (1933) saw management very much as a science, believing that successful managerial practice required the application of theoretical principles derived from objective research and analysis. Urwick (1933) asserted the importance of novel and dynamic forms of organisation, based on robust findings but never held back by tradition, adapting instead to the ever-changing needs and knowledge of consumers. Although primarily influenced by principles of scientific management, Urwick (1933) discerned the need for an overarching, critical theory of management that acknowledged and incorporated useful ideas from various sources. As such, he called for courses in management at university level, and co-edited a comprehensive collection of essays, *Papers on the Science of Administration* (Gulick et al., 1937), which includes diverse work by thinkers from various cultures and industries, such as James Mooney, Henry Dennison and Henri Fayol.

A leading figure in French managerial thought, Fayol's (1949) experience as a highly successful managing director in the latter half of the nineteenth century brought a practical focus to his writings. Fayol (1949) was also an eminent scientist and engineer, whose positivist, process-based approach placed the manager at the centre of business, and categorised five types of managerial activity: forward-thinking, organisation, coordination, leadership and quality control. First published in 1916, his Fourteen Points of management borrow elements from both the mechanistic and humanistic approaches, tempering a hierarchy of discipline and central command with employee equality and fair wages. Fayol's influence ensured that France led the way for business education and research into the mid-twentieth century (Callender, 2008). Fayol and Urwick's focus on the manager's place and practices within a carefully structured and openly communicative organisation came to be understood as the 'administrative theory' of management, and remains utilised as an alternative to Taylor's task and efficiency-centred approach (McLean, 2011).

In Germany, the first generation of business graduates was engaged in similar debates, with Heinrich Nicklish, Fritz Schonpflug, Eugen Schmalenbach and Joseph Schumpeter discussing the human elements of management, and the obligations of businesses towards the community. From an industry perspective, Walther Rathenau also found aspects of scientific management dehumanizing, arguing that businesses should strive towards egalitarian ideals, with employees treated fairly, and offered training that facilitates progression. The reification of workers in the name of efficiency came to inform Max Weber's 'bureaucratic theory' of management, which shares with administrative theory the principle of a firm organisational hierarchy governed by stable, transparent rules. Broadly speaking, administrative theory offers a more detailed, practical, and optimistic examination of business practices than bureaucratic theory, focussing on the managerial role. In contrast, as a philosopher and sociologist, Weber was deeply critical of the drive towards mechanistic efficiency at the expense of individuality and emotion, and warned against accepting this through more general observations of society and the political economy.

Witzel (2012) writes of a general decline in British, German, and French managerial thought from the 1920s onwards, due to a lack of management education in Britain, the socio-political upheaval of Nazism in Germany, and the Depression in France. Again, much of the management thinking of the twentieth century comes from the US, where the philosophy of Mary Parker Follett, Elton Mayo's Hawthorne Studies of the early 1920s, and the associated human relations movement together formed a significant intervention into the efficiency/humanity problem.

■ Human Relations

Follett's (1918; 1942; 1930) philosophical writings on society and politics focussed on dismantling bureaucratic institutions and redistributing the powers of central government to smaller communities. A crucial theoretical notion of Follett's is integration, whereby the allegedly disparate viewpoints of traditionally conflicting groups are re-examined and reconciled. By placing individual and group dynamics at the centre of discussions of power and conflict, Follett became known as the founding figure of the 'human relations' theory of management. Follett's approach calls into question the notion of single, objective (or universal) truth that lies at the hearts of both scientific management and administrative theory, instead valuing and exploring the outcomes of diverse experiences and multiple perspectives. Entirely opposed to central control, Follett argues that being in a small group empowers the individual members to better understand their needs and wants, with each group articulating temporary instances of control that leaders at several levels must work to bring together and coordinate. These principles of collective consultation and peer group controls bear considerable resemblance to those emerging around the same time in the early stages of industrialisation in Japan, from thinkers such as Ohara Magosaburo, and from Arabic and Persian thinkers of the late nineteenth century, such as Muhammad 'Abduh, Muhammad Rashid Rida, and Jamaluddin al-Afghani (Witzel, 2012).

Despite an emphasis on subjectivity, the human relations school of thought found itself backed by science, specifically Elton Mayo's experiments at the Hawthorne plant of the Western Electric Company. Beginning as experiments on the effects of lighting on the productivity of workers, Mayo (1949) soon discovered a more significant measure in the interactions between employees and scientific investigators. The opportunity for staff to open up to these supposedly impartial observers about personal and social matters led to conclusive findings about the positive impacts of cohesive group dynamics and individual emotional wellbeing upon productivity (2003). As evidence of the practicality of Follett's theories for management, the Hawthorne Studies further established the human relations principles of facilitating team cohesion, open consultation with and between workers, and business as a social system. These principles continue to be recognisable in the twenty-first century.

■ Organisation theories

Following the success of the Hawthorne Studies, the connections between science and management became both stronger and more diverse, with the findings of psychological and sociological experiments of the 1940s and 1950s further attesting to the significance of individual motivations, group dynamics, and cultural change. This research on individual and group behaviours was developed by thinkers such as Keith Davis, Abraham Maslow, Frederick Herzberg, and Douglas McGregor. At the same time, the Second World War brought with it the necessity of developing increasingly efficient methods of production, and the practical application of human relations theory was challenged by this renewed emphasis on efficiency and organisational control. The imagined threat of communism of the 1950s, 60s and beyond led to an academic scramble for scientific certainties, one of which was the necessity of strengthening capitalism, through the application of mathematical systems and financial economics (Witzel, 2012). These repeated attempts at scientific optimisation were again criticised by those in the social sciences, such as Herbert Simon (1947), Ludwig von Bertalanffy (1968) and Joan Woodward (1965), who argued that striving towards rational ideals ignores the fact that organisations are composed of people and communications, and so inherently susceptible to irrationality. These thinkers developed organisation theories in order to better understand these human systems.

Simon's (1947) principal contribution to understanding the organisation was the concept of 'bounded rationality': that the limitations on what an individual can comprehend at any one time render it impossible for any one person to make a truly rational choice. As such, organisations of people allow us to effectively process a wealth of collective information and knowledge, towards informed decision-making. At the same time, even the largest organisations cannot take into account all information, nor predict all outcomes, and so organisations too are subject to this bounded rationality. The decision made can only be that deemed the best at the time and place, rather than the perfect, rationally realised ideal.

Von Bertalanffy's (1968) theory of the open system views the interactions of the constituent parts of an organisation as a whole, in contrast to the closed system of scientific management, which attempts to analyse and optimise each function individually. Open system organisational theory characterises the organisation as constantly in flux, variously responsive to external and internal forces. This emphasis on evolution and unpredictability poses serious problems for any attempt to describe and predict the actions of an organisation through scientific observation, and led to the idea of organisational cultures that develop and change over time (Vickers, 1967).

The contingency theory developed by Woodward (1965) works towards an understanding of the ways in which an organisation chooses a structure and system of control. Contingency theory argues that the structural and systemic evolution of organisations is dependent on various internal and external factors, such as the use of technology in processes of production (Witzel, 2012). Contingency theory continued to develop into the 1980s, before postmodern management thought cast doubt on any and all attempts to create overarching theories of organisation and management.

Readers may notice that much of the managerial thought of the twentieth century has been described in relation to the scientific management approach most successfully articulated and implemented in the United States. Yet throughout the twentieth century the role of manager came to be enacted quite differently in different cultural contexts. Indeed, attempts to simply transplant (typically Western) managerial theory and practice across national borders without consideration for (typically non-Western) theoretical and practical equivalents are very likely to end in failure. It is absolutely vital that approaches to management continually respond to the cultural contexts of which they are (to some extent) products. That which is entirely valid and successful in one culture will not be immediately replicable in another. This is not to conflate national and organisational cultures, the former being enduring and far more difficult to change than the relatively transient latter. It is also important to understand that the following are broad and not universal differences, generally apparent into the late twentieth and early twenty-first centuries.

Managers in the US continue to be seen as aspirational and motivational figures, with management referring to a group of people as well as a process (Hofstede, 1993). Hofstede (1993) characterises late-twentieth century US managerial thought as emphasising competition between individuals, and focussing on managers over other workers. This may be seen, for instance, in Peter Drucker's (1974) popular and accessible writings on the manager as an individual. Echoing Fayol's (1949) assertion of a hierarchical system of management, with employees reporting to a single boss, late-twentieth century France continued to reject Taylor's (1911) idea of splitting management into eight specialist bosses (Hofstede, 1993). Meanwhile, much of Germany's highly skilled workforce progressed through the nationally recognised apprenticeship system, and therefore managers in Germany are more simply seen as those with technical expertise who assign tasks (Hofstede, 1993). As mentioned earlier, this focus on workers over management can also be found in Japan, where employees tend to consult each other when tackling smaller issues, only consulting managers over larger decisions (Hofstede, 1993). Whilst the vast majority of managerial thinking still comes from US practitioners, theorists, and institutions, this only testifies to the increasing need to pay attention to those voices both from diverse and often vilified cultural contexts, such as those related to Islamic societies, and suppressed within (former) colonies, such as North America, parts of Africa, and Australia (Tsui, 2004; Tsui, Nifadkar, & Ou, 2007).

So is it an art or a science?

To conclude, let us return to the question posed at the beginning of this chapter: "Is management an art or a science?" Well, normally, art is considered to be an inborn talent usually involving imaginative or technical skill that can be refined through learning and practice. That could be true about management, and it could also be considered as the art of getting things done through people. Science is the systematic body of knowledge that is universally accepted in a given area of study. As you read earlier in this chapter, Taylor is considered the father of scientific management, and was perhaps the first person to regard management as a science. He was of the opinion that management should conduct their business affairs by following certain well-established standards.

This is not to suggest that management should be considered one of the physical sciences studying non-living systems such as, for example, astronomy, physics, chemistry and mathematics or even a life science – which study living organisms – like bioethics, biology or even neuroscience. It is most accurately compared with the social sciences, which focus on society and the relationships among individuals within a society, and include economics, political science, human geography, and in a wider sense, anthropology, archaeology, history, law and linguistics. Contemporary managers can draw on all of those disciplines to inform their current practice.

That said, even this is an oversimplification. An organisation could easily be compared to a living organism, and a good manager, like an artist, should be practical and dynamic, with emphasis on results rather than activities. However, managers also need to be focused on how staff perform their tasks and understand the job knowledge (formal and informal) that they have, and must work with them to find ways to improve performance. Managers must codify new methods of performing tasks into written work rules and standard operating procedures; as proposed in Taylor's *Principles of Scientific Management* (1911). As St. Benedict observed, if staff do not have the skills or equipment to carry out their duties then managers are to blame, and staff must be fully resourced and supported by the management team.

References

al-Mulk, N., & Darke, H. (1994). *Siyar al-mulūk* (Siyāsat'nāmah): Scientific & Cultural publications.

al-Muqaddasī, M. A. ([946]/1877). كتاباباسناتلقاسیمیفرامتفهاتلقلم Brill: Lugduni Batavorum.

al-Tabarī. ([838]/1989). تایرخلارسولواولملاوكـ Albany: State University of New York Press.

Archivum Secretum Vaticanum. (2007). *Processus Contra Templarios*. Status Civitatis Vaticanae: Scrinum.

Bodenhorn, H. (2002). *State Banking in Early America: A New Economic History*: Oxford University Press.

Bryce, D., O'Gorman, K.D. and Baxter I.W.F. (2013) 'Commerce, Empire and Faith in Safavid Iran: The Caravanserai of Isfahan' *International Journal of Contemporary Hospitality Management*. Vol. 25, No. 2 pp. 204-226, 2013

Burton, F. G. (1899). *The commercial management of engineering works*: Scientific Publishing Company.

Cadbury, E. (1914). Some Principles Of Industrial Organisation. *The Sociological Review, 7*(2), 99-117.

Callender, G. (2008). *Efficiency and Management*: Taylor & Francis.

Cassis, Y., Crouzet, F., & Gourvish, T. R. (1995). *Management and Business in Britain and France: The Age of the Corporate Economy*: Clarendon Press.

Casson, H. N. (1908). *The Romance of the Reaper*: Doubleday, Page.

Casson, H. N. (1910). *The history of the telephone*: Books for Libraries Press.

Casson, H. N. (1911). *Ads and Sales: A Study of Advertising and Selling, from the Standpoint of the New Principles of Scientific Management*: AC McClurg & Company.

Casson, H. N. (1935). *How to Get Things Done: A Book of Suggestions of Executives*: Efficiency Magazine.

Child, J. (2012). *British Management Thought (Routledge Revivals): A Critical Analysis*: Taylor & Francis.

Chinon Parchment. (1308). *Archivum Secretum Vaticanum Call No.: Archivum Arcis Armarium D 217*.Unpublished manuscript, Status Civitatis Vaticanae.

Chodes, J. (1998). 'Dr. Andrew Ure: Pioneer Free Trader- An Unsung Proponent of International Trade and Internal Industry.' Freeman New York Foundation for Economic Education 48: 604-606.

Elbourne, E. T., Home-Morton, A., & Maughfling, J. (1914). *Factory Administration and Accounts: A Book of Reference with Tables and Specimen Forms, for Managers, Engineers and Accountants*: Longmans, Green, and Company.

Emerson, H. (1911). Philosophy of Efficiency. *New York*.

Emerson, H. (1912). *The twelve principles of efficiency*: Engineering magazine.

Evans, J. N. (2013). *Great Figures in the Labour Movement: The Commonwealth and International Library: History Division*: Elsevier.

Fayol, H. (1949). *Administration générale et industrielle*, 1916. English translation by Storrs, G., General and industrial management, Pitman & Sons, London.

Follett, M. P. (1918). *The New State: Group Organization the Solution of Popular Government*: Pennsylvania State University Press.

Follett, M. P. (1930). *Creative Experience*: Longmans, Green and Company.

Follett, M. P., Metcalf, H. C., & Urwick, L. F. (1942). *Dynamic administration*.

Gulick, L. H., Urwick, L. F., & Pforzheimer, C. H. (1937). *Papers on the science of administration*. New York: Institute of Public Administration, Columbia University.

Hall D. L., & Ames R. T. (1987) *Thinking Through Confucius*, SUNY Press.

Hofstede, G. (1993). Cultural constraints in management theories. *The Academy of Management Executive*, **7**(1), 81-94.

Hooker R. (1966) *Glossary of World Cultures: European Enlightenment-Capitalism*: Pullman: Washington State University, .

ibn Abd al-Hakam, A. ([1014]/1922).کتاب فتوح میسر واہب آریا New Haven: Yale University Press.

Inquisitiones contra Templarios in Romana Curia. (1308a). *Archivum Secretum Vaticanum Call No.: Archivum Arcis Armarium D 208*.Unpublished manuscript,

Status Civitatis Vaticanae.

Inquisitiones contra Templarios in Romana Curia. (1308b). *Archivum Secretum Vaticanum Call No.: Archivum Arcis Armarium D 209*.Unpublished manuscript, Status Civitatis Vaticanae.

Inquisitiones contra Templarios in Romana Curia. (1308c). *Archivum Secretum Vaticanum Call No.: Archivum Arcis Armarium D 210*.Unpublished manuscript, Status Civitatis Vaticanae.

Kennedy, C. (2002). *Guide to the Management Gurus: The best guide to business thinkers*: Random House.

Marsh, E. R. (1975). Research Notes. The Harmonogram of Karol Adamiecki. *Academy of Management Journal,* **18**(2), 358-364. doi: 10.2307/255537

Mayo, E. (1949). *Hawthorne and the Western Electric Company*.

Mayo, E. (2003). *The Human Problems of an Industrial Civilization*: Taylor & Francis.

McLean, J. (2011). Fayol – standing the test of time. *Manager: British Journal of Administrative Management, Spring*, 32-33.

O'Gorman, K.D. (2010) 'Historical Giants: Forefathers of Modern Hospitality and Tourism'. *In:* Butler, R.W. and Russell, R. (eds) *Giants of Tourism*. CABI, Oxford. pp.3-17.

O'Gorman, K.D. (2010) *The Origins of Hospitality and Tourism*. Goodfellow, Oxford.

O'Gorman, K.D. and Beverage, E. (2012) 'The Crusades, the Knights Templar and Hospitaller: A combination of religion, war, pilgrimage and tourism enablers' *In*: Butler, R.W. and Suntikul, W. (eds) *Tourism and War: A Complex Relationship*. Routledge, London. pp.39-48.

Rowntree, B. S. (1921). *The Human Factor in Business*: Longmans, Green and Company.

Sheldon, O. (1923). *The Philosophy of Management*: Sir I. Pitman.

Simon, H. A. (1947). *Administration Behavior: Study of Decision-making Processes in Administrative Organization*: Macmillan.

Sinclair, U. (1906). *The Jungle* (1946 ed, reprinted 1971). Cambridge, MA: R. Bentley. Harmondsworth.

Solvay, E. (1900). *Notes sur le productivisme et le comptabilisme : études sociales*. Bruxelles: H. Lamertin.

Taylor, F. W. (1911). *The Principles of Scientific Management*: Harper & Brothers.

Towne, H. R. (1886). The engineer as economist. *Transactions of the American Society of Mechanical Engineers,* **7**, 428–432.

Tsui, A. S. (2004). Contributing to global management knowledge: A case for high quality indigenous research. *Asia Pacific Journal of Management,* **21**(4), 491-513.

Tsui, A. S., Nifadkar, S. S., & Ou, A. Y. (2007). Cross-national, cross-cultural organizational behavior research: Advances, gaps, and recommendations. *Journal of Management,* **33**(3), 426-478.

Urwick, L. F. (1933). *Management of Tomorrow*: Nisbet and Company, Limited.

Vickers, G. (1967). *Towards a Sociology of Management*: Basic Books.

von Bertalanffy, L. (1968). *Organismic Psychology and Systems Theory*: Clark University Press.

Webb, S. (1917). *The Works Manager To-day: An Address Prepared for a Series of Private Gatherings of Works Managers*: Books for Libraries Press.

Witzel, M. (2002). A short history of efficiency. *Business Strategy Review,* **13**(4), 38-47.

Witzel, M. (2012). *A history of management thought*: Routledge.

Woodward, J. (1965). *Industrial Organization: Theory and Practice*: Oxford University Press.

Woodward, J., Dawson, S., & Wedderburn, D. (1965). *Industrial Organization: Theory and practice* (Vol. 3). London: Oxford University Press.

Woodward, R. (2005). Merchant guilds. *Encyclopedia of World Trade from Ancient Times to the Present*. New York: ME Sharpe, 3, 631-638.

2 Strategic Management

Robert MacIntosh

Organizing has been central to the evolution of our species. From our earliest days as hunter gatherers, humans have worked collaboratively to achieve things which might be impossible when acting alone. Long before the emergence of formal organizations such as armies or religious groups, people have acted strategically and our history is littered with the names of those who are remembered for the quality of their strategic thinking. One simple definition is that strategy is the craft of collectively rising to a significant challenge and accomplishing more than might be reasonably expected (MacIntosh and MacLean, 2015: 3). Defined in this way, it is easy to spot strategy wherever unexpected outcomes are achieved. In military terms, leaders such as Alexander the Great occasionally triumph against the odds. They do so by being strategic in deploying their troops or by outsmarting their rivals. In political terms, leaders such as Nelson Mandela or Mahatma Ghandi galvanise efforts to overcome seemingly impossible circumstances and effect regime change where others have failed. In commercial terms, small start-ups go on to dislodge larger competitors and establish a dominant position.

On first inspection, David should never defeat Goliath, yet this assessment of advantage and disadvantage overlooks the critical role of the strategist. The lowly shepherd boy would almost certainly have lost had he engaged in hand-to-hand combat with a larger, more experienced and more skilled warrior. Instead, David chose to use a particular skill, accuracy with a sling shot, to change the dynamic of the competitive encounter. In order to achieve more than might reasonably be expected, strategists must draw on resources that are often hidden from their opponent's sight. Knowledge of their unique skills might allow them to achieve things which their opponent would find difficult. A deep sense of resolve might allow them to endure things which others would find unpalatable. A capacity to develop a deep understanding of their context might allow them to spot opportunities and threats in their environment long before others have had the chance to respond. An acute sense of timing might allow them to act decisively when circumstances confer maximum advantage and not a moment too early or too late. Finally, a creative capacity to weave resources, skills, environmental conditions and timing into a strategy which is inherently cunning can allow good strategists to overwhelm better resourced, longer established and seemingly invincible opponents just as David overcame Goliath.

Why develop strategy?

Given that strategy has helped groups and individuals across the ages to build empires, the topic has been studied in military and political contexts for centuries. Modern studies of strategy substitute corporations for nation states and measures like market share or profitability are the contemporary means of assessing conquest. Strategy itself has become something of an empire supporting a multibillion dollar consulting industry. Academics may debate nuanced points relating to the nature and value of strategy, but its status as a significant social practice is largely taken for granted. Strategies are developed by individuals and organizations on a regular basis and it is worth considering the motivations that may lie behind a desire to develop a new strategy.

There are three poor motives for developing a new strategy. First, strategists may be driven to develop a new strategy simply because the existing strategy covers a time period which is drawing to a close. Most strategy documents cover a defined period. If your organization's strategy covers the period 2013-2018, there will be significant social pressure to replace this strategy as the year 2018 draws nearer. A common distinction between strategy and tactics is that the former relates to the medium to long term, whilst the latter relates to immediate and short term priorities. Five to ten year periods are typical in Western organizational practice though it is also worth noting that the perception of what constitutes long-term is influenced by the pace at which individual industries move. Computer gaming tends to evolve far more quickly than ship building or mining. Regardless of the time frame set by the existing strategy, drawing close to the end of the period in question tends to imply a need to renew or refresh strategy. This, in and of itself, is not a good enough reason for developing a strategy unless significant change has taken place in either the organization, its operating environment or both.

The second poor motivation for developing a strategy is the perceived pressure to mimic other organizations. This process of copying the behaviour of other organizations is sometimes referred to as mimetic isomorphism (Di

Maggio and Powell, 1983). Noticing that other organizations in your peer group appear to have a strategy, a Twitter feed, an international office or any other feature is not a good enough reason for investing the time and energy into these activities. In the specific case of strategy however, it is not uncommon to find that a desire to fit in drives a tendency to produce relatively homogenous strategy documents. As an experiment, pick three or four organizations of the same type (e.g. universities, software firms, financial service providers, etc.) and compare their public domain strategy documents. You will often find striking similarities and a strong sense of "me-too" about such documents, particularly when they are drawn from the same sector. Strategy is of vital importance; it is not a fashion accessory or a way of fitting in with your peers.

The third poor motivation for developing strategy is because you have been coerced. Particularly when organizations grow or move into new markets they can be required to produce a strategy by regulators, accrediting bodies, funders, customers or potential investors. Whilst it is reassuring to note that such groups or individuals value strategy enough that they might reasonably expect that a well run organization should possess one, this is not a compelling enough reason to develop a strategy.

At its heart, strategy defines everything about an organization from its mission, to the products and services offered, target customers and competitors, the basis on which to compete, the kinds of skills required and measures of eventual success. For this reason, strategy is often seen as the capstone topic in business school curricula. Strategy's rightful place at the top of the functional food chain means that marketing, operations, human resources and finances should only be developed once clarity over the broad strategic direction has been set. Developing strategy is therefore not something to be undertaken lightly. Indeed, there is only one justifiable reason for developing a strategy, namely to overcome a difficulty that has been identified. The starting point for strategy development should therefore be the diagnosis of a particular difficulty, challenge or opportunity facing the organization. Strategies should be developed in response to problems rather than habit, fashion or coercion.

Furthermore, we tend to discuss strategy as a singular concept in that organizations are usually seen to have *a* strategy. If an organization faces multiple challenges, it may actually require a suite of strategies to overcome these problems. This introduces the potential for conflict between strategies which we will return to later in the chapter. At this stage, it is sufficient to note that the definition of strategy used here relates to the coherence of the alignment of broad intentions, environmental circumstances and available resources but that the process of assessing alignment should be done in relation to a perceived challenge, opportunity or difficulty.

Spotting strategic intent

Having introduced the concept of strategy, it is now possible to develop some criteria by which to assess whether organizations, or individuals, are behaving in a way that is strategic (see Table 2.1). Happily, most of us recognise the hallmarks of focused strategic intent in business. In Europe, the airline Ryanair has established a dominant position from a starting point of relative disadvantage. Starting as a young, small, regional and generally unprofitable airline, Ryanair needed a clear strategy to overcome better resourced, more established competitors. Ask yourself, what is the first thing that comes to mind when you think of Ryanair? The answer for most people is something to do with pricing. Ryanair has worked hard to establish a reputation for low cost travel.

In terms of identifying strategy, this sense of consistency is an important marker. If you ask a selection of people to describe the organization in one word or in one sentence you should get a high degree of consistency if the organization has been pursuing a clear strategy. Persistence tends to flow from a clear and consistent sense of purpose. Where an organization appears confusing to its customers and competitors there is a high likelihood that it is, itself, confused. A second marker for strategic behaviour is that the consistent and persistent behaviour of the organization relates to a relatively well-defined problem. For Ryanair, this was how to achieve the combination of scale and profitability that appeared to have eluded most other airlines.

A further characteristic of strategic behaviour is that the strategy itself is subject to major revision only infrequently. Since strategy relates to the medium to longer term, decisions which are genuinely strategic in nature occur rarely. Day to day pricing decisions, which individual member of staff to recruit or promote as part of a regular process, or which suppliers to use, are examples of operational decisions that are taken frequently. In contrast, genuinely strategic decisions are so rare and so important that they typically have no past-precedent that could be followed. In the absence of asking themselves "what do we normally do?" strategists are forced to engage in higher order thinking that challenges existing assumptions and calls for careful analysis. Once made, strategic decisions typically bear significant consequences for other aspects of an organization's operations. For a firm like Apple, the decision to introduce an iPhone with greater storage capacity or a better camera would be routine and would not qualify as a strategic decision. The decision to allow other manufacturers to develop products that use Apple's operating system would mark a significant shift in that they have not done this before, it would highly consequential for other product and business model decisions within the firm and it would be difficult to put the genie back into the bottle once such a decision was made.

1. Appears to be addressing a defined difficulty or problem
2. Develops a consistent and persistent set of priorities and actions
3. The strategy is revised relatively rarely
4. The strategy bears measurable consequences for a range of lower order decisions
5. The strategy sets a particular direction of travel which would be hard to reverse

Table 2.1: Criteria for spotting strategic intent

How organizations frame the problem they are addressing is critical, and effective strategists tend to begin by framing the challenge they face in creative ways. In 2012 when internet streaming service Netflix began making its own content, setting aside a $300M budget for original programming, Chief Content Officer Ted Sarandos was clear: "our goal is to become HBO faster than HBO can become us." The development of popular series such as *House of Cards*, *Better Call Saul* and *Orange is the New Black* indicate that Netflix has begun to produce high quality content that is attracting a loyal audience. Netflix has experimented with major innovations such as releasing a whole box set simultaneously or drip-feeding one episode per week in the same manner as traditional broadcasters. Another example of the importance of framing is Amazon's early 'get big fast' philosophy (*Management Today*, 2012) which clearly prioritised growth over profitability in the belief that the internet retail market was likely to be a huge opportunity where one firm would secure first mover advantages. If Amazon had worried about profitability rather than growth in the early years it may well have been another firm that have secured the dominant brand and reputation that are now amongst the most valuable aspects of Amazon.

These examples, and many others, tend to populate strategy text books. They do, however, have a heroic feel where clear, perhaps even cunning, thinking led to decisive advantages. For every successful strategic move there are other counter moves which have proven disastrous. Arriving with the right technology before a market is ready to recognise or accept it is a recipe for disaster as Sir Clive Sinclair discovered when launching an electric vehicle in 1985. Strategies do not always work. Winston Churchill concluded that no matter how beautiful the strategy, occasionally it is necessary to look at the results being delivered. Similarly, from the oldest recorded writings on military strategy, Sun Tzu notes that it is possible to know how to conquer without actually having the capacity to execute the plan. Both Churchill and Sun Tzu point to important tensions. Strategy is ultimately judged on results delivered and those results must be deliverable by you rather than by some hypothetical or fantasised version of you.

Malcolm Gladwell (2013) offers an excellent overview of the challenges facing marginalised or disadvantaged competitors. Arguing for the advantage of disadvantages, Gladwell suggests that success often flows from reconceptualising competitive engagements. Large armies can be undone by guerrilla tactics, imposing physical strength can be disabled by speed and agility, established social networks can be disrupted by innovations from the periphery. For Gladwell, everything from dyslexia to poverty can be turned from a source of disadvantage to a source of advantage in certain circumstances.

Author George Orwell claimed that whoever was currently winning is often perceived as invincible, yet no empire, organization, technology or individual in the history of civilization has ever dominated indefinitely. In the early years of computing it was difficult to imagine anyone threatening the dominance of computer manufacturers such as IBM. Yet Microsoft led a shift from hardware and circuitry to software and operating systems. In so doing, Microsoft became dominant to the point where it controlled over 90% market share for operating systems. Manufacturers were left making commodity products at low margins. Whilst Microsoft is still a major player, it is clear that the ground is shifting again with firms such as Google and Apple pursuing new strategies which are in danger of marginalizing Microsoft just as they marginalized IBM and other computer manufacturers. The inescapable fact is that strategies and strategic management practices themselves have a shelf-life. The ability to create, dismantle and recreate strategic order is the domain of the strategist. As individuals, strategists lead their organizations, sometimes directly, sometimes indirectly and as we move into progressively more global, more networked and more challenging times it appears that the role of the strategist is changing.

Types of strategist

Thus far, the emphasis has been on the role of strategy in organizational or individual success. Yet this overlooks one key point; whilst strategy matters, strategists matter more. A sculptor can produce intricate three-dimensional surfaces from a block of stone using only a hammer and chisel. Simple tools are of course indispensable but the craft and inspiration come from the sculptor. Whilst other onlookers may only see a block of uncarved stone, the sculptor may see a figure trapped within the flat surfaces and regard themselves as engaged in releasing the figure from their entrapped position. If strategists are similarly sculpting their organization's future, it is the individual and situated strategist that must be able to see how to overcome a perceived obstacle, difficulty or disadvantage where others cannot. An honest and detailed assessment of you, your circumstance and your disposition are therefore critical. There is little point observing that you could run a sub-four minute mile only if you trained consistently, had better diet and had access to world class coaching or physiotherapy. If you do not have access to these resources, this is ultimately not a workable solution. Simply copying someone else's strategy is rarely successful since you are always playing catch up.

Research indicates that the way in which individual strategists approach the task of developing strategy varies in much the same way that individual handwriting, personality or other traits vary from one person to the next. MacIntosh and MacLean (2015) identify three distinct strategy styles. **Intent-driven strategists** place greater emphasis on those parts of strategy which relate to objectives, goals and intentions. If you are an intent-driven strategist, you will tend to focus on ambitious targets or noble aspirations to generate inspiration and a sense of shared purpose amongst others. In 1961, John F Kennedy set the ambitious target of sending a man to the moon. He had little or no knowledge of whether this was achievable and significant challenges lay ahead but his public call to action played an important role in developing NASA's strategy. When the UK won the rights to host the 2012 Olympics in London, the national sports agency set Team GB the target of securing the highest ever medal haul from a single Olympics. Whilst there were already a number of established star athletes who might be medal hopefuls, a step change would be required to deliver against this ambitious target. In the seven years between winning the right to host the games and the games themselves, the target of producing the best medal outcome galvanised a huge range of activities. In the end, Team GB came third in the medal table behind the US and China. In so doing, the medal target was met and expectations exceeded. Both the lunar landings and the 2012 Olympics represent good examples of intent-driven strategy.

A second strategy style focuses on developments, opportunities and threats in a firm's environment. **Trend-driven strategists** scan the horizon looking for advance notice of future tastes, trends and technologies. Using the market intelligence that they gather, they are able to position their organizations to capitalise on opportunities before others have time to react. Like surfers, trend-driven strategists are constantly looking for the next wave of change that will sweep through their industry in order to time their run and maximise the momentum which they can exploit. Steve Jobs moved Apple[1] into the music industry with the release of iTunes and the iPod. Now it seems an obvious fit but at that point in time, Jobs was looking at developments in a number of key areas. Hard disks were becoming smaller, cheaper and had higher capacity. Digital music had been widely available in the form of CDs but technology developments meant there was a real possibility of convergence occurring between consumer electronics firms making stereos and computing firms. Apple's launch of the iPod and iTunes was decisive. It opened significant new revenue streams for the firm and introduced a whole new group of customers to their products and services. The momentum gained by this move swept Apple toward unprecedented growth and profits. Just as in surfing, all waves eventually dissipate and Apple has effectively withdrawn the iPod which has been rendered all but obsolete with the convergence of mobile telephone handsets and MP3 players. However, trend-driven strategists tend to manage the ebb and flow of technological, business model and regulatory change. Apple has recently announced a move into music streaming and wearable technology in the hope of catching the next wave of change. Steve Jobs approached strategy in a way that foregrounded change and he is seen as being largely responsible for the spectacular results achieved by Apple. It is, of course, worth noting that early signals are often hard to read. Throughout the book are salutary tales of strategists who have guessed wrong, leading their organizations to over-invest or come to market too early.

A third strategy style relates to those who pay attention to the internal skills, resources and capabilities of their organization. **Resource-driven strategists** look for opportunities to deploy existing skills and know how. Operating with a mind-set that argues "if we build it, they will come" resource-driven strategists tend to focus efforts on the progressive refinement of capability. Tennis champion Andre Agassi succeeded in an era where technology and coaching meant that the serve had become the dominant weapon in men's singles match play. Agassi himself was not a powerful server. From a young age he trained daily, returning hundreds of balls fired at him from a 'robot' on a court at their home. Both the court and the robot were built by his father. The result, over years of practice, was that Agassi developed a superb service return. Hand-eye coordination, nimble footwork and supreme endurance meant that he could return the powerful serves of tall, athletic players such as Pete Sampras and Boris Becker. This is a classic case of turning disadvantage to advantage. Powerful opponents serving at speeds of around 130 miles per hour would win most points either direct from their serve or quickly thereafter when opponents struggled to make an effective return. However, faced with a return which was deep, accurate and low, the server would find themselves at a distinct disadvantage as they struggled to reset their feet in order to strike the ball cleanly. In organizational terms, Honda is often quoted as an example of a firm with a clear capability in engine technology. Whether the eventual product is a lawnmower, an outboard motor, a car or a motorbike, there are key aspects of Honda's skill set which are being deployed and developed. Lessons learnt from one context are fed back into other contexts and strategy is in some ways the continuing search for opportunities to exploit core skills. It is no accident that Honda has run an advertising campaign that claims "everything we do goes into everything we do." Resource-driven strategists tend to have a patient approach where skills developed over an extended period are difficult to imitate and produce sustainable advantages. The downside can be that it is relatively difficult to adapt a deeply embedded skill set when a major disruption occurs as a result of technological, regulatory or other changes.

There is no definitive or correct way to build strategy. Rather, individual strategists have default preferences and frame strategy work to foreground some issues whilst overlooking others. A sensible starting point is to recognize the strengths and limitations of your own biases in relation to strategy.

> Discover your strategy style: Knowing your own preferences can help you become a more effective strategist. There is a free app available at www.stridesite.com

Why is it difficult to build strategy?

For commercial organizations, strategy requires the answer to some simple questions: which products or services should we offer? Which kinds of customer(s) are we looking to build a relationship with? Who might we therefore compete with, and what will be the basis of that competition? Conceptualising as a set of answers to such questions, strategy seems a rather simple affair. If however, it were this simple, few organizations would fail. Since public, private and charitable organizations do fail, it is clear that difficulties must arise in a number of ways.

First, those inside the organization may not address these simple questions. This could be an oversight, a lack of skill or a perceived lack of need. Some businesses, some of the time, hit upon a happy coincidence of circumstance such that they are successful without trying or even in spite of their own efforts. However, as we shall see, such circumstances rarely last. A second difficulty may be that the tools and techniques of analysis are not adequate for the job at hand. As business schools professionalised in the 1960s, strategy became a key topic area and scholars such as Kenneth Andrews (1971) developed tools like SWOT analysis to help managers analyse the strategy of organizations of the time. Many of the commonly used strategy tools such as SWOT, five forces and strategic group analysis emerged over 30 years ago and the competitive environment has changed almost beyond recognition, with revolutions taking place in terms of internationalization, deregulation, innovation and communications. Tools developed for a context where the competitive environment was relatively stable and simple can seem somewhat inadequate when whole industries collide in ways which are difficult to predict and where the pace of change can seem relentless, to the extent that Richard D'Aveni describes the process as *hypercompetition* (1994).

A third reason for the relative failure of strategy is the concept of strategic drift. Here, strategists typically have developed a clear answer to the basic questions set out above, at least at one point in time. Through a gradual process, attention tends to migrate from making these fundamental decisions to coordinating the myriad set of activities involved in delivering the strategy. Organizations can become inward looking, such that the dominant conversation is "are we delivering the strategy as agreed?" rather than the more important question "are we delivering the right strategy?" In the short term, little tends to have changed in the operating environment and delivering the original strategy remains a valid purpose. Over time, gradual changes in the environment can gather pace, previously separate trends may begin to reinforce each other to drive the pace of change faster still and the net result can be a mismatch between the strategy as agreed and the strategy that is required by the current circumstance. Because of this paucity of attention, small signals of change in the external environment can be overlooked and by the time the need for change is fully recognised a dramatic strategic adjustment is needed. This sense of losing touch with customers, competitors or technologies is present in many accounts of organizational failure. From the outside looking in, it can seem odd that no-one noticed but from within the situation those involved explain away key issues without realising their significance at the time. Hence, it is observed that "the signs of an impending crisis are often hidden in plain sight" (MacIntosh and MacLean, 2015, p. 56).

A fourth reason for difficulties with strategy can result from what the economist, John Kay, terms *obliquity* (2011). Kay argues that complex goals are often best approached indirectly. Ask someone who is explicitly trying to be happy whether they are in fact happy and the answer is often 'no'. However, ask someone engaged in something about which they are passionate such as a hobby or cause, and they may well answer 'yes'. Experience suggests that powerful statements of organizational intent are set within some deeper sense of purpose which captures the 'why' of the organization. Articulating the purpose behind your own organization's very existence can be a helpful first step in shaping a statement of intent. For some, the underlying purpose can be to win at all costs or to maximize profits. For others it can be a desire to make a difference in the world and in so doing, inadvertently almost, the organization makes a profit. Sceptics might point to the functional use of doing the latter in order to achieve the former. Ryanair periodically presents itself as a "no fares" airline emphasizing its role in stimulating economic development and tourism for regional airports. However, it is also a highly profitable organization which has reported profits of hundreds of millions of Euros. Perhaps the most heavily cited strategy scholar is Harvard Business School's Michael Porter. His recent interest in the development of shared value is driven by the same observation that a focus on short term financial outcomes produces poorer results in the longer term (Porter and Kramer, 2011).

Finally, a fifth reason that it can be difficult to develop strategy relates to the perceived sense of being too busy running the current organization to have the time to stop and think about future direction. When the late Stephen Covey (2005) suggested that there were key habits that underpinned successful leadership, one of his pieces of advice was that if he had a fixed amount of time in which to saw down a tree, he would spend a significant period of time ensuring that the sharpening the saw before starting with the tree itself. What this advice teases out is the relationship between a sense of busyness and business sense. The latter centres on what is required to make the organization effective at the delivery of its intended purpose or 'core business'. The former can often relate to the sense of being frantically busy in the day to day conduct of business. If however, you are busy with a series of tasks it is vital to ask whether these tasks are simply a reflection of accumulated habits rather than the best way of approaching the task. It could be that you are sawing with all your might but using a blunt saw. More significantly, it could be that there is no longer a need to cut down trees. Perhaps the most important signifier of strategic behavior is the conscious choice of which things to stop doing. Habit is no excuse and the one of the most valuable weapons in the strategist's armoury is the simple phrase 'no'.

Strategy as fantasy

Scholars differ in their conceptualization of strategy. Historically, many have viewed strategy as an artefact such as a document, report or plan. Others argue that this narrow view of strategy overlooks the very process of strategizing (see Johnson et al., 2003). In many respects both views are in danger of overlooking the influence of individual perceptions of strategy. If strategies are developed by strategists, it is important to understand the world as viewed from the perspective of those individuals or groups responsible for crafting strategy. One recent contribution to the research literature on strategy takes seriously the idea that strategy itself can be viewed as socially constructed. From the perspective of strategy as fantasy, it matters little whether observations about markets, competitors, collaborators, customers or colleagues are 'true' since even misinformation can be real in its effect.

MacIntosh and Beech (2011) report on in-depth studies of two different organizational contexts, one a private organization, the other a large public organization. In both contexts, senior figures based strategic decisions on a mixture of factual analysis and their interpretations of the motives of others. In one example, a large corporate organization undertook the acquisition of a series of smaller, independent firms as part of a major strategic move into a new area of business. Managers from the corporate headquarters of the parent company were clear that they did not really understand the dynamics of the industry in which their newly acquired firms operated. Further, they were clear that they did not want to supress the creative, entrepreneurial spirit of the management teams within each of the acquired businesses. One director from the parent company commented "they [the management teams on the acquired businesses] know the customers and the markets, they're the ones best placed to figure this [the future strategy] out." In parallel, the management teams of each of the acquired businesses met up periodically trying to figure out how they would fit within the corporate structure that they had joined. Their view was that the parent company clearly had a hidden agenda in making the acquisitions and that this master plan would shortly be revealed to them. One Managing Director from one of the acquired businesses commented "they [the corporate HQ staff] obviously have some view of how all of this is going to work and I expect that we don't all feature in that future. Bits of each acquired business will be kept and other bits ditched. I'm not sure where that leaves us. We're paralysed until they let us in on the next step."

The two quotes detailed are from interviews undertaken separately but within weeks of each other. What is clear is that each group or individual is dealing with a fantasised view of what the other is thinking or doing. The acquiring parent company had no masterplan beyond allowing talented people to continue doing what they had always done and looking for opportunities to build scale, scope and synergy as this happened. There was therefore no specific plan to hide or reveal. The management teams of the acquired companies were convinced that there was a concrete plan which would eventually be revealed and therefore began to avoid any major decisions until the supposed plan was communicated to them. The net result was that both groups grew increasingly frustrated with each other and no major decisions were taken for an extended period of time. From the outside looking in, it is clear that neither group was dealing with a complete picture of the situation yet both acted on the basis of a partial, fantasised and uncorroborated view of their situation.

The social meaning created by individuals engaged in strategy work can be real in its effect even if it is not founded in any verifiable 'truth.' For this reason, strategy development tends to develop in a cyclical fashion where strategists begin with discussion of possible and desirable future states. This tends to generate a carefully crafted strategic plan (MacIntosh and MacLean, 2015 suggest that this plan comprises 12 key elements). When this plan encounters the harsh reality of delivery there are often difficulties which mean that many plans are abandoned. The research literature suggests failure rates for formal strategic plans that can be as high as eighty percent. However, the very process of struggling to implement the agreed plan drives a process of experimentation and improvisation where strategists begin to develop a view of plausible strategic moves. They make sense of these moves in relation to both historic and current circumstances before moving again to think about possible future states, how attainable these might be and what form of plan might be effective in delivering this desired future to the organization. Figure 2.1 sets out the key stages of the strategist's journey. The ways in which individuals and groups make sense of current circumstances, recent events and possible future states is driven largely by the processes of sensemaking (Weick, 1995) and social construction (Berger and Luckman, 1967).

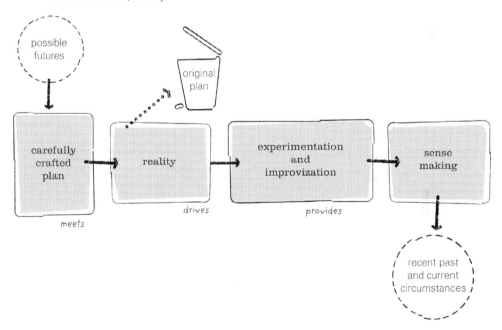

Figure 2.1: The Social Construction of Strategy (adapted from MacIntosh and MacLean, 2015)

References

Andrews, K. R. (1971). *The Concept of Corporate Strategy*, Homewood Irwin.

Berger, P. & Luckman, T. (1967). *The Social Construction of Reality*, New York, Doubleday.

Covey, S. R. (2005) *The Seven Habits of Highly Effective People*, London: Simon and Schuster

D'aveni, R. (1994) *Hypercompetition*, New York, Free Press.

DiMaggio, P. J., & Powell, W. W. (1983). The Iron cage revisited: Institutional isomorphism and collective rationality in organizational fields. *American Sociological Review*, **48**: 147-160.

Gladwell, M. (2013) *David and Goliath: underdogs, misfits and the art of battling giants*, London: Allen Lane

Johnson, G., Melin, L. & Whittington, R. (2003). Micro strategy and strategizing: Towards an activity-based view. *Journal of Management Studies*, **40**, 3-22.

Kay, J. (2011). *Obliquity: why our goals are best achieved indirectly*, London, Profile Books.

MacIntosh, R. & Beech, N. (2011). Strategy, strategists and fantasy: a dialogic constructionist perspective. *Accounting, Auditing & Accountability Journal*, **24**, 15-37.

MacIntosh, R. and MacLean, D. (2015) *Strategic Management: strategists at work*, London: Palgrave

Management Today (2012). The rise and rise of Amazon.com. *Management Today* [Online].

Porter, M. E. & Kramer, M. R. (2011). Creating shared value. *Harvard Business Review*, **89,** 62-77.

Weick, K. E. (1995). *Sensemaking in organizations*, Thousand Oaks: CA, SAGE.

3 Marketing and Consumer Behaviour

Gillian Hogg, Keith Gori & Wendy Hisbent

Exercise 1: Before reading this chapter take a few minutes to write down some notes detailing your existing understanding of what marketing is and why it is important for management: What does marketing do and how? What processes are involved? How important is it to business or organisational success?

In today's highly complex market economy an understanding of marketing is essential for businesses to succeed. Long-term business success is dependent on meeting consumer wants and needs using the company's resources through offerings which create value for customers. Those businesses which do not create value for their customers cannot expect to achieve long-term success. Such is the scale of the topic several introductory management textbooks avoid engaging with it and there are a vast number of large textbooks devoted to the discipline alone. This chapter will attempt to briefly explain why marketing is important and how its core features have developed, before outlining the central relationship between producer and consumer and the importance of the exchange of value that occurs between them. It is this exchange that marketers aim to deliver and enhance in their work.

What is 'marketing'?

Trying to define marketing simply is a difficult task. Despite this, introductory chapters or text-books on marketing often begin from such a definition and aim to build up an explanation of this vast field from there. Wide debates have taken place in the marketing field over attempts to create an accepted definition for scholarly use (Mick, 2007; Sheth & Uslay, 2007; Zinkhan & Williams, 2007).

Three such definitions are provided below to highlight the inconsistencies in attempts to define marketing.

■ The action or business of promoting and selling products or services, including market research and advertising. (Oxford Dictionaries, 2015).

■ The process by which companies create value for customers and build strong customer relationships to capture value from customers in return. (Kotler, Armstrong, Harris, & Piercy, 2013, p. 5)

■ Marketing is the activity, set of institutions, and processes for creating, communicating, delivering, and exchanging offerings that have value for customers, clients, partners, and society at large. (American Marketing Association, 2013).

As the three definitions above highlight there is no accepted definition of marketing; rather definitions found across dictionaries, scholarly publications and marketing association materials are vague, contradictory, and sometimes both. To compound this problem, people not involved in studying or practicing marketing often characterise it merely by the elements which are most commonly encountered in public: sales and advertising (Kotler et al., 2013). It is important at the outset of this introductory chapter then, to try and better understand what it is we are referring to when we discuss marketing and its related concepts. Actually, trying to attempt to offer a concise yet informative definition is not overly helpful; rather we ought to consider how and why marketing develops.

■ Where did marketing come from?

Clearly marketing is related to trade and therefore we can safely assume that, though the term marketing is likely a relatively new label, it has a long history. Scholars have attempted to trace its starting-point with some arguing that marketing is as old as trade itself and has important roots in ancient civilisations such as Mesopotamia (Demirdjian, 2005) and others suggesting the development of a systematic model of activities common within contemporary marketing began in Greek and Roman antiquity (Shaw, 2015). It is clear however that the activities now understood under the rubric of marketing have developed over a long period of time. The practice of marketing is best understood as an effort to increase the efficiency of trade, and as accompanying the lengthy development of the socio-economic conditions in which we now live.

For example, Shaw (1995) argued that much of the debate across marketing, economics and sociology surrounding the integration of the economy into society can be found in the work of Plato, for whom states came into existence in order to fulfil the varied needs of citizens: food, shelter, clothing and so forth. Though he obviously did not use the modern marketing vernacular,

Plato outlined the foundations of a market system. At one point each person would have laboured to produce what was required to fulfil each of these needs and produced food, shelter and clothing. Plato observes however, that in time it becomes clear that some are suited to one role more than another and can produce much more by focussing on this area, for example producing food, whereas someone else is more skilled in building structures to provide shelter. Due to the comparative advantages between people a division of labour occurs in which people commit all their time and effort to one trade. In such a system each person produces a surplus (efficiency in production) of one or a small number of outputs and must trade their surplus with other types of producers in order to satisfy all of their needs. So, for example a farmer trades his surplus food with a carpenter in order to attain shelter and with a cloth maker to attain clothing. In this scenario all traders are required to meet other traders in order to satisfy all their needs but the division of labour separates them and makes trade onerous. If all traders are able to meet in the same location at the same time these exchanges are made much more efficient (market exchange) though they must still cease production in order to sell reducing efficiency (opportunity cost). In time a system, which allows for producers to continue producing whilst their products are sold, exists through the development of specialist sellers, further increasing efficiency in exchange.

In summary, Plato has shown that *comparative advantage* leads to a *division of labour* resulting in *efficiency in production*. But the division of labour also results in a separation of producers and consumer. To bridge this gap *market exchange* is required. The exchange process requires work, work takes time, and time has an *opportunity cost*. Hence, marketing institutions emerge because of increased *efficiency in exchange*. (Shaw, 1983, p. 147)

Shaw (2015) argues that during antiquity trade underwent its greatest development in its long history – from the Stone Age to modernity – as a result of the introduction of three factors which underpin the earliest marketing systems: centralised marketplaces, sedentary retailing, and coined money. Marketplaces matched supply with demand, sedentary retailers allowed for efficient exchange for buyers and sellers, and coined money provided a commonly accepted store of value and means of payment. Though this development is of such importance, it was largely taken for granted until the turn of the twentieth century when it became a field of academic study. Now marketing is a central part of both business education and research (with most business or management schools containing marketing courses or departments), and of business practice (with most companies devoting considerable time and resources to the practice). In the short review above of how the basic market systems developed we can see a central theme, the exchange between buyer and seller. Though this is traditionally viewed in terms of a business transaction – the processes that allow for exchange of goods and services for payment – there are also arguments that favour consideration of marketing in broader terms as the processes which allow for any exchange of value between two parties, be they business exchanges or social exchanges. This debate was at its height in the 1960s and 1970s with those that favoured the 'broadening' side seemingly having been more successful (Kotler, 1972, 2005). It is along the lines of the broadened conception of marketing that most marketing education is delivered and in which this chapter will now proceed. This jump ignores a huge period in the development of trade which has seen the world become extremely interconnected, and seen the development of mass production and consumption, to cite only two developments. This is not only a huge jump in the history of trade but also in the history of marketing, the entirety of which can of course not be covered in this chapter, though both marketing history and the history of marketing thought have received considerable scholarly attention in recent years (see Jones & Tadajewski, 2016; Shaw & Jones, 2005).

Understanding marketing

The section above highlights that although marketing systems developed over several millennia, interest in marketing as a discipline really only took hold in the twentieth century. As a result it is often argued that marketing developed over this short period, with particular emphasis on periods in which marketing focussed on production, followed by a focus on sales, before evolving into a focus on marketing itself (Keith, 1960), though this periodization has been widely questioned (Fullerton, 1988; Hollander, Rassuli, Jones, & Dix, 2005). Others argue that this evolution continued into the development of a relationship marketing era more focussed on developing long-term relationships with customers and continuing business (Dibb, Simkin, Pride, & Ferrell, 2001) and onto the development of a *marketing orientation*. A marketing orientation is defined as a business model that focuses on delivering products designed according to customer desires, needs, and requirements, in addition to product functionality and production efficiency (Kohli & Jaworski, 1990).

This shift from marketing which looked to create the 'correct" products in an efficient manner allowing for profitable exchange, to a system in which a holistic orientation based around providing value, is perhaps best illustrated through the evolution of the 'marketing mix' concept which is often used to introduce new students to marketing. This has evolved to embrace the more service-based elements of a business organisation, following arguments that all companies are service-based regardless of their product(s) (Kotler et al., 2009).

■ The marketing mix

As mentioned above many people consider marketing to be merely the act of selling a product or its promotion to customers. Actually it is often now considered to involve the entire lifecycle of a product from its planning, design and creation, through promotion and sales, and includes after sale services such as returns, replacement and repair. In order to cover this larger perspective, marketing is most often introduced to students through the concept of the marketing mix developed in the 1950s and 1960s by Borden (1964). He argued that marketers used a mix of elements in order to best facilitate increased trade. These elements were organised into four groups organised according to their type – *The 4 Ps*: product, price, place and promotion – by McCarthy (1960). Various scholars have adapted this approach over the decades to include more service oriented tools, with the product group updated to include services and the addition of three further groups: people, process, and physical evidence (Magrath, 1986). Figure 3.1 shows the tools with which each of the seven 'P' group is addressed and the core concerns of the seven outlined in the Table 3.1.

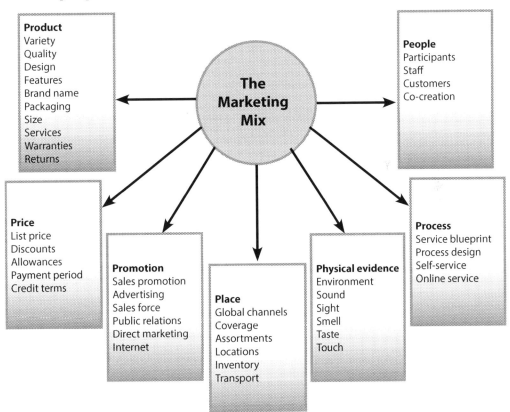

Figure 3.1: The 7Ps components of the marketing mix (adapted from Kotler et al, 2009).

Product	Production of a need-satisfying offering – either goods or services
Price	The cost accepted for sale of the offering
Place	Considerations of channels through which the offering is made available
Promotion	Communication to target customers of the availability & merits of the offering
People	The participants involved in the delivery of the offering
Process	The planning and systems which underpin the delivery of the offering
Physical evidence	The special features of the space in which the offering is provided

Table 3.1: Outline of the 7Ps of Marketing

Exercise 2: Think of a company you admire or engage with quite regularly: Which features of the Marketing Mix do you think they are good at and which could they improve on?

Understanding consumers and value

Key to marketing is an understanding of consumers, be they individuals or organisations. We all consume, and therefore understanding how and why consumers make choices, what motivates these decisions and how they are implemented is central to marketing. Without consumers exercising choice, there would no need for modern marketing. The study of consumer behaviour is therefore central to marketing; it guides our understanding of how consumers will react to a new product offering, a new advertising campaign, or the introduction, or withdrawal, of a service. It informs the design of buildings such as shopping centres and restaurants and more recently internet sites. Marketing helps explain the rise of Facebook; the decline of products such as VHS recorders, services such as video rental shops, and brands such as Blockbuster; or even the outcome of elections. There is almost no part of twenty-first century life that does not rely on an understanding of consumers. Central to marketing, and central to understanding consumers, is an understanding of *value*.

Value is what is received in exchange for what is given. In an exchange relationship a consumer receives something of value in return for giving something of value. In its simplest terms that can be money, the consumer wants to buy a bar of chocolate and gives money in exchange. This does not need to be money however; it could be a vote, for example. The key to an exchange relationship is that both parties receive something of value. Understanding how consumers, in different circumstances, define value and what they are prepared to give in exchange is central to understanding consumer behaviour. Good marketing starts from an understanding of what consumers value (marketing research and consumer behaviour), the development of goods and services that will deliver that value (product development), the communication of that value (advertising, branding) and the delivery of that value via retailers, internet etc (customer relationship management). We must recognise however that not all consumers are the same and they do not all value the same things.

Consumers have different resources at their disposal. The main resources that impact on consumption decisions are temporal (how much time they have available), cognitive (how much mental effort that can or are willing to put into the decision), economic (how much money they have) and emotional (how much they care about the decision). If we take the example of the purchase of a new laptop, some consumers will be interested in the technology and are willing to spend time and effort considering features, processors, etc and are willing to pay more for the laptop that they think will deliver greater value to them. Others may simply want a laptop that connects to the internet and can be used for simple tasks. They will therefore not invest much time or effort in comparing alternatives. Added to this is the way in which consumers interact with products that they perceive reflect their identity and choose products, brands or service providers that they feel reflect this identity, so for example they may decide to buy an Apple laptop, because they associate this brand with a particular identity. How consumers express their identity through the goods and services they buy is an important part of understanding consumers.

We also need to consider how consumers reflect their personal *values* in their consumption decisions, choosing to buy – or not buy – goods or services from organisations that fit with their own principles or beliefs. So some consumers will not purchase clothing that they believe was not produced to their ethical standards, will choose a washing up liquid that they believe does not damage the environment or will only buy meat that has been slaughtered in line with their religious beliefs. The relationship between *value* and *values* is complex as individuals are not necessarily consistent in their views and will use different criteria in different circumstances. This is the basis of segmentation in marketing, how consumers either as groups or individuals make choices.

In general however we can assume that to make consumption decisions, consumers have three requirements (Zeithaml, 1981):

■ Information about the alternatives available

■ Criteria on which to evaluate the alternatives

■ Motivation to make a choice

The economic view maintains that consumers have advanced computational abilities that allow them to make informed decisions regarding consumption preferences based on the capitalization of utilitarian attributes, and are subsequently highly rational decision makers who navigate the consumption process with precision. Orthodox economic theories suggests consumers are able to navigate choice by processing information based on functional attributes and ordering preference – e.g., if a consumer has a choice of the leading sportswear brand and four alternative brands they will be able to weigh up the functional attributes of those brands, order them by preference based on the information gathered and make a decision based on the identified attributes. We know however, that the cognitive process relating to consumption is not merely one of perception, preference and process rationality (McFadden, 1999). Human beings cannot process information in a perfect computational form when making choices, so we need to consider how they acquire information, what choice criteria they use and what motivates them.

When a consumer needs information the first source is internal – memory, what did I buy last time and was I happy with the choice? Naturally this is a highly credible source of information and is very difficult for the marketer to influence. It is however essential for the marketer to do whatever possible to discover, and much of marketing research is based on understanding why consumers liked, or disliked certain products. If memory is deficient, because for example this is a new or unusual purchase, the consumer will search for more information. The easiest information to acquire is word of mouth – the opinions of other people who have purchased that good or service before. Word of mouth information is very powerful as it is regarded as more credible than information provided by marketers. This type of information has undergone a massive transformation in the last 10 years with the rise of internet and social media. 25 years ago if you were unhappy with a purchase you might tell a few people you knew; today everyone is a critic, a reviewer or a commentator and the audience is no longer geographically restricted. Consumers are encouraged to review every purchase – books, restaurants, hotels, washing machines, etc. – and to share this information with potential purchasers using media such as Twitter, Facebook and Trip advisor; every internet site now has a 'reviews' section. Today, faced with a decision to buy a new vacuum cleaner, for example, it is possible to see what hundreds of other consumers have thought of the choice they made, both of the product and the retailer or channel they used. This explosion of word of mouth information is the greatest challenge to traditional marketing methods. Whereas consumers used to rely on marketer produced information and a small circle of previous purchasers, they now have the world to consult.

There are of course problems with this information: not all is as genuine or impartial as consumers think. Evidence has emerged of marketers posting reviews as if they were independent when they are actually not – and even of organisations providing a service of apparently impartial reviews. However, in general consumers find this type of information very powerful and influential when evaluating alternatives.

In addition to the decision-making information, it is also recognized that consumers require motivation. The motivation research of the 1950s concentrated on the symbolic nature of consumption, and attempted to illustrate the reasoning behind choice based on symbolic attributes (Hirschman and Holbrook, 1982). This was a step away from the traditional view that goods were consumed primarily for utilitarian purposes of economic benefit and product value, whereby products were purchased due to their ability to maximize utility. Abbott (1955) contends that "People want products because they want the experience-bringing services which they hope the products will render." (Abbott, 1955, p. 40).

The motivation research of the 1950s was the precursor to the approach that emerged several decades later. Put simply, consumers do not always consume on functional or rational grounds but for emotional, symbolic and experiential reasons – or fantasies, feelings and fun (Hirschman & Holbrook, 1982; Holbrook & Hirschman, 1982). The experiential/symbolic nature of the purchase becomes the dominant decision making tool for the consumer, regardless of the brand's superior or inferior utilitarian value. However, a study conducted by Bhat and Reddy (1998) demonstrates that consumers are willing and able to make choices based on both utilitarian/cognitive and symbolic/experiential aspects; the sportswear brand, Nike, was construed by consumers taking part in the study as functional, prestigious, and expressive.

This chapter has made reference to 'consumer wants and needs' several times thus far and so it is perhaps worth exploring what we mean by this a little further. As highlighted above Plato argued that a state comes into existence because of need to fulfil human needs, and Shaw (2015) outlines the role of efficiency in this fulfilment in the development of a marketing system. The most fundamental element underlying marketing remains to this day the provision of basic human needs through a market economy. These include those demands alluded to by Plato: food, clothing and shelter but according to Kotler et al (2009) include the social human need for belonging and affection, and the individual human need for knowledge and self-expression. Wants are different to needs in that they are human needs shaped by the culture in which an individual exists and their personal characteristics. Addressing consumer wants therefore means understanding that not only does a consumer want to be able to have shelter and a place to live, but wants that shelter to have a set of accompanying features which differentiate it from other available shelter; a consumer does not want any house but wants their perfect home, with their view of perfection shaped by individual taste and circumstance and the cultural norms and values by which they are surrounded. Of course there are instances in which consumers perhaps do not need something, but want it nonetheless. Marketing succeeds when it either best fills a consumer's needs (and need related wants), creates a product that consumers want without needing, or one which consumers want so much they convince themselves they need. When such needs and wants are facilitated by marketers and backed with consumer buying ability, marketers have successfully created demand for their offerings (Kotler et al, 2009).

Exercise 3: Think about your entire life as a consumer: What has changed in the way you purchase and consume products? What has driven these changes? Can you think how your purchasing practices might change in the years to come?

The relationship between consumers and products is therefore complex and multi-faceted and before drawing any conclusions about marketing in the 21st Century, we need to consider the nature of products, goods, services or the combination that are bundled together to deliver value to the consumer.

Understanding products

As highlighted above, the development of marketing has seen emphasis move from saleable goods to include the provision of services and the service-related aspects of products. A product is a bundle of benefits that the consumer perceives will provide a solution to a problem. The product is the central part of the value exchange between consumer and provider; a good product must deliver value to the consumer and marketing lies at the heart of this. A product is that deliverable 'thing' – goods, services, ideas, policies, experiences – which is exchanged with the consumer for money or some other form of value (Baines, Fill, & Page, 2008). Products which are marketed can be tangible objects which consumers can touch and feel, intangible services or consumer experiences which often combine a combination of the two. They offer value through not only their functionality and it is this added value that marketing seeks to provide and highlight.

In order to deliver value, products must address a problem – an actual one experienced by consumers or one created by marketers. Successful products provide a solution to this problem in a manner which goes further and provides additional value. A number of processes within marketing combine to allow this to be successful and, as highlighted above, this chapter can only begin to touch on some of the core aspects of this. In relation to how a product is understood within the value exchange marketers seek to engage in, the section below details the levels that combine to create a valuable product. These are referred to as three levels of a product, the 'product onion', the augmented product concept and other terms in marketing literature (Baines et al, 2008; Kotler et al, 2013).

- 'Core' product: here the focus is on the central benefit provided whether it be functional, emotional, or both.

- 'Actual' product: this is the physical good or service delivered and which provides an expected benefit and includes features such as durability, design, packaging, and brand name. This is also sometimes referred to as the 'embodied' product.

- 'Augmented' product: including the core and embodied levels along with any factors necessary to support its purchase and use.

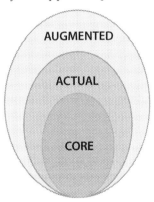

Figure 3.2: The three levels of a product

Using a car as an example, Baines et al (2008) highlight the 'core' level is a combination of a functional means of travel and an emotional or symbolic means of expression; the 'actual' or 'embodied' level covers the variety of styles and features specific to different models of car; and the 'augmented' level includes the purchasing schemes and offers, warranties and guarantees and other services which often accompany the purchase of a car. Through facilitating each of these product levels, value is provided which allows producers to compete with others who produce products with the same central offering; through the additional value provided these products compete in the marketplace.

Exercise 4: Consider a recent product purchase: how does the product levels concept above apply to the product you purchased? Which levels does the product best achieve and how could marketing improve others?

Developing products is an important process in any business, as without them there is no business. The marketing orientation was discussed above, and it is often within this model that businesses develop; however other businesses choose to focus more attention on product development rather than understanding consumer wants and needs. These organisations are driven by a belief that their innovation will drive sales because they will produce offerings clearly better than their competitors. This is referred to as the product concept, but is often seen as a risky strategy and one which can leave companies with an exceptionally well executed offering but no consumer base to which they can sell it, because they have not invested the time in either understanding consumer wants and needs, making their product available or informing customers of its existence. Rather Kotler et al. (2009) outline eight steps which allow for product development within a marketing orientation:

1 **Idea generation**: brainstorming of product ideas (in line with an analysis of consumer needs, wants or problems).

2 **Idea screening**: ideas filtered in order to retain strongest and limit chance of failure

3 **Concept development and testing**: develop specific product concepts and begin market testing through, for example, focus groups to discuss consumer needs and product ideas.

4 **Marketing strategy development**: craft marketing plan which includes target market, production and distribution channels, communications etc. using the marketing mix

5 **Business analysis:** evaluate the marketing plan with cost analysis, sales projections, etc. Products must pass this stage or are dropped.

6 **Product development**: prototype products produced

7 **Market testing:** actual product tested on real consumers

8 **Commercialization or new product launch**: scaling up of product in line with marketing plan according to three essential questions: when, where and how.

It is important to remember, however, that products must deliver value. The consumer must perceive that value and marketing messages explain how the product features will solve their problem. Take for example, the purchase of a washing machine. A washing machine is not a thing of beauty; it provides a service to the consumer by delivering clean clothes. The value the machine delivers is convenience, but it may have some augmentations that particular consumers value, e.g. higher spin speed = less drying time; fast wash = less electricity used. Designing marketing strategy for washing machines is dependent on identifying what the various consumer groups will find of value and ensuring they receive those messages.

There is, however, another layer around the product which is the brand. Branding is a topic which deserves a chapter of its own, but for our purposes brand is a cue, a shortcut that the consumer can use to assist. Branding can be used to imply missing information, you want your washing machine to be reliable and Hotpoint has been a reliable brand in the past; you want it to be eco-friendly and you believe Bosch to be an environmentally conscious brand. The consumer does not know in advance of purchase how reliable a product will be, but brand provides a cue. Branding is particularly important in the age of internet shopping as it replaces physical presence when making choices.

Marketing in the 21st century

The exponential growth of technology creates particular challenges for marketers, some of which have been described already in the chapter. It is however, worth considering some of these challenges for developing marketing strategy.

The time when a market place was physically defined is long gone. Today's markets are international and there is an increasing emphasis in marketing texts on the global nature of the marketplace. Consumers are increasingly well informed, internet information is cheap and the cost of acquiring multiple quotes for goods and services in terms of both money and time has reduced. At one time a marketer would be confident that the effort involved in acquiring information meant consumers were likely to restrict their information search to a few key products in the category. Now they can search hundred at the click of a mouse – and if they don't want to do it themselves there are sites such as GoCompare that will do it for them. In store, smart phones can read barcodes and QR codes for instant price comparisons. This makes the traditional marketing mix, where a marketer could set a price, or design a promotion, challenging.

One impact of digital consumption has been the ability of marketers to collect and aggregate more detailed behavioural data, and, through personalization and data analytics, provide increasingly personalized and adaptive consumption environments. There are excellent examples of how data can be used, dunnhumby Ltd, founded by Edwina Dunn and Clive Humby, turned the information collected through the Tesco club card scheme into market intelligence that helped Tesco become the leading supermarket in the UK. This technology enabled Tesco to record every promotion, cross-reference with possible variables like the weather, other promotions, what else was purchased time of day, etc and develop an understanding of marketing based on customer data that outstripped its rivals. Based on previous purchases and location, Amazon is able to deliver personal offers to consumers on a daily basis. But this comes at a price and there are consumers who find the information stored on them both unwelcome and unsettling.

Another impact of in the internet and social media in general is upon the shared context of consumption. The increased connectivity between consumers, and their ability to collaborate with, and learn from each other, has created virtual communities of shared interest and connected individuals, and places individual consumption in a highly social context. This in turn impacts upon the creation of shared beliefs about products, services and brands, and the development of truly collaborative forms of consumption (Denegri-Knott & Molesworth, 2013). Consumers now Blog, Tweet and Post their likes and dislikes and instantly share their experiences. There is evidence that consumers are more likely to believe the internet than traditional sources of information so, for example, patients will look up their symptoms on the internet before visiting the doctor or check their diagnosis or prescription. This has a fundamental effect on the relationship between doctor and patient, lawyer and client, as the conventional relationships are altered (Laing & Hogg, 2008).

In conclusion, an understanding of marketing is essential for any business. In order to design marketing strategies, marketers need to understand the concept of value and how consumers, either as individuals or organisations perceive value. They then need to design goods and services based on that value, communicate the value to their consumers and deliver what they have promised. This remains constant regardless of the variety of ways in which consumers now interact with products and organisations.

Exercise 5: Take some time to repeat the first in-text exercise from the beginning of this chapter and compare your writing from the beginning of the chapter with that just completed: How much of your original answer do you still stand by? What are the key differences in your answers?

References

Abbott, L. (1955). *Quality and Competition*. New York: Columbia University Press.

American Marketing Association. (2013). Definition of Marketing. Retrieved June 2015, from https://www.ama.org/AboutAMA/Pages/Definition-of-Marketing.aspx

Baines, P., Fill, C. and Page, K. (2008). *Marketing*. Oxford: Oxford University Press.

Bhat, S., and Reddy, S. K. (1998). Symbolic and functional positioning of brands. *Journal of Consumer Marketing*, **15**(1), 32-43.

Borden, N. H. (1964). The Concept of the Marketing Mix. In G. Schwartz (Ed.), *Science in Marketing*. New York: John Wiley.

Demirdjian, Z. S. A. (2005). *The Rise and Fall of Marketing in Mesopotamia: A Conundrum in the Cradle of Civilization*. Paper presented at the The Future of Marketing's Past: Proceedings of the 17th Conference on Historical Analysis and Research in Marketing, Long Beach, CA.

Denegri-Knott, J. and Molesworth, M. (2013). Redistributed consumer desire in digital virtual worlds of consumption. *Journal of Marketing Management*, **29**(13-14), 1561-1579.

Dibb, S., Simkin, L., Pride, W. M. and Ferrell, O. C. (2001). *Marketing: Concepts and Strategies*. Boston, MA: Houghton Mifflin Company.

Fullerton, R. A. (1988). How Modern is Modern Marketing? Marketing's evolution and the myth of the "production era". *Journal of Marketing*, **52**(1), 108-125.

Hirschman, E. C. and Holbrook, M. B. (1982). Hedonic consumption: Emerging concepts, methods and propositions. *The Journal of Marketing*, **46**(3), 92-101.

Holbrook, M. and Hirschman, E. (1982). The experiential aspects of consumption: consumer fantasies, feelings and fun. *Journal of Consumer Research*, **9**(2), 132-140.

Hollander, S. C., Rassuli, K. M., Jones, D. G. B. and Dix, L. F. (2005). Periodization in Marketing History. *Journal of Macromarketing*, **25**(1), 32-41.

Jones, D. G. B. and Tadajewski, M. (Eds.). (2016). *The Routledge Companion to Marketing History*. New York: Routledge.

Keith, R. J. (1960). The Marketing Revolution. *Journal of Marketing*, **24**(3), 35-38.

Kohli, A. K. and Jaworski, B. J. (1990). Market Orientation: The Construct, Research Propositions, and Managerial Implications. *Journal of Marketing*, **54**(2), 1-18.

Kotler, P. (1972). A Generic Concept of Marketing. *Journal of Marketing*, **36**(2), 46-54.

Kotler, P. (2005). The Role Played by the Broadening of Marketing Movement in the History of Marketing Thought. *Journal of Public Policy & Marketing*, **24**(1), 114-116.

Kotler, P., Armstrong, G., Harris, L. C. and Piercy, N. (2013). *Principles of Marketing* (Sixth ed.). Harlow, Essex: Pearson Education Limited.

Kotler, P., Keller, K. L., Brady, M., Goodman, M. and Handsen, T. (2009). *Marketing Management*. Essex: Pearson Educational Limited.

Laing, A. and Hogg, G. (2008). Re-conceptualising the professional service encounter: information empowered consumers and service relationships. *Journal of Customer Behaviour*, **7**(4), 333-346.

Magrath, A. J. (1986). When marketing services, 4Ps are not enough. *Business Horizons*, **29**(3), 44-50.

McCarthy, J. E. (1960). *Basic Marketing: A Managerial Approach*. Homewood, IL: Richard D. Irwin.

McFadden, D. (1999). Rationality for economists? *Journal of Risk and Uncertainty*, **19**(1-3), 73-105.

Mick, D. G. (2007). The end(s) of marketing and the neglect of moral responsibility by the American Marketing Association. *Journal of Public Policy & Marketing*, **26**(2), 289-292.

Oxford Dictionaries. (2015). 'Marketing', from Oxford Dictionaries website. Retrieved June 2015, from http://www.oxforddictionaries.com/definition/english/marketing

Shaw, E. H. (1983). *Plato and the Socio-Economic Foundations of Marketing: An Historical Analysis in the Development of Macro-marketing Thought*. Paper presented at the First North American Workshop on Historical Research in Marketing, East Lansing, MI.

Shaw, E. H. (1995). The first dialogue on macromarketing. *Journal of Macromarketing*, **15**(1), 7-20.

Shaw, E. H. (2015). *On the Origins of Marketing Systems*. Paper presented at the Crossing Boundaries, Spanning Borders: Voyages Around Marketing's Past: Proceedings of the 17th Conference on Historical Analysis and Research in Marketing, Long Beach, CA.

Shaw, E. H. and Jones, D. G. B. (2005). A history of schools of marketing thought. *Marketing Theory*, **5**(3), 239-281.

Sheth, J. N. and Uslay, C. (2007). Implications of the revised definition of marketing: from exchange to value creation. *Journal of Public Policy & Marketing*, **26**(2), 302-307.

Zeithaml, V. A. (1981). How consumer evaluation processes differ between goods and services. In J. Donnelly & W. George (Eds.), *Marketing of Services* (pp. 25-32). Chicago: American Marketing.

Zinkhan, G. M. and Williams, B. C. (2007). The new American Marketing Association definition of marketing: An alternative assessment. *Journal of Public Policy & Marketing*, **26**(2), 284-288.

Exemplar paper

Laing, A. & Hogg, G. (2008) Re-conceptualising the professional service encounter: information empowered consumers and service relationships. *Journal of Customer Behaviour*, **7**(4), 333-346.

4 Operations and Performance Management

Umit Bititci and Ihssan Jwijati

When global firms launch new products, a complex chain of suppliers, raw materials and distribution helps deliver them to customers. It is not uncommon for complex products like Apple's iPhone to sell several million units in over 50 countries within the first few days of launch. Thereafter, there is the challenge of ensuring that supplies are replenished and customer demands continue to be met. Ensuring that manufacture, assembly, testing, delivery and support work effectively and efficiently is the realm of the modern operations manager.

Operations management

Operations management is the management discipline that deals with the design and management of products, processes, services and supply chains. It considers the acquisition, development and utilization of resources firms need to deliver the goods and services their customers want. Basically, all organisations, whether they are industrial, manufacturing, service or public sector organisations, have operations. They all have to organise their resources to deliver products and services to their customers on a day-to-day basis.

In a nutshell, operations management is about translating and executing an organisation's objectives, policies and strategies in day-to-day operations and ultimately delivering the performance objectives of the organisation. Therefore, it is important that, before we go in to too much detail on how to manage business operations, we understand how organisations perform. For this reason this chapter provides an overview of the origins and evolution of operations management, explains how businesses (organisations) perform, and discusses how operations management can contribute towards overall organisational performance.

Above we defined operations management as *the management discipline that deals with the design and management of products, processes, services and supply chains. It considers acquisition development and utilisation of resources firms need to deliver the goods and services their customers want.*

If we elaborate on this definition, then operations management is really about products and services and the processes we use to deliver those services to our customers. We also recognise that organisations are not islands; they don't exist themselves. Thus, in managing operations, we are not just coordinating the resources inside the organisation, we are also coordinating resources of organisations outside our own, including: suppliers, suppliers' suppliers, customer and customers' customers, i.e. the supply chain. Here suppliers could be supplying materials, equipment, transport services (e.g. somebody who's taking our products and distributing them to our customers' premises), information and so on.

The second part of this definition also considers acquisition, development and utilisation of resources. So, if you are in the business of making bottled water you have to buy the appropriate equipment, you have to have appropriate equipment to actually make those bottles of water efficiently and effectively. Questions regarding who we buy them from, their specification, how fast they operate, and their reliability, are all important and need to be considered in managing operations.

An important function of operations management is the day-to-day co-ordination and orchestration of the organisational resources (materials, people, equipment, information and knowledge) to efficiently and effectively deliver to its customers the products and services they want, on time, to budget, and to agreed specifications, while at the same time making sure that the organisation is operating within its own budgets, delivering profit and growth objectives to its shareholders.

Background and evolution

Operations management is an ancient discipline. For example the construction of the Great Pyramid of Giza Egypt (2650 BC) and the Great Wall of China (*c.* 700 BC) are all achievement of ancient operations management practices and skills. However, as a distinct field of study operations management had its foundation in the Industrial Revolution. Some would argue that operations management as a discipline gained traction with Henry Ford's Ford Model T which, in 1903, was the first mass produced car in the world. Today, Toyota's production system, the Toyota Production System (TPS), is heralded as the best example of contemporary operations management practices.

The First Industrial Revolution significantly changed almost every aspect of society. In Europe, from about the High Middle Ages (*c*.1300) to the eve of the Industrial Revolution in 1750, almost everyone lived and worked in the countryside. There were some pre-industrial cities like Florence, Salamanca or London that were the hubs of learning, craft production, the beginnings of mechanics and markets. However, it was the evolution in the transportation infrastructure that was to play a large part in the change that followed. For example, in 1285, King Edward II enacted the first legislation, since the departure of the Romans in around 480 A.D., that dealt with the maintenance of roads. By about 1350, some degree of safety having returned to the roads, travel and trade increased. Roads were to improve dramatically again from 1706 with the first turnpike trusts. With the evolution of the roads came the revolution of transportation. In the pre-industrial age manufacture was limited to the small scale artisans and craftsmen, the carpenters, blacksmiths, weavers and tailors. Even today some textiles are still made by pre-industrial processes in village communities in Asia, Africa and South America.

The Industrial Revolution began in Great Britain in about 1750, spread to Western Europe and North America within a few decades and lasted until sometime between 1820 and 1840. The Second Industrial Revolution, often referred to as the Technological Revolution, spanned from the mid-nineteenth century to the First World War; from the introduction of Bessemer steel in the 1850s to the initial electrification of factories, mass production and the introduction of the production line.

Originally, the factories and mass manufacturing severely limited customer choice; producers made the goods and customers bought what was available. This is epitomised by Henry Ford's famous quote "you can have any colour you want as long as it is black," which is often cited to characterise this product-driven economy of the technological revolution. Ford is also heralded as the earliest example of mass production, and was the first recorded use of a moving conveyor belt system, where the worker stood still and the product moved past them.

An overview of the development of operations management, from the time of Ford into the modern management discipline it is today, is given in Figure 4.1. In short, operations management developed as a management discipline as the sophistication of markets developed through the years. When Frederick

Taylor wrote *Principles of Scientific Management* in 1911 (Taylor, 1998), he studied what was happening in the early factories and described it as 'specialisation of labour'. No longer was a skilled craftsman making the whole product. Now there was a fast moving production line with a number of workers organised along the line, in such a way to maximise the throughput (flow of work) on the line. Each person wass specialised in a limited range of operations such as hanging a door; putting the windows in; putting on the door handle and so on.

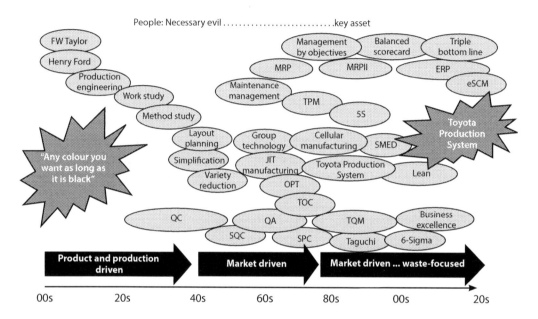

Figure 4.1: Evolution of operations management

Production engineering was borne from this line of thinking, where the key objective was *productivity*. The basic principle behind productivity is to get as much value-added work as possible from a unit of resource. Early production engineering/operations management techniques such as *work study, method study* and *time-motion study* were developed to study how a particular task was carried out in order to eliminate wasted motion or activity so as to improve productivity. However, as markets started to become more sophisticated and the economic power started shifting from the producer to the consumer (i.e. a market driven economy) we have seen the increase in *variety* of products that are being produced. For example, today there are over a thousand variation of a Ford Transit Van depending on the model, engine and other options customers can specify. Consequently we have seen development of techniques such as *layout planning, simplification* and *variety reduction* to deal with this increasing variety and complexity.

Layout planning was concerned with how we design or lay out the factory/ workplace to optimise flow. Whilst production lines are good for producing the same product in high quantity, they are not very efficient in producing high variety of goods in smaller quantities. Techniques such as *group technology* and *cellular manufacturing* were developed to group products with similar manufacturing requirements so that dedicated production cells (mini production lines) could be created to produce these products more efficiently.

Simplification and *variety reduction* were concerned with reducing the complexity of the variety of the products a factory had to produce. This was primarily achieved by reducing the variety of component parts used in different end-products. For example, today the indicator stalks of all new Volkswagen cars are the same. You will also find the same indicator stalk in the VW-owned Seat and Skoda range of cars. This line of thinking led to further development of *Just-In-Time manufacturing* (JIT) and optimised production technology (OPT) that culminate in the *Toyota Production System* (Womack et al., 1990) and today's modern operations management practices including *Lean Management* or *Lean Thinking* (Womack et al., 2010).

With these developments we have also seen more specific disciplines developing within operation management. *Quality management* as a field has emerged out of operations management, initially as *quality control* (QC), where the focus was to find and separate the defective (out of specification) parts from the good ones. This then evolved into *quality assurance* (QA), where the focus became prevention. Here the objective was to design the production system in such a way to prevent defective parts being produced in the first place. The concept of *total quality management* (TQM) extended this line of thinking from the production lines into everything we do in the workplace. In support of these approaches a number of statistical techniques also evolved to help organisations better measure and manage quality. These include *statistical quality control* (SQC) *statistical process control* (SPC), *Taguchi* and *6-sigma* methods.

In a similar manner, *maintenance management* also evolved from *reactive maintenance* through *planned maintenance* to *total preventative maintenance* (TPM). Today the *5S* approach (Sort, Set in order; Shine; Standardize; Sustain) forms the foundations of all good housekeeping and maintenance management practices.

In operations management the increasing accessibility and functionality of information and communication technologies (ICT) has been widely exploited. Manual methods for materials and inventory management gradually evolved in to computer supported systems for *materials requirements planning* (MRP), which then evolved beyond materials to include all other manufacturing resources including: capacity, equipment, tooling, people, transportation – i.e.

manufacturing resources planning (MRPII) – which when integrated with financial planning and analysis capabilities evolved in to *enterprise resource planning* (ERP). Today, ERP systems extend beyond organisational boundaries connecting supply chains (eSCM) and enable *collaborative planning, forecasting and replenishment* (CPFR).

At the outset we stated that ultimately operations management was about delivering the strategic goals and objectives of the organisation. Thus in operations management, we need to interface with strategic management and deploy an organisation's high level goals and objectives into various operational areas. We also need to ensure that these operational areas are designed, configured and operated in such a way as to maximise contributions towards these high level organisational goals and objectives. In other words, *continuous improvement* of these operational areas is a key responsibility of operations management. A number of techniques that emerged from the strategic management field, such as management by objectives, policy deployment and balanced scorecard, are commonly used to deploy high level organisational performance objectives to operations and feedback operational performance information for tactical and strategic planning purposes.

How do companies compete?

■ Understanding competitive factors

The bottom line is that a business exists to create wealth for the shareholders. If it fails to create wealth for the shareholders, then they will take their money and go somewhere else, and the business will cease to exist. Thus any business needs to fulfil its shareholders' expectations. In a business that means the creation of wealth. In a public sector organisation we need to look at stakeholders in a wider sense and fulfil their requirements.

So, a business exists to create wealth for the shareholders. It does so by being competitive in a number of different areas. A business creates wealth for its shareholders by being competitive in its chosen market. It identifies a demand for products or services in a market; it develops products and/or services to meet that need; it generates orders for these products and/or services and fulfils these orders. In doing this it generates positive returns. The following are the typical competitive factors organisations use to compete in its selected markets:

- Quality
- Cost
- Functional performance

- Delivery time
- Delivery reliability
- After sales support
- Styling design
- Image
- Innovation
- Flexibility
- Responsiveness

Various studies conducted over the years suggest that although these competitive factors rarely change, the way customers use them can change significantly in short spaces of time, depending on social, economic and political conditions. Essentially customers use these factors to make two kinds of buying decisions: *Order qualifying* decisions and *Order winning* decisions.

Order qualifiers are the minimum criteria you must deliver to qualify to go on the customers' shopping lists, i.e. for customers to consider buying from you. Order winners are the criteria by which the customers make the actual buying decision. For example, if you are going shopping for a family car and you want a premium brand name, you want reasonable performance and comfort and you want to pay a particular price. Suddenly you have a set of criteria that a number of cars will fulfil. So your shopping list may include BMW, Mercedes, Audi, Lexus, Jaguar, etc. These cars have met your qualifying criteria and now they are on your shopping list. You then go along and take test drives, look at specifications; performance figures, economy figures and so on. You eventually buy one of these cars. In making your decision you may have gone through a complex thinking process, making some trade-offs. You may say *"I have bought the BMW as it gives the best performance, it's a bit more expensive than the Audi but slightly cheaper than the Mercedes, and its fuel economy is better."* So, you use a subset of your order qualifying criteria, or maybe some other factors, to make your eventual buying decision.

Intelligent management of organisational performance requires an understanding of the ways in which customers make buying decisions. Figure 4.2 illustrates the S-curve which describes the competitive dynamics of organisations. The five points represents how a particular company is positioned with respect to its competitors for a particular competitive criterion. Although the x-axis, i.e. competitive criteria, could represent any of the criteria listed in the previous page, we will use 'quality' as an example to illustrate the use of this curve.

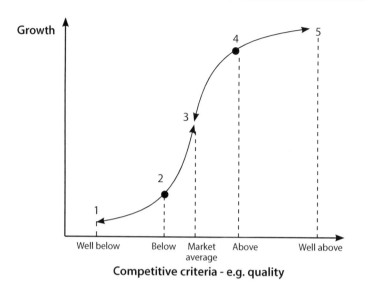

Figure 4.2: Competitive dynamics

What the S-curve says is that if our quality is market average (i.e. the steepest point of the curve – point 3), then any improvement in quality performance, however small, will help to differentiate our product from the competitors' products, giving us larger gains (e.g. increasing sales because we have improved quality). Similarly, a slight deterioration of quality with respect to our competitors will make us less competitive, i.e. losing sales. The shape of the S-curve suggests that the biggest opportunity for improvement is between points 2 and 4, at the steepest point; so small changes here could have significant impact on our competitive position. In contrast, if our quality levels are well below market average (i.e. point 1) we need to achieve significant improvements before we see any benefits. Similarly, beyond point 4 towards point 5 we have differentiated ourselves and we are so much better than our competitors that any more differentiation is only going to give us marginal benefits.

Over the years, as our understanding of how organisations compete improved, organisations became better and more mature in how they manage their competitive positions. For example, the 1970s and 1980s are usually typified as the *just-in-case era*. Organisations were not very good at predicting what may happen in the future and faced with the increasing complexity caused by the market demanding greater levels of variety and functionality they adopted a just-in-case strategy. They had more stock than they needed; they employed more people than they needed; they used more space than they needed; and so on. They needed to have the spare capacity to enable them to respond to the unpredictable changes. During this period most organisations tried to be good at all the competitive criteria previously listed, but failed to excel in any one of these. This dynamic is captured and explained by Treacy and Wiersema (1997) and Porter (2008).

Moving forward into the 1990s, we've seen a big difference in the way organisations managed their operations. There were two drivers behind this change. *First*, the development of information technology enabled better data processing, which in turn enabled better forecasting and planning. *Second*, the worldwide recession of the early 1990s forced organisations to cut waste from their operations. This period is typically characterised as the *lean era*. Here, organisations, fuelled mainly by the *just-in-time-manufacturing philosophy* focused on delivering what the customer wants whilst minimising waste. We started to focus on the processes that delivers value to the customers and anything that did not add value is classified waste. This line of thinking led to: flattening of organisation structures; multiskilling of workforce; delegation of responsibilities further down the organisational hierarchies; investments into flexible automation; adoption of cellular manufacturing systems; creation of flexible workforce and processes; concurrent engineering of products and processes. Consequently, organisations started to focus and differentiate their offerings, in an attempt to position themselves in a unique way in the markets they were trying to serve. Some focused on delivering the best quality, others the best price, the best service and so on. In effect they were focusing on one specific competitive criterion and trying to different themselves by being better than everyone else on that particular criterion whilst maintaining the other order qualifying criteria around market average.

In the 2000s we witnessed another change in the way organisations compete. Whilst the lean era continues, today organisations are becoming more connected, more focused and more dynamic. It is no longer sufficient to be lean; organisations also need to be agile. They need to be good at sensing what is happening in the outside world, identify any significant opportunities and threats, come up with innovative responses and then change faster than their competitors, Today, what makes an organisation stand out from the others is the agility by which it can bundle and configure the competitive criteria in unique and innovative ways offering customers value that they have not experienced before. We can characterise today's competitive environment as the *agile era*.

In summarising how organisations compete, the 1980s was about fat, lazy, just-in-case organisations. The 1990s saw the emergence of the lean organisation focusing on customer needs whilst reducing waste. Today we are in the *agile era*, focusing on unique ways of creating value for our customers and markets. But what is value?

■ Understanding value

The concept of value creation becomes quite fundamental to how we manage our operations. The concept of *value* goes back as far as 400 BC to Socrates and Aristotle from which a number of theoretical frameworks have emerged, such as: exchange theory; utility theory; labour theory; theory of price; theory of supply and demand; theory of value chains and value systems. In this chapter we will refrain from going into these theories. We can define value from a number of perspectives. Figure 4.4 which is based on Livesey's definition of high value manufacturing (Livesey, 2006) effectively illustrates these perspectives.

We have already provided the list of criteria that customers typically use to make buying decisions. However, research suggests that the value we offer to our customers can be classified into a number of value propositions, which effectively bundle these criteria to create unique value offerings, also known as *value propositions*. Originally Treacy and Wiersema (1997) developed the three generic value propositions as:

■ Product leadership – best product

■ Operational excellence – best price

■ Customer intimacy – best solution

	Financial perspective	Strategic perspective	Social perspective
Country perspective	GDP impact	Sustainable employment	
Investor perspective	Return adjusted for risk Long term growth	Adaptibility Sustainability	Ethical action
Employee perspective	Pay, wages Funding of retirement	Life long learning Opportunities for growth	Personal development Social interaction Work-life balance
Customer perspective	Price Cost of ownership	Performance (quality, delivery) Reliability, responsiveness, innovation, flexibility, etc.	Trust Relationship Collaboration

Figure 4.3: Perspectives of value

Others developed this concept further to develop the value matrix, which essentially extends the Treacy and Wiersema's three generic value propositions by differentiation between tangible value drivers (e.g. price, quality, delivery, functionality) and intangible value drivers (e.g. image, feelings, convenience). Figure 4.4 illustrates the resulting six generic value propositions (Martinez and Bititci, 2001).

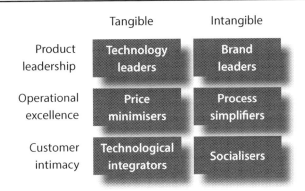

	Tangible	Intangible
Product leadership	Technology leaders	Brand leaders
Operational excellence	Price minimisers	Process simplifiers
Customer intimacy	Technological integrators	Socialisers

Figure 4.4: Six generic value propositions

Product leaders are either technology leaders or brand leaders. Technology leaders invest in research and development, develop next generation of products; they offer technological products never seen before. Brand leaders have marketing or design led products; most of their leadership comes from the image, the quality and the name. They invest significantly in marketing and brand development.

Operational excellence can be about being a price minimiser or being a process simplifier. Price minimisers have the most efficient manufacturing and distribution processes and are able to provide the products/services at the best possible price. Process simplifiers simplify the customer's life and take hassle away. They have customer-facing processes so slick that their customers find it easy to deal with them.

Customer intimacy can be about technological integrators or socialisers. Customer-intimate organisations tend to work with a very few customers and really understand what the customers' businesses are about. Technological integrators are experts in using latest technologies to deliver customer-specific solutions. Socialisers understand their customers' short and long term business needs; they have intimate and trusting relationships with their customers. Usually they are the first port of call for their customers.

These six value propositions can be characterised by using the six pillars of value propositions (Finkelstein et al., 2006). Figures 4.5 and 4.6 illustrate the typical footprint for technology leaders and brand leaders respectively.

Price	Features	Quality	Service & Support	Availability	Reputation
1 Premium	1 Original	1 Excellent	1 Comprehensive	1 Restricted	1 Prestigious
2 Premium/ Competitive	2 Original/ Customized	2 Excellent/ Average	2 Comprehensive/ Standard	2 Restricted/ Selective	2 Prestigious/ Respected
3 Competitive	3 Customized	3 Average	3 Standard	3 Selective	3 Respected
4 Competitive/ Leader	4 Customized/ Basic	4 Average/ Acceptable	4 Standard/ Minimal	4 Selective/ Universal	4 Respected/ Functional
5 Leader	5 Basic	5 Acceptable	5 Minimal	5 Universal	5 Functional

Figure 4.5: Footprint of a typical technology leader using the six pillars.

Price	Features	Quality	Service & Support	Availability	Reputation
1 Premium	1 Original	1 Excellent	1 Comprehensive	1 Restricted	1 Prestigious
2 Premium/ Competitive	2 Original/ Customized	2 Excellent/ Average	2 Comprehensive/ Standard	2 Restricted/ Selective	2 Prestigious/ Respected
3 Competitive	3 Customized	3 Average	3 Standard	3 Selective	3 Respected
4 Competitive/ Leader	4 Customized/ Basic	4 Average/ Acceptable	4 Standard/ Minimal	4 Selective/ Universal	4 Respected/ Functional
5 Leader	5 Basic	5 Acceptable	5 Minimal	5 Universal	5 Functional

Figure 4.6: Footprint of a typical brand leader using the six pillars.

In summarising how the competitive maturity of our organisations developed, we could say that our competitive maturity developed from trying to be good at everything, but failing to deliver on all fronts, to one of differentiation and focus and then bundling of competitive criteria to develop unique customer value propositions. As we move further into the 21st century organisations need to be more innovative in how they bundle and combine their resources to create unique value offerings to their customers and markets. They also need to be able to configure and reconfigure their operations, responding to opportunities and threats faster than their competitors. In short, organisations compete by:

- Understanding what customers value and how they make buying decisions.

- Understanding order winning and order qualifying criteria.

- Configuring value propositions that are attractive to customers and markets.

- Collaborating with complementary enterprises to create value proposition bundles.

- Organising their operations to ensure that these value propositions are delivered to the customers and markets efficiently and effectively.

Measuring and managing performance

■ Measuring performance

The foundations of performance measurement lie in the organizational and management control theories that emerged from general systems theory. Performance is defined as *the efficiency and effectiveness of an action*. At the most fundamental level an action has inputs and outputs. Turning inputs to outputs consumes some resources. Controls set goals, objectives and policies within that govern the action. If the action is effective then the output meets the specification or requirements. If the action is efficient then it uses minimum resources to produce the required out. In short, performance has two dimensions: efficiency and effectiveness as illustrated in Figure 4.7.

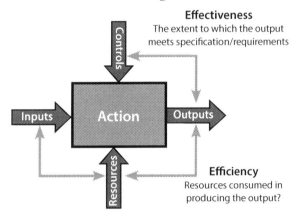

Figure 4.7: Two dimensions of performance: efficiency and effectiveness.

Although it's easy enough to talk about performance as the efficiency and effectiveness of an action, when we try to apply this to an organisation it gets a bit more complicated. Consequently, we've seen the emergence of a number of different performance measurement frameworks and models. In this chapter we do not have the space to cover all these. It is sufficient to say that out of these models and frameworks, the Balanced Scorecard (Kaplan & Norton, 1996) has emerged as the most widely cited and applied framework for managing organisational performance. This is because since its inception in 1996 it has been continuously developed and refined (Kaplan & Norton, 2001, 2006). An interpretation of the Balance Scorecard is illustrated in Figure 4.8.

The Balanced Scorecard defines four perspectives of performance around the central them of strategy – Financial, Customer, Process, and Learning and Growth. It suggests that any organisation should balance its performance measurement and management around these perspectives. The measures contained within each perspective are aligned with both short and long term strategic goals of the organisation as well as informing the evolution of these strategic goals. Essentially, long-term sustainable financial results are a function of: satisfied customers that keep coming back and referring new customers (1) and internal processes that are so efficient that generate over-average returns (2). In turn, satisfied customers are a function of effective processes that deliver repeatable products and services to all customers reliably (3). Here, process excellence is defined as processes that are highly efficient whilst being highly effective.

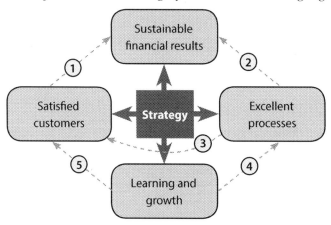

Figure 4.8: Balanced scorecard

The Learning and Growth perspective is all about what we invest in now that will develop our capabilities for the future. For example, investing in education, technology and improvement projects today will make our processes more efficient and/or effective in the future (4). Similarly, investing in new technology and product development initiatives today will serve to make our products and services more attractive to customers in the future (5).

Organising the four perspectives into a hierarchy as illustrated in Figure 4.9 gives us the strategy map, which is a tool used for deploying organisational goals and objectives to processes and growth initiatives. For example, from the bottom layer of Figure 4.9, developing and implementing a better sales and operations planning (S&OP) process will improve plan adherence (an internal process), which in turn will result in improved delivery reliability and reduced customer complaints (two key measures the customers use), which in turn will improve sales.

Today, tools and techniques such as the balanced scorecard and strategy maps represent the state of the art in managing performance of organisations. We take the top level objectives and deploy them through these different perspectives into things that we need to do today. As we do these things we expect, over time, process performance to improve, customer performance to improve and the financial results to improve.

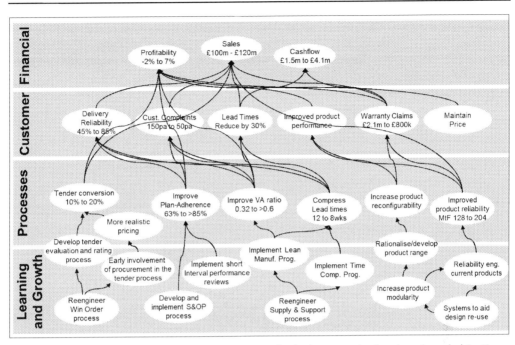

Figure 4.9: Balanced scorecard base strategy maps deploying organisational goals and objectives.

◼ Managing performance

An organisation is defined as a network or group of people coming together for a particular purpose. In organisations people do things. People do things with machines, with other people, with pen and paper, with computers, with raw materials, with information, and so on. When you string what people do end-to-end you get processes. If these processes work well you get good performance. If they don't work well you get bad performance. In short, in organisations people operate processes that deliver good or bad performance. So in managing performance of organisations we cannot forget about the people component, we need to get a balance between managing processes and managing people.

In managing processes, the most important thing about a process is flow. A business process is defined as *a series of continuous or intermittent cross-functional activities connected together for a particular purpose.* They are connected together because work flows through these activities for a purpose, such as to develop a new product; to fulfil a customer order; to develop a business plan; and so on. In measuring and managing performance of these processes we need to measure the efficiency and effectiveness of the work-flow through the process.

The graphs in Figure 4.10 contain three different performance reports. Here the detail is not so important. What is important is that they show three completely different performance dimensions of a process: customer complaints (top-left); recordable accidents (top-right); delivery performance (bottom). It is important to note how they show performance against time, which makes it possible to observe whether performance has been improving or deteriorating over time. It is also important to note the use of annotations that explain the cause of performance problems. For example, in the bottom graph one can see that the delivery problems between weeks 36 and 45 has been due to raw material supply problems.

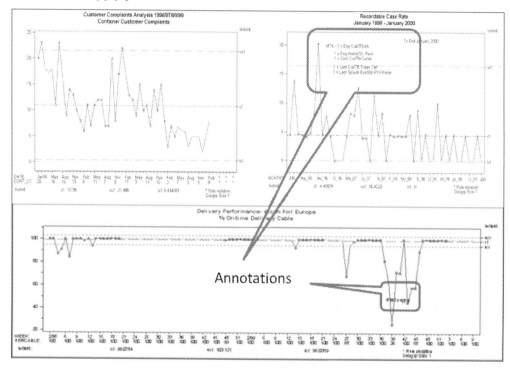

Figure 4.10: Examples of effective performance measures.

In operations management such performance information is commonly used. The important point here is that the information is consistent, easily understood and openly communicated. In today's modern workplaces (factories, offices, call centres, banks and so on) it is commonplace to see similar performance charts on walls and boards. Often people will huddle around them once a day, once a week, depending on the nature of the business, to have a conversation about: what went right; what went wrong; what is the cause; what needs to be done; who is going to do it; what can we learn from this. The real purpose behind such performance measurement approaches is to identify and permanently fix the causes of the problems as well as engaging people in a conversation about the performance of the process.

In managing people, however, many organisations don't use these measures the right way. We end up demotivating and disengaging people from the work and the organisation they are there to do. Take a call centre as an example. In a call centre you will have around eight minutes (or some similar target) to deal with an incoming call from a customer. Many of us may have experienced the situation when we are told *"sorry, sir/madam, the computer systems are down at the moment; can you please phone back in 20 minutes"*. Maybe you waited for 20 minutes on the line and told them what you're phoning for and they said *"oh, sorry, you've come to the wrong department; I'll put you through to the right department"* and you wait another 20 minutes before you talk to someone (sound familiar?). It is quite common that they have simply put you back on the same queue. In the first example, there was probably nothing actually wrong with the computer system but by getting you off the phone they finished the call under a minute. If the operator had spent more than 8 minutes dealing with the last few calls these are just some of the tactics they will use to catch up with their target. It is not necessarily the right thing to do, but it means that they achieve their target.

This is typical of the sort of behaviour you get when people are being managed by a single efficiency focused measure. What you get is people working to measures, even if it means doing the wrong things. There are many other such examples from the healthcare, education, financial and public sectors. The point here is that it is not what we measure but how we use these measures that make people and organisations behave in different ways.

Understanding organisational controls

Management in general, and operations management in particular, is about configuring and controlling organisational resources in such a way to maximise performance. The organisational behaviour literature identifies two kinds of organisational control:

- Technical controls – the type of control exercised through mechanistic and rational management practices, such as: vision statements; plans, policies, procedures, performance measures and targets, performance reviews, and annual development reviews.

- Social controls – the type of control exercised through cultural, behavioural and interpersonal interaction between people, such as: having shared purpose and values, trust, respect, benevolence, transparency and fairness.

These types of controls are not mutually exclusive as illustrated in Figure 4.11. The organisational behaviour literature classifies organisations according to how they deploy these two types of control.

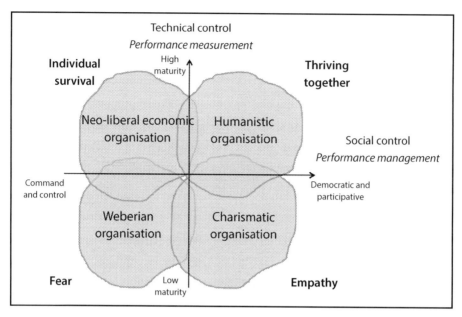

Figure 4.11. Two dimensions of organisational control.

- **Weberian organisations**, where: jobs are narrowly prescribed; work is closely supervised and governed by tight rules and standard procedures; workplace lacks the emotional component; the performance measurement systems are usually not so well developed, with a small group of powerful bureaucratic managers acting as judges following procedures. Quite often fear of discipline and job security drives performance.

- **Charismatic organisations**, where: job enrichment, autonomous work-groups, participation and industrial democracy are the norm; often a semi-divine leader lays down fundamental values, gives the vision, while the followers responded eagerly; the performance measurement systems are usually not so well developed, and a charismatic leader can ignore due process, and makes decisions personally. Employees are usually engaged, they are team players, empowered by the vision. They work over and above the call of duty, regardless of work–life balance. Quite often it is empathy with the purpose and the leader that drives performance.

- **Neo-liberal economic organisations**, where principles of free enterprise are used to drive performance. The performance measurement systems are usually well developed and the senior managers' incentives are closely aligned with shareholders' interests. CEOs and managers are appointed on contracts with very specific performance indicators with challenging targets that are closely monitored. There is usually tough internal competition and internal groups/divisions have to compete with outside providers. Employees are put in a weak position with casual, short term and sometimes zero-hours contracts with minimal commitments. Quite often it is the energy for individual survival and advancement that drives performance.

■ **Humanistic organisation**, where: there are well-developed performance measurement systems aligned with a shared purpose that often emerges from the values and views of the individuals; human relations, job enrichment, autonomy, participative working and industrial democracy are valued; diversity in gender and culture and equality in pay and stakeholder power are encouraged. In such organisations, quite often the driver of performance is growth of the organisation as an entity working towards a common purpose.

When we ask the question – *which one of the above organisations would you like to work in?* – almost everyone chooses the humanistic organisation, with a few also choosing the charismatic organisation. However, the reality is somewhat different and there are differing opinions as to which organisational form is most suitable for which context.

The world we live in is changing rapidly, both socially and economically. We have to deal with increasingly complex and demanding global challenges that include environmental protection, an ageing population, energy shortages, and food scarcity. The future holds challenges that we cannot yet imagine. In the meantime, continuing developments in almost all areas of science and technology are opening new opportunities and providing us with the means for dealing with these challenges. In response to these challenges and opportunities, we are trying to develop a high value-added economy that will be based on leading-edge research, technological development and innovation, built upon knowledge-based innovating sectors, underpinned by a workforce and society that encourages experimentation, change, risk-taking and learning. With this in mind, there is a growing opinion that in order to succeed in the modern society we need to create humanistic organisations using highly developed technical control systems whilst having open, democratic and participative social controls (Bititci, 2015).

Operations management contribution to overall performance

Earlier in this chapter we intimated that operations management is about managing people and processes. In fact, in many organisations the majority of people work for operations doing operational jobs. Consequently, getting the right balance between managing people and managing processes becomes an important consideration for operations management. We need to ensure that operations make a sustainable contribution to overall performance.

So how do operations contribute to overall performance in a sustainable way? At the simplest level, in operations management performance is measured by using two types of measures: customer facing measures and internal process facing measures. These are equivalent to the customer and process perspectives of the Balanced Scorecard. Table 4.1 provides some examples of the commonly used performance measures under these headings.

Table 4.1: Common performance measures used in operations management.

Customer facing measures *How do our customers measure our operational performance?*	**Internal process facing measures** *Are our processes working efficiently and effectively?*
Customer satisfaction Customer Satisfaction Customer Complaints Net promoter score Customer retention rate	**Product development** Time to Market Product development cycle time Design re-use Plan/schedule adherence
Delivery reliability On-time delivery to request On-time delivery to promise On-Time-In-Full Delivery Perfect order fulfilment	**Resource productivity and process flow** Cost of goods sold / ownership Productivity Throughput Value add ratio Change-over time Overall Equipment Effectiveness (OEE) Tact Time
Responsiveness and flexibility Delivery lead-times Turnaround time Response times Fill rates Flexibility	**Planning** Forecast accuracy Schedule adherence Inventory turns/levels Inventory accuracy Supplier performance
External quality Many different measures all quantifying the number or % of defects and failures experienced by the customer.	**Internal quality** Various quality rates First pass yield

Operations management uses the principles, tools and techniques discussed earlier to optimise the performance of operations. Performance measures such as those sited in Table 4.1 are used to maximise its contribution to overall organisational performance. For example:

- Designing and operating efficient and effective administrative and manufacturing processes and using lean management principles will improve the flow of orders and products improving delivery performance and responsiveness, in turn improving customer satisfaction and customer retention, and ultimately sales revenue. Efficient processes will also improve value-added productivity and thus the profitability of the organisation.

- Using appropriate supply chain management techniques such as strategic procurement and collaborative supplier development will increase the reliability of the supply base, which in turn will reduce costs, lead times and response times, further contributing towards growth and productivity objectives.

- Using quality management techniques such as statistical process control and 6-sigma will improve the reliability and repeatability of our processes. Reducing internal and external quality defects increases capacity, reduces costs, increases customer satisfaction, once again making a contribution towards the growth and productivity objectives of the organisation.

In conclusion, operations management is an important management discipline that plays a vital role in the achievement of both short and long term organisational goals and objectives. Although operations management as a discipline is focused on the use of various tools and techniques to measure and manage the performance of organisational processes, the people component remains equally critical.

References

Bititci, U. (2015). *Managing Business Performance: the Science and the Art*, John Wiley & Sons, Inc..

Finkelstein, S., Harvey, C. & Lawton, T., (2006). *Breakout Strategy: Meeting the Challenge of Double-Digit Growth*, McGraw-Hill Professional.

Kaplan, R. S., & Norton, D. P. (1996). *The Balanced Scorecard: Translating strategy into action*. Harvard Business Press.

Kaplan, R. S., & Norton, D. P. (2001). The strategy-focused organization. *Strategy and Leadership*, **29**(3), 41-42.

Kaplan, R. S., & Norton, D. P. (2006). *Alignment: Using the balanced scorecard to create corporate synergies*. Harvard Business Press.

Livesey, F. (2006). *Defining High Value Manufacturing*. CBI.

Martinez, V., & Bititci, U. (2001). The value matrix and its evolution. In EurOMA Conference, Bath, UK, June.

Porter, M. E. (2008). *Competitive Strategy: Techniques for analyzing industries and competitors.* Simon and Schuster.

Taylor, F. W. (1998). *The principles of scientific management.* 1911.

Treacy, M., & Wiersema, F. D. (1997). *The Discipline of Market Leaders: Choose your customers, narrow your focus, dominate your market.* Basic Books.

Womack, J. P., Jones, D. T., & Roos, D. (1990). *Machine that changed the world.* Simon and Schuster.

Womack, J. P., & Jones, D. T. (2010). *Lean Thinking: Banish waste and create wealth in your corporation.* Simon and Schuster.

5 Managing People: Practice and Theory

Abigail Marks and Gavin Maclean

It is often observed that people are an organization's most valuable resource. Without the ingenuity, creativity and willingness of individuals to perform assigned tasks, organizations would not function. Human Resource Management is the formal mechanism that many organisations use to manage and develop the people that they employ. Teamwork is central to the way in which most contemporary organisations deliver their goods and services and an examination of teamwork can help on different approaches to work. Sometimes work can be structured to exploit employees. Throughout the text, key words from the wider field of human resource management are identified in a bold font. The intention is to alert you to the need for independent research to help define the ways in which these terms are used in the literature.

Human resource management

Wilton (2011, p4) describes human resource management (HRM) as

> "the term commonly used to describe all those organisational activities concerned with recruiting and selecting, designing work for, training and developing, appraising and rewarding, directing, motivating and controlling workers. In other words, HRM refers to the framework of philosophies, policies, procedures and practices for the management of the relationship that exists between an employer and worker."

Prior to the 1980s, HRM was a term rarely used in the UK. Earlier writing practices had focused on the personnel department of the organization. Indeed, the Chartered Institute for Personnel and Development (CIPD) still uses that terminology. '**Personnel management**' was used by British companies to denote the area of managerial activity, most usually a distinct department, that was concerned with organising the workforce, providing training, ensuring legal compliance and importantly, managing the relationship between the company and trade unions. In many organisations, personnel management was historically a support function operating on the periphery of the workplace, and the personnel department would have no representation within the strategic decision making forum (Redman and Wilkinson, 2013). However, from the late 1980s the people management function of the organisation started to develop greater strategic ambitions.

In the broader context of social, political and economic changes associated with **Thatcher's government** in the UK and Reagan's presidency in the USA, HRM emerged to displace personnel management (Guest, 1990; Harley and Hardy, 2004). HRM has been promoted over the past thirty or so years as the alternative to the perceptions of the conflictual employment relations of the past, seen to be marred by strikes and disputes. However, some writers (e.g. Guest, 1984) argue the HRM might be little more than the re-naming of personnel management. In fact, some organisations made subtle changes to practice and started to use the terms human resource manager/department instead of personnel manager/department. Other organisations embraced HRM as a mechanism for changing the way in which an organization manages its people (or human resources). Traditionally personnel management was focused on the relationship between employees and **trade unions**. However, as Tichy et al. (1982) note, HRM is concerned with four generic processes: recruitment and selection, appraisal (or performance management), rewards and development.

Recruitment and selection

Recruitment and selection are often considered as the same process. However, they should be examined separately as many argue that recruitment is the single most important HRM activity (Taylor and Collins, 2000). Recruitment is the process of finding the most qualified and most suitable candidates for a job. Recruitment needs to be scrupulously thought out in order to attract the right candidate for the job. Attracting unsuitable candidates is not financially sensible for the organisation concerned and, in the long run, might be regarded as unfair on those candidates who are recruited despite a poor fit in terms of skills, attitude, values, etc.

The amount of money that an organisation spends on selection depends often on the nature of the labour market. If there are many skilled people available for work, as is common when the country is in recession, then an organisation will probably needs to spend less money on its recruitment process. However, if there are fewer skilled (or relevantly skilled) people available for work, then the organisation may have to invest significant time and effort in designing appropriate recruitment processes.

When designing a recruitment process it is important to look at the factors that attract people to apply for a job. A YouGov survey (2006) found the factors that were most important to job applicants are location of work, holiday entitlement, flexible working, salary and bonuses and the workplace culture. Opportunities for promotion and development came a long way down the list. In order to recruit successfully, it is important to understand what is important to candidates and equally, if not more importantly, whether the criteria of suitability for the role are explicit and relevant. This process is often via a job analysis. The cost of making a poor recruitment decision can be disastrous for all concerned over the medium term.

A **job analysis** is the process used to collect information about the duties, responsibilities, necessary skills, outcomes and the work environment of a particular job. You need as much data as possible to put together a job description that is the frequent outcome of the job analysis and forms the basis for both advertising the job and designing selection tools. There are many different methods of job analysis that can involve discussing the role with current job incumbents or independent observation.

Incorrect assumptions about class, gender, ethnic group or physical ability, or any other type of discrimination, can potentially impact on objectivity when recruiting for a particular role. Employers may face legal action and employment tribunals if their recruitment practices do not comply with current legislation. Discrimination is illegal and is covered by specific legislation in the UK. The Equality Act 2010 is an Act of Parliament of the UK and forms the basis of anti-discrimination law in the UK, protecting against discrimination in employment on the grounds of religion or belief, sexual orientation and age as well as disability, gender reassignment, marriage and civil partner status and race.

The job analysis is used to develop a job or person specification and this in turn is adapted to create a brief profile of the ideal candidate and job description. The job description will be used to describe the duties and responsibilities of the jobholder. This information is then used as the basis of any job advert. The job advert can be posted in a number of outlets depending, in which one is viewed as appropriate, taking into account the nature of the work. Possible outlets for such adverts include:

- Job centres
- Recruitment agencies
- Executive search agencies
- Newspapers and trade/professional magazines

Additionally, recruitment can flow from cold callers and word of mouth.

Selection can be viewed as the final stage of the recruitment process that leads to the decision as to who the successful candidate(s) will be. This should also comply with the anti-discrimination law described previously. It is argued that selection should be undertaken in an impartial manner, but this is not always possible when people are involved! As much as we try to be unbiased, often we recruit and select on the basis of underlying biases (including recruiting in our own image). There are many tools used for selecting employees including interviews, psychological tests, work-based tests, assessment centres, references, biodata, graphology, polygraphy, telephone screenings and the Internet. All of these will be covered in more detail in future years of your degree. However, for the purpose of this introduction to people management we will look at the most popular techniques – interviews, psychological tests and assessment centres. We will also look at how the Internet has changed both recruitment and selection.

Interviews remain the most popular way for selecting employees. These can either be one-to-one or by interview panel. Interviews can either be used as a single selection method or be part of a broader selection process, for example an assessment centre. Interviews are popular because they are reasonably inexpensive and present a genuine opportunity for potential employees and employers to exchange information. This allows both parties the possibility of making an informed judgement about person-job fit and person-organisation fit.

Many forms of interview are viewed as having low validity and represent a limited opportunity to select the correct candidate. However, they continue to be a popular selection technique because many managers would not appoint a candidate without meeting them first (Klehe, 2004). There are ways in which interviews can be made both more valid and reliable. This includes using structured interviews (Van der Zee et al., 2002), using situational interviews (Huffcutt et al., 2004), competency-based interviewing (Newell, 2006) and patterned behaviour description interviewing (Huffuctt et al., 2013).

Psychological tests, or psychometric tests as they are frequently known, include both personality tests and intelligence tests. They are frequently used in employee selection because it is believed that they represent a 'valid' and 'scientific' way of selecting employees. Selection tests are most popular for the selection of junior and middle management and are particularly popular for assessing graduates (Newell and Shackelton, 2000).

Psychometric tests that are designed to measure mental ability can include general tests of intelligence, or tests to examine verbal, numerical and special ability. There are even tests that focus on clerical speed, computer aptitudes and sales skills (Toplis, 2014). Those that measure personality are based on 'trait' or 'type' theories and try to identify independent and enduring characteristics that are seen as important for a particular role. The tests are often centred on the 'Big Five' personality factors (openness to experience, extroversion, agreeableness, conscientiousness and emotional stability).

There are potentially a number of problems with using psychometric tests. Professional bodies including the British Psychological Society (BPS) and the Chartered Institute of Personnel and Development (CIPD) have expressed concerns about the emergence of unregulated providers and untrained assessors interpreting the findings. Moreover, some academic research has indicated that some tests maybe discriminatory, particularly against ethnic minorities and women (Newell and Shakleton, 2000).

Psychometric tests are frequently included within assessment centres. According to the CIPD about one third of companies use assessment centres to select employees (mainly professional and managerial appointments). Assessment centres usually involve a series of activities that are supposed to represent the full range of skills required in the job and have been suggested as being one of the most accurate ways to select someone for a job (Smith, 2002). Moreover, when assessment centres are run professionally they are generally seen as fair and providing equal opportunities. Assessment centres make the candidate feel as if they are being invested in (assessment centres are often run in hotels and involve an overnight stay) and give the candidate some feel as to the character and culture of the organisation, as the job applicants get to meet potential colleagues and undertake 'real' work assignments.

Frequently, the first step of selection is undertaken in the virtual realm, with shortlisted candidates being asked to complete competency-based assessment questions and psychometric tests by logging into a website. This allows the organisation to screen potential applicants at a relatively low cost and in large numbers. The rise in the use of the Internet for both recruitment and selection is probably the most significant develop in personnel practice over the last ten years. Various surveys suggest that online recruitment is the preferred way of attracting applicants for many companies (IRS, 2005). The CIPD (2007) suggests that 75 per cent of organisations are using their website as the most common method of advertising vacant posts (CIPD, 2007). However, there is no evidence that the Internet produces better candidates (Crail, 2007). What the Internet does, is make it easier for people to apply, therefore increasing the applicant pool. However, as the Internet makes it easier and faster to apply for jobs, more people are applying for more jobs, making it harder for employers to sift through the increasing volume of applications.

Performance management

Performance management, as a term, emerged with the development of Human Resource Management. Performance management has been defined as 'a process which contributes to the effective management of individuals and teams in order to achieve high levels of organisational performance. As such, it establishes shared understanding about what is to be achieved and an approach to leading and developing people which will ensure that it is achieved' (Armstrong and Baron, 2004). The main feature of performance management is to merge the objectives of the organisation with the targets of individual employees. Consequently, formal appraisal is placed at the centre of the approach. Performance management practices are centred on the alignment of processes with organisational objectives and formally attempt to align discussion and accountability across the organisation. Armstrong and Baron (2004), argue that performance management is actually about establishing a culture where all employees take responsibility for continuous improvement; sharing expectations between managers and individuals; improving communication and interrelationships and enabling measurement of performance of all employees and teams.

A performance appraisal is the process by which organisations assess the performance of employees and is central to the performance appraisal process. If we examine performance appraisal as the key resource in the tools of performance management, it can be viewed as having a number of purposes. It can be used to set targets for employees, to assess performance in an objective manner and to provide appropriate feedback to employees.

Training

Training has always been an important issue within organisations as, however successful the recruitment and selection processes, it will typically be important for a company to equip individual employees with the skills necessary to be able to function effectively within the organisation. Moreover, as the nature of work and technology changes, the individual will have to update their knowledge through training activities. Within an increasingly service-based economy, training has started to focus on 'soft skills' training, which involves equipping employees with the appropriate inter-personal skills for the job as a mechanism for improving competitive advantage.

Part of the focus on soft skills lies within a framework of developing a 'quality culture', which represent a broader training and development issue (Mabey and Salaman, 1995). In recent times, companies have sought ways to control costs.

Sometimes initiatives include stripping out middle-management layers. For the remaining managers and supervisors, their roles have increased in scope. They have become responsible for a wider range of functions and a larger number of employees. Frequently, words such as 'flexibility' and 'teamwork' enter the organisational narrative when talking about training, as many organisations introduced teams when they were stripping out managerial layers. Teamwork often requires the training of the team and the development of multi-skilling in order that the members of the team can undertake all the tasks within the group.

Teamwork

Groups and teams have traditionally been a major focal point of psychological and sociological theory and research. An understanding of groups is necessary for almost every analysis of social behaviour, including, leadership, majority-minority relations, status, role differentiation and socialisation (Levine and Moreland, 1998). Furthermore, small groups provide important contexts within which other behaviours occur, for example attraction, aggression and altruism (Geen, 1998, Batson, 1998). At a functional level, people spend much of their lives in collectives of some kind; e.g. families, school classes and sports teams, and these groups provide members with vital material and psychological resources.

Yet, the formal use of teams in organisations is a relatively recent phenomenon. Traditional work arrangements attempted to remove the power of the informal team and preferred a more individualised form of work organisation. This can be traced back to Adam Smith and his discussion of the benefits of the division of labour. Smith, in his 1776 work, *An Inquiry into the Nature and Cause of the Wealth of Nations*, argued for the splitting of broad tasks into subtasks, each of which was to be assigned to an individual employee who would specialise in carrying out that subtask. He believed that the concentration and specialisation of workers on a single subtask would lead to increased skill and greater productivity.

Adam Smith's ideas influenced the work of Fredrick Winslow Taylor, the man generally considered to be the founding father of Scientific Management. Taylor argued that the application of scientific methods to workers could greatly improve productivity. Taylor promoted the use of time and motion studies to determine the most efficient method for performing each work task, a piece-rate system of compensation to maximize employee work effort, and the selection and training of employees based on an analysis of their personalities and skills. Hence, under scientific management, work was designed to be precisely measured and repetitive, with workers having little control or discretion over their work. One of the desired outcomes of this way of organising work was to reduce 'soldiering'. This was described by Taylor as manifesting itself in two forms. The first, from the nature instinct and tendency of men to take it easy – termed natural soldiering. The second form of soldiering – systematic soldiering – was viewed as being more intricate, and evolving from interactions with other men (Taylor, 1947, p.19). Taylor was recognising the occurrence of naturally formed workgroups and was concerned with their elimination. He believed that 'collusion' between employees reduced productivity.

Some supporters of Taylor applied scientific management in work settings, other than manufacturing, including the office (e.g. Gilbreth and Gilbreth, 1917). However, research on the development of manufacturing within the USA found that the application of Taylorism was by no means commonplace (Hounshell, 1984). In fact there are some writers who believe that Taylorism was, in reality, a failure (e.g. Palmer, 1975, Edwards, 1979). For the most part, Taylorism was difficult to introduce due to employee resistance and employer suspicions. This has produced arguments that Taylorism is only significant as a management ideology (Burawoy, 1979). Indeed, the power of the informal workgroup that Taylor wished to break down, failed to be eliminated from the industrial environment.

The use of teams and workgroups within organisational settings has rapidly increased within the Western industrialised world (Waterson et al., 1999). The rise of quality circles in the UK in the 1980s and the subsequent prevalence of self-managing teams have come to embody this movement in terms of work organisation. This transition was predominantly a response to lack of flexibility in more Taylorised forms of work, which led to decreased competitive ability. Teamwork was primarily introduced in order to find a more effective way to recruit and better utilise employees to achieve organisational goals. Teamworking was also viewed to fulfil the needs of employees for control over their work environment (Doorewaard, van Hootegem and Huys, 2002).

Teamwork is frequently described amongst the package of practices included in Human Resource Management (HRM). Indeed, the message behind the move from traditional personnel management to an HRM agenda was based on the notion that Western employers should copy the Japanese approach, by integrating flexible production and quality management practices with related employment practices. These include the development of a workforce willing and able to learn new skills and an emphasis on teamworking (Sisson, 1993). Teamwork was seen as allowing individual workers to share their knowledge and skills and develop them in a way that enhanced economic success. Teamwork was not only perceived as being able to help the firm's achievement, but also to ensure employment security (West, 1994). More recently, management 'fads and fashions' such as business process re-engineering (BPR), total quality management (TQM), lean production, socio-technical approaches and HRM, have each in their own way supported the core principles of team-based work (Benders and van Hootegem, 1999; Womack et al., 1990).

There are a number of ways in which the literature interprets teamwork. The popular literature tends to focus on the creation of successful teams and the relationship with productivity and effectiveness (Proctor and Currie, 2002). An alternative approach is to examine the broader experience and meaning of teamwork for employees. Further struggles lie in teamwork research. Some accounts of teamwork view it as a powerful force that brings the benefits of political democracy into the workforce (e.g. Dachler and Wilpert, 1978). However, contradictory versions posit that teamwork is just another management technique to control workers (e.g. Barker, 1993). Sociologically informed writers believe that by fostering a sense of participation in the organisation on the part of the employees, there is a destruction of collective solidarity among workers, which makes them vulnerable to high levels of management control (Edwards, 1979; Burawoy, 1983). Despite the vast quantity of writing on teamwork, these distinct and even contradictory research itineraries have materialised, with very little assimilation of the understandings of each other. As Batt and Doellgast (2004, p.156) note, "at a time when firms have embraced team structures to break down the bureaucratic organisation, academic researchers have continued to operate in disciplinary and theoretical silos."

Nonetheless, some attempts have been made at combining differing approaches. Both Marchington (2000) and Thompson and Wallace (1996), have developed integrated frameworks in order to understand teamwork. Specifically, Thompson and Wallace's exploration and definition of the technical, normative and governance dimensions of teamwork has received considerable empirical attention and validation (e.g. Findlay et al., 2000a, 2000b; McCabe, 2000).

The Team Dimensions Model (TDM) could be described as a pragmatic mechanism for the evaluation of teamwork and, as such, has influenced a number of other writers (e.g. Delbridge et al., 2000; McCabe, 2000; Bélanger and Edwards, 2002), as it enables researchers to develop an assessment of teamwork without being forced into defining teams according to pre-existing classifications. Like other similar frameworks (e.g. Marchington, 2000) this model has acknowledged the results from an evaluation of the broader teamwork literature and accepts that the overwhelming rationale for the introduction of teams by organizations is instrumental and realistic. There is, therefore, a strong focus on what can be described as the technical dimension, such as the application of knowledge and employee flexibility. This is based on the origins of the model which drew on manufacturing experiences. Mulholland (2002) used the TDM to show the focus on technical control – as well as gender politics and exploitation of emotional labour – in a call centre.

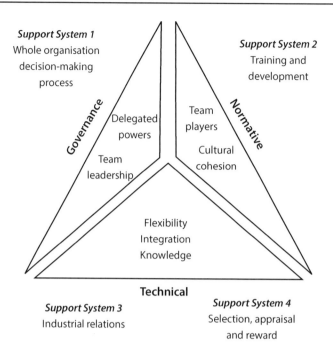

Figure 5.1: The Team Dimensions Model (Thompson & Wallace, 1996; Findlay et al. 2000a, 2000b)

Labour ProcessTheory: Examining work critically

Critical writers often view teamwork as the latest in a succession of management fads or as a covert mechanism by which management intensify their control over labour (e.g. Barker, 1993; Sinclair, 1992). It is instructive to therefore use teamwork as a way of examining work from a critical perspective.

The expansion of capitalism developed the widespread study of work organisation. This interest was stimulated by two groups of individuals. First, those who by broadly scientific methods sought to improve the effectiveness of production (Smith, 1937; Babbage, 1963; Taylor, 1964); and second, those who criticised the processes of capitalism due to its perceived negative impact on employees' skills and experiences, and have challenged the rhetoric of those who claimed that the development of capitalism benefits all (Marx and McLellan, 2000; Braverman, 1974; Edwards, 1979; Friedman, 1977). It is within the latter perspective that Labour Process Theory (LPT) is located.

The labour process was defined by Marx as comprising three elements, independent of any particular social formation. These are first, purposeful activity (that is work itself); second, the object on which work is performed; and last, the instruments of that work (Marx and McLellan, 2000). The human and technical elements interact during the labour process and require the worker to concep-tualise how to perform the required task, prior to its commencement. According to Marx, the conscious purpose of human labour is its defining characteristic – differentiating it from animal labour (Marx and McClellan, 2000).

In brief, Marx claims that through work humans lose their 'humanness' and become an object in themselves. They become alienated from the social world that they have created. The product of work becomes a commodity, and because of waged work, the employee himself becomes a commodity. The wage worker becomes a slave of his own product. Waged work, therefore, alienates humans from their product and productive activity. Waged work also contains a social alienation, where humans become **alienated** in their relations to other humans. In the end, humans also become alienated from society, even though society is borne of human actions. Society thus becomes a power, which develops on its own, and that no one is able to control.

Although the original work of Marx was not specific to organisationally based work, Marxist-influenced theory and research has dominated criti-cal research on work over the last four decades. This was broadly due to the publication of *Labour and Monopoly Capital* by Braverman (1974), which came after a "long and largely barren period when work became a forgotten issue" (Thompson, 1989, p. 67). The impetus for revised interest in the labour process came at a time when industrial conflict was increasing across Europe. However, its focus moved to qualitative issues such as the quality of working life (QWL). This increase in the levels of dissatisfaction with work came at a time when critical researchers were writing about the ever-increasing skill levels required from modern work. To Braverman such a contradiction required investigation and provided a motivation for his research.

The contribution made by Braverman essentially highlighted two main theoretical concerns. First, work under the capitalist mode of production is increasingly degrading and dehumanising to the people who perform it in order to survive. Second, such an organisation of work results in an ever increasing number of workers who are subjected to these tendencies and which results in the emergence of two classes, one that is 'powerful and whole' and another 'scarred and angered' (Sattel, 1978).

In developing Marx's notion of control, Braverman provides an insightful review of Taylor's version of scientific management. He describes Taylorism as the dominant approach utilised by the owner of the means of production to maximise control over the labour process in search of surplus value (the dif-ference between the value of the product produced by workers and the actual employment costs paid out in wages). For Braverman, Taylor promoted the issue of managerial control over production to unprecedented dimensions and asserted management's right to dictate to workers the precise manner in which work should be performed.

Partly as a response to the widespread emergence of teamwork over the last two decades, it is the nature of change within these control structures that has more recently formed a key debate from a labour process perspective. Friedman, who examined the evolution of managerial strategies as a response to transformation in work organisation due to labour market changes, believed that there are two ways that employers can control the labour process; termed 'responsible autonomy' and 'direct control' (Friedman, 1977). In the former, workers are given some freedom to make decisions on their own, but are then held responsible for their actions by management. The latter follows the Taylorist model, simplifying the job so that it can be more tightly controlled by management.

As already stated, pressures of global competition and **deregulation** have led many companies to develop new forms of organisation and adapt alternative models for managing people: Taylorist or Fordist production regimes are often incompatible with market demands. Restructuring processes can lead to a new balance of power. The decrease of direct control (Friedman, 1977; Edwards, 1979) and explicit forms and bases of power (e.g. authority) do not imply the disappearance of power itself. There is a shift towards a new control structure in team-based organisations based on responsible autonomy (Friedman, 1977). This new control structure can be labelled as 'participatory regulation', meeting the organisational demands to cope with permanent 'dynamic complexity' (Chouraqui, 1993).

Conclusion

The purpose of this chapter was to introduce some of the key concepts used when looking at the management of people from both a practitioner and a 'critical' academic perspective. When studying work and the organisation of work, it is important to understand that sometimes the actions of management can be detrimental to the wellbeing of employees. Whilst some activities may be deemed strategically good, they may not be viewed as being to the advantage of individuals working in the organisation. A number of issues that are central to the understanding of the experience of people at work have not been given sufficient attention in this chapter, but will become part of your examination of work over the next few years. These include trade unions, equality and diversity, the impact of non-work (unemployment) and the experience of contemporary work.

References

Armstrong, M. and Baron, A. (2004) *Managing Performance: Performance management in action*. London: CIPD.

Babbage, C. (1963) *On the Economy of Machinery and Manufactures*. New York: Kelly.

Barker, J. (1993) Tightening the Iron Cage: Concertive Control in Self-Managing Teams. *Administrative Science Quarterly*, **38**, 408-437.

Batson, C. D. (1998) Altruism and prosocial behavior. In *The Handbook of Social Psychology*, 4th edition, eds. D. T. Gilbert, S. T. Fiske, & G. Lindzey., p.. 282-316. Boston: McGraw-Hill.

Batt, R, and Doellagst V. (2004) The Organization of Work. In *The Oxford Handbook of Work and Organization*, eds. S. Ackroyd, R Batt, P. Thompson, and P. Tolbert. London: Oxford.

Bélanger, J and Edwards, P. (2002) The conditions for social compromise in the workplace. Drawing lessons from teamwork. Special Seminar. Free University of Berlin.

Benders, J., and Van Hootegem, G. (1999) Teams and their context: Moving the team discussion beyond existing dichotomies. *Journal of Management Studies*, **36** (5), 609-628.

Braverman H. (1974) *Labor and Monopoly Capital: The Dedagradation of Work in the Twentieth Century*. New York: Montly Review Press.

Burawoy, M.. (1979) *Manufacturing Consent: Changes in the Labor Process Under Monopoly Capitalism*. Chicago: University of Chicago Press

CIPD (Chartered Institute of Personnel and Development) (2007) Recruitment, retention and turnover. Annual survey report 2007. CIPD, London.

Crail, M. (2007) http://www.personneltoday.com/hr/online-recruitment-delivers-more-applicants-and-wins-vote-of-most-employers/

Dachler H.P. and Wilpert B (1978) Conceptual dimensions and boundaries of participation in organizations: a critical evaluation. *Administrative Science Quarterly*, **23**, 1-39.

Delbridge, R., Lowe, J. and Oliver, N. (2000) Worker autonomy in lean teams: evidence from the world automotive components industry. In *Teamworking*, eds, S. Proctor and F. Mueller. Houndmills: Macmillan.

Doorewaard. H., Van Hootegem, G., and Huys, R.(2002) Team responsibility structure and team performance. *Personnel Review*, **31** (3), p. 356-370.

Edwards, P. (1979) *Contested Terrain*. New York : Basic Books

Findlay, P., McKinlay, A., Marks, A. and Thompson, P. (2000a) In search of perfect people: Teamwork and team players in the Scottish spirits industry. *Human Relations*, **53** (12), 8-31.

Findlay, P, McKinlay, A, Marks, A, and Thompson, P (2000b) Flexible when it suits them: the use and abuse of teamwork skills. In *Teamworking*, eds, S. Proctor and F. Mueller, p. 222 -243. Houndmills: Macmillan.

Friedman, A. L. (1977*) Industry and Labour*. London: Macmillan.

Geen, R. G. (1998) Aggression and antisocial behavior. In *The Handbook of Social Psychology*, eds. D. T. Gilbert, S. T. Fiske, and G. Lindzey, 4th edition, p. 317-356. Boston: McGraw-Hill

Gilbreth, F.B. and Gilbreth, L.M. (1917) *Applied Motion Study: A collection of papers on the efficient method to industrial preparedness*. New York: MacMillan

Guest, D. E. (1990) Human resource management and the American dream, *Journal of Management Studies*, **27**(4).

Harley B and Hardy C. (2004) Firing Blanks? An analysis of discursive struggle in HRM, *Journal of Management Studies*, **41** (3), 377 - 400.

Hounshell, D.A. (1984) From the American System to Mass Production 1800-1932: *The Development of Manufacturing Technology in the U.S.* Baltimore: Johns Hopkins University Press.

Huffcutt, A. I., Conway, J. M., Roth, P. L., & Klehe, U. (2004). The impact of job complexity and study design on situational and behavior description interview validity. *International Journal of Selection and Assessment*, **12**, 262–273.

IRS Employment Review (2005). *Survey on online recruitment*. IRS Employment Review.

Levine, J. M., & Moreland, R. L. (1998). Small groups. In D. Gilbert, S. Fiske, & G. Lindzey (Eds**.),** *Handbook of Social Psychology* (4th. ed., Vol. 2, pp. 415-469).

Klehe, U.-C. (2004). Choosing how to choose: Institutional pressures affecting the adoption of personnel selection procedures. *International Journal of Selection and Assessment*, **12**, 327-342.

Mabey, C. and Salaman, G. (1995) *Strategic Human Resource Management*. Oxford: Blackwell Business

McCabe, D. (2000) The team dream: the meaning and experience of teamworking for employees in an automobile factory. In *Teamworking*, eds, S. Proctor and F. Mueller, p. 202-222. .Houndmills: Macmillan.

Marchington, M (2000) Teamworking and employee involvement: terminology, evaluation and context. In *Teamworking*, eds, S. Proctor and F. Mueller, p. 60-80. Houndmills: Macmillan.

Marx , K. and McLellan, D. (ed). (2000). *Karl Marx: Selected Writings*. New York: Oxford University Press.

Mulholland, K (2002) Gender, emotional labour and teamworking in a call centre. *Personnel Review*, **31**(3) 283-303.

Newell S. and Shackleton V. (2000) "Recruitment and Selection" in Bach S. and Sisson K., *Personnel Management: A Comprehensive Guide to Theory and Practice*, Blackwell, Oxford, p. 111-136

Palmer, B. (1975) Class, conception and conflict: the thrust for efficiency, managerial views of labor and the working class rebellion, 1903-22. *Review of Radical Political Economy*, **7**, 31-49.

Procter, S. and Currie, G. (2002) How Teamworking Works in the Inland Revenue: Meaning Operation and Impact. *Personnel Review* **31**(3), 304-319.

Redman, T. & Wilkinson, A. (2013). *Contemporary Human Resource Management: Text and Cases*. Pearson Education.

Sattel, J, (1978) The Degradation of Labor in the 20th Century: Harry Braverman's Sociology of Work. *The Insurgent Sociologist*, **8** (1), p 35 - 50.

Sinclair, A. (1992) The tyranny of a team ideology. *Organization Studies*, **13**, 611-626.

Sisson, K. (1993) In Search of HRM? *British Journal of Industrial Relations*, **31**(2) 201-210.

Smith, A (1937) *The Wealth of Nations*. New York: Random House.

Taylor, M. S., & Collins, C. J. (2000). Organizational recruitment: Enhancing the intersection of theory and practice. In C. L. Cooper & E. A. Locke (Eds.), *Industrial and Organizational Psychology: Linking Theory and Practice*. 304-334. Oxford, UK:Blackwell.

Taylor, F.W. (1947) *Shop Management and Principles of Scientific Management*. New York: Harper & Row

Taylor, F. W. (1964) *Scientific Management - Comprising Shop Management, The principles of Scientific Management and Testimony before the Special House Committee*. Harper and Row

Thompson, P. (1989) *The Nature of Work*. Basingstoke: Macmillan

Thompson, P. and Wallace,T. (1996) Redesigning production through teamworking. *International Journal of Operations and Production Management*, **16**(2), 103-118.

Tichy, N. M. (1982). Managing change strategically: The technical, political, and cultural keys. *Organizational Dynamics*, **11**, 59-80.

Van der Zee, K. I., Van Oudenhoven, J. P., & De Grijs, E. (2002). Personality, threat and cognitive and emotional reactions to intercultural situations. *Journal of Personality*.

Waterson, P. E., Clegg, C. W., Bolden, R., Pepper, K., Warr, P. B. and Wall, T. D. (1999) The use and effectiveness of modern manufacturing practices: a survey of UK industry. *International Journal of Production Research*, **37**, 2271–2292.

West, M. (1994). *Effective Teamwork.* Leicester: British Psychological Society.

Wilton, N (2011) *An Introduction to HRM*, Sage, London

Womack J, Jones, D, Roos, D (1990) *The Machine That Changed the World*. New York: Maxwell MacMillan International.

Further reading

Marks, A., and Richards, J. (2012) 'Developing ideas and concepts in teamwork research: Where do we go from here?' *Employee Relations*, **34**(2), 228-234

Findlay, P., McKinlay, A., Marks, A. and Thompson, P. (2009) Collective bargaining and new work regimes: too important to be left to bosses. *Industrial Relations Journal*, **40**(3), 182-197

Torrington, D. and Hall, L(2014) *Human Resource Management*, 9th Edition, FT Pearson.

6 Managing Change

Robert MacIntosh, Kyle Andrews and Josh McLeod

One of the mantras that we hear today is that change is the only certainty. Further, we are often told that we are living through a period of unprecedented change driven by globalisation, the internet, deregulation and the rate of technological innovation occurring. Previous eras may be able to lay claim to rapid and radical change but there is little doubt that technological advancements mean that we are living through a second industrial revolution (MacIntosh, 2003). Most of the time, most organizations are managing change through the deliberate selection of organizational structures, processes and practices which they hope will produce particular results. This is often called change work (Beech & MacIntosh, 2012) and can emanate from within the organization, be driven by shifts in the external environment or through a combination of both. Change may therefore be opt ional or unavoidable, rapid or slow, radical or evolutionary.

Some changes are **driven by a regulator** for example, the Telecommunications Act in the United States deregulated the radio broadcast industry in 1996. This regulatory change significantly loosened ownership restrictions by eliminating the national ownership cap. Some firms were then able to expand, driving consolidation in the industry. Clear Channel moved from owning 36 radio stations across the US before the regulatory change to owning 1,225 by 2003 (Prindle, 2003).

In contrast, Amazon has both been driven by and has driven **technological change**. The very existence of the firm relies on high levels of internet usage amongst its customers. Without the rapid technological change which has occurred in the last 20 years, the firm's business model would not be workable, but having achieved profitability, the firm is beginning to invest significant resource in pushing future changes from its own innovations. Currently, Amazon is exploring the permissions required by aviation authorities if it begins to deliver packages to customers via unmanned aerial drones. By using drones, the company believes it may be able to deliver packages directly to the costumer in 30 minutes or less. It is easy to see how this technological change would affect not only Amazon but also other delivery firms such as FedEx, UPS, and Royal Mail.

Some firms approach change as both **rapid and all-encompassing.** Danish hearing aid manufacturer Oticon did precisely this when it introduced the so-called 'spaghetti organization' (see Beech and MacIntosh, 2012 for a detailed case study) and removed almost all vestiges of formal, hierarchical or function-based organization. This new, structureless approach was introduced as they moved to a new office building, and used project teams as a means of organizing. Instead of getting rid of old employees and hiring new ones, the company moved from what it called mono-job to multi-job thinking where everyone was involved in several projects to increase productivity and generate new ideas. The idea of holacracy (Robertson, 2015) is based on a similar, self-managing philosophy.

In contrast, some aspects of organizational change occur in ways which are more **gradual and evolutionary**. When Apple's then CEO Steve Jobs identified potential areas of technological development, the organization's product portfolio expanded slowly from computers to music listening devices (iPod), phones (iPhone), tablet computers (iPad) and the online sale of digital content such as movies, music and apps (iTunes). Now making watches and continuing to innovate, Apple has experienced a series of gradual shifts which cumulate over time to radically reposition the firm as something significantly more than the simple computing business which it had originally been.

The ability to manage change effectively is a crucial skill for managers but as the examples above demonstrate, no one approach will work in all circumstances. The real skill of change management is based on the ability to judge situations, selecting and adapting from prior practices and deploying workable solutions in a manner sensitive to the context in which the change is taking place.

Change agents and change models

Over many years, we have asked senior managers from a range of public, private and third sector organizations to characterise their approach to change. A sample of responses is given below:

Q. What is your approach to managing change ?

A1. Don't ____ about. Bish, bash, bosh. Get in there. Job done (CEO FTSE100 business)

A2. I don't subscribe to the 'let's just let it happen' school of change. That might happen in a web design set up in San Francisco but, trust me, it doesn't work in Stoke-on-Trent on a wet Monday morning (senior partner in management consultancy firm)

A3. I think of change in the way that a sheep dog herds sheep. If the dog has to actually bite the sheep there's been a failure somewhere. Change is working best when the very presence of the dog encourages the sheep to move off in a particular direction without any actual contact. It creates a much more fluid sense of how change happens,   but it is how I approach it (director, large public organization)

Clearly these individual responses differ from each other. This is likely one part personality and one part context. Figure 6.1 below sets out five dimensions on which to compare change contexts.

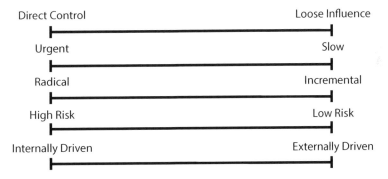

Figure 6.1: Dimensions of change contexts

The first of these dimensions relates to the attitude to control which prevails in either the organization where the change is taking place or the individual responsible for the change process. Some contexts are highly regulated and control is rightly seen as important where safety is a major issue, such as nuclear power plants, healthcare, etc. In contrast, design or other creative industries thrive on the spontaneity of innovative and unexpected ways of working. Some individual change managers have strong preferences for detailed micro-management whilst others prefer a hands-off approach. In combination, contextual factors and individual preferences might produce an approach to change which is more directed and controlling or more loosely structured and enabling.

A second dimension relates to the pace at which change can, should or needs to proceed. In a failing organization there may be significant urgency, whereas a successful setting may afford a longer time horizon to be seen as appropriate. Contrast for example the preparations for a regulatory change which is known many years in advance, such as the introduction of the Euro as a physical currency in 2002. The earliest sight of the Euro occurred in legislative form over a decade before giving retailers, banks and many other organizations time to prepare for the change. In contrast, other changes occur in a very short time period. The introduction of free email services such as Hotmail in 1996 quickly signalled the demise of paid for email services such as those offered by AoL in the early days of the internet.

A third dimension of change is to consider whether what is proposed represents a modest or incremental adjustment or a more fundamental and radical rethink of the product, service or business model. Incremental changes such as small-scale reorganization of structures or the gradual changes caused by growth are usually described as evolutionary in nature. They do not challenge fundamental assumptions about the nature and type of organization required, but they are nonetheless more than simply the continuation of business as usual. Radical change on the other hand tends to rupture current ways of working and require new structures, new processes, new people, new skills and/or new business models. The advent of web-based provision of financial services meant that many existing providers had to rethink their high street presence. This combined with the global financial crisis has produced a wave of consolidation. When two existing organizations merge, there are often radical change outcomes where lines of reporting, product portfolios and incentive systems are harmonised. The more radical the change, the more likely it is to involve challenges to the existing culture of the organization.

The next dimension on which to compare change contexts relates to the perceived risk attached to it. Some changes represent a small side bet whilst others are wholesale, bet-the-company type changes. An example of a successful high-risk change is the photo-sharing application Instagram. Instagram originally started as Burbn, a relatively popular check-in app that had a number of gaming features alongside its photo-sharing feature. However, the creators were concerned that the app was too cluttered with different features and would never properly excel in its current format. They decided to risk stripping all the features but one: photos. This risky change clearly paid off, Instagram is now the third most downloaded app of all time and was sold to Facebook for $1bn in 2012 (Nazar, 2014).

The final dimension on which to compare change contexts relates to the starting point for the change. If your competitors have introduced a new product or service which renders your own offering largely redundant, the driver can be said to be external to your own organization. Similarly, if a legislative change forces you to alter your organization in order to comply, this too would be described as emanating from beyond the organization. If however, the change process were instigated by a new management team, or from an analysis of current poor performance by the existing management team, these would be described as internally driven. At one point in its history Microsoft was developing a new product (MSN) which was originally seen as a safe, paid for, alternative to the internet. Bill Gates, then still CEO of Microsoft, realised that this was unlikely to work and asked all staff working on other product lines (such as Word, Excel and Powerpoint) to rethink their offering as something that could be web-enabled. The resulting change brought significant differences in both products and the ways in which Microsoft organized, but the genesis of the change came from within the organization. In contrast, when the UK regulator insisted that BAA sell off one of its Scottish hub airports, the change driver was clearly external to the firm.

By characterising any given change context using these, or similar dimensions, it is possible to heighten one's sensitivity to the types of change challenge that might be faced. Clearly some of these dimensions are interlinked. More radical change is often perceived as higher risk and is sometimes undertaken in circumstances where there is significant time pressure, perhaps because earlier, more incremental and slower approaches to change have failed to deliver the desired outcomes.

Having given some thought to the type of change facing the organization, change agents sometime choose to be guided by a model or framework from the large literature on the topic. One commonly cited example is John Kotter's framework which suggests that change proceeds in eight steps, as described in Figure 6.2 below:

1   Establish a sense of urgency – create a compelling reason for the change

2   Form a coalition with enough power to lead the change

3   Create a vision to direct the change

4   Communicate the vision throughout the organisation

5   Empower others to act on the vision – remove barriers, encourage risk-taking

6   Plan for and create short-term wins

7   Consolidate improvements, reassess changes, make necessary adjustments

8   Reinforce the changes by demonstrating the relationship between new behaviours and organisational success

Figure 6.2: Kotter's Eight Step Model for organizational change (from Kotter, 1996)

Kotter's framework recognises that meaningful organisational change will not occur without the cooperation of employees and other affected stakeholders. As a result, step 1 of the model suggests that creating a sense of urgency for a change initiative is the first action leaders must take to gain the cooperation of stakeholders. Persuading employees that the change is in their best interests will help to achieve this. Leaders must also convince employees that the change needs to be enacted quickly to avoid detrimental consequences.

The success of a change initiative largely depends on the quality of the people leading it. Step 2 of Kotter's model proposes that senior leaders must empower a coalition of people to drive the change and keep it on target through its various stages. It is also important that senior leaders stay actively engaged with the coalition to help them counter inevitable resistance from elsewhere inside the organisation. This ensures so-called leadership from the top.

A critical responsibility for any business leader is setting the future direction of an organisation. Thus, step 3 for Kotter suggests that leaders must take responsibility for creating the vision and strategy for change. The change vision will provide stakeholders with a picture of what the organisation will look like in the future. It also tells stakeholders why they should let go of the past, and follow the vision of the leader.

Step 4 of Kotter's model concerns communicating the vision to employees. If the vision is communicated effectively, an organisational understanding will be established that acts as a foundation for gaining the commitment of employees and managers. These vital stakeholders will not only understand the reason for change, they will be committed to making it happen.

Encouraging others to get behind the change initiative is important. Many change efforts fail because too many people within the organisation have strong ties to the status quo. Thus, step 5 advocates empowering broad based action. This involves first identifying why employees resist change, then taking steps to convert them.

Large-scale organisational changes often fail because of a lack of early success, with employees becoming demoralised at the lack of progress. Step 6 suggests that, to sustain a change effort, an organisation must create short-term wins. Short-term wins are organisational improvements that can be implemented within 6-18 months. Generating such improvements will help prevent loss of momentum.

Step 7 suggests that improvements from earlier short-term wins must be consolidated to prevent the organisation from sliding into complacency. Reassessing changes will also help to counter any continuing resistance to change. Essentially, this step is a tool to prevent the organisation from reverting to its old way of doing things.

Change within an organisation will not last unless it is aligned with the organisational culture. To anchor the new changes into the culture, the change effort itself must have brought positive results. Once the new changes have been shown to promote organisational success, employees will accept the change as normality. Recognition from stakeholders that the change has led to success is the final step in Kotter's framework.

Many people like the structure and implied sequence that Kotter's model entails. Kotter himself contends that skipping "even a single step" almost always creates problems (1996, p. 23). However, having dealt with each step in turn, it may be oversimplifying to suggest that you have then dealt with that task and can move on to the next. Rather, it may be helpful to think of the eight steps as a series of tasks which must be attended to in parallel with each having some consequence for the other steps. For example, creating short-term wins (step 6) may play a vital role in creating, or perhaps maintaining, the coalition of support needed to see the change project through to successful completion (step 2).

For this reason, there are other models in the literature which adopt a more iterative and processual approach. One such example is the Enquiry-Action framework (see Figure 6.3 below) which sets out three key areas of activity that change managers undertake. This more processual approach to change focuses on questioning and understanding the context, content and process of change, as well as developing a repertoire of alternative ways of enacting change.

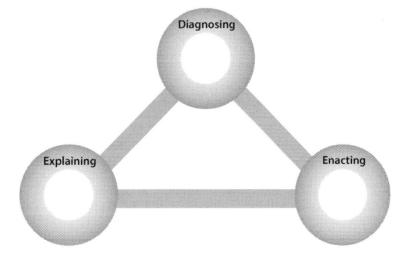

Figure 6.3: The Enquiry-Action Framework (reproduced from Beech and MacIntosh, 2012)

Diagnosis often focuses on understanding the current and desired future state(s) of the organization. Diagnosis can be about setting a clear purpose, but on other occasions it can be about understanding the different interpretations that people make of that purpose and recognizing the consequences (both positive and negative) of such ambiguity. It can concentrate on how far people are (potentially) engaged with a change or the state of play politically and whether stakeholders are aligned or not. Equally, diagnosis may need to uncover the cultural context of change, and people's established habits and ways of thinking, in order to recognize where it is possible an desirable to introduce innovations.

In **enacting** change it is rarely the case that one form of action will work well for all aspects of the change and for all those who are involved. It is therefore important to establish a repertoire of options for action. This means embarking on change with a combination of options and enough flexibility to be able to cope with the unexpected events, tensions and paradoxes that arise. Hence the second focal area entails the change agent and other participants making informed choices about a set of interventions which can involve different foci. Choices for enacting change might include changing the structure of the organization; exploring and engaging with a new identity for the organization, i.e. who we are as a group and what we see ourselves doing as a result of who we are; it may also entail choosing customers and competitors, changing processes, aligning people and their activities, fostering learning and development or developing a new narrative within the organization. Of course, the specific circumstances of any change situation may require a blend of more than one set of actions and the diagnostic work undertaken elsewhere in the framework might help to highlight complementary courses of action.

The third area of change work involves a switch in emphasis from enactment to **explaining**. Communication is often cited as being central to organizational life in general and to change in particular (one expression of this is Kotter's observation that we under-communicate 'by a factor of ten" in change situations, 1996). Yet communication is too often considered as the mono-directional transfer of instructions or explanation of the change typically from senior figures to more junior members of the organization. Similarly, the idea of piloting a new process in one area and then 'rolling it out' across the organization can be experienced by those who receive the roll-out as an imposition of ideas developed elsewhere. Overcoming this 'not-built-here' reaction is important in overcoming perceived resistance to change. The ways in which people respond to change is at least in part coloured by their reactions to evidence either that the change was necessary, or that it is working or that it will create new opportunities for groups or individuals. Such evidence is rarely simple and is usually subject to multiple interpretations.

The enquiry-action framework suggests that change can start in three different areas. In some cases enactment is underway and it is helpful to explain what is going on and then to diagnose because the change is having unintended consequences. Alternatively, it is possible to start by explaining things and in so doing to recognize the need to analyse and then act in a new way. Equally, the sequence can reverse and explanation can lead to a realization that a particular line of action is needed.

The matter of best practice in change management is a contentious one. For some, it is simply a question of adhering to a reasonably prescriptive set of advice such as Kotter's model. For others, a more processual orientation is required to establish what might work in specific circumstances. Given the complex and multi-faceted nature of change, there is no one right or best way to approach the problem. Indeed, as Henry Mintzberg wryly observes, when change fails "those at the top of the hierarchy blame it on implementation lower down. 'If only you dumbbells appreciated the brilliance of the strategy we created' … those down below might respond 'If you're so smart, why didn't you take into account the fact that we are dumbbells?'" (1994, p.25)

Why change is difficult

Research on change management indicates that change is often seen as problematic. One element of folk wisdom is that 'people resist change' and this observation underpins the development of models such as Lewin's force field analysis (Lewin, 1951). Using such an approach, those managing change are supposed to be able to identify in advance whether a particular initiative is likely to be successful or not based on an assessment of the balance of pros and cons. Other scholars would contend that this very conception of change is problematic since it assumes that the normal state of affairs is that organizations are not changeful, but for concentrated periods change can be effected through deliberate or inadvertent actions. Hari Tsoukas and Robert Chia turn this logic on its head by suggesting that organizations are naturally and perpetually changeful in their orientation. For them, organization is an achievement (Tsouka and Chia, 2002), achieved through the deliberate actions of managers who try to impose structure and ways of doing things which produce a temporary sense of stability. This line of argument brings the relationship between repetitiveness and newness. Most organizations come across these dilemmas from time to time and the themes of culture and learning can help in analysing the perceived choices of whether and how to persist or to change.

Culture and change

Organizations are inherently social and when we use turns of phrase such as "the government is asking us to ..." we are guilty of anthropomorphising organizations because governments, companies or other forms of organization don't ask, tell or instruct. It would be more precise to say that individuals working within an organization do the asking, telling or instructing. In doing so, these individuals draw on sources of power which relate to the collective rather than the individual. One key aspect of our sense of collective is the notion of culture. We each know that those organizations in which we participate have distinct characters and ways of conducting business. We pick it up in the first few moments of interacting with members of the organization and culture is therefore often defined as "how we do things round here" (Drennan, 1992; Hall, 1976)

When senior managers have a larger office, this tells us something about the culture of the organization concerned and this goes beyond the practicalities of that office being used as venue for meetings. The meanings associated with cultural symbols can vary. For example, some might regard a large office as something to aspire to and a mark of achievement, whilst others might see it as symbolising the separation of senior managers from the rest of the workforce. The ascription of such meanings is beyond the control of management yet will have an impact on how people behave. A singular description such as entrepreneurial, rigid or innovative is unlikely to capture every aspect of the organization, or to be universally true. Nevertheless we often develop such caricatures as a form of shorthand for use with those inside and beyond the organization. If nothing else, such descriptions help us make sense of the organization, particularly as a newcomer. New members of an organization must establish what is acceptable in their new surroundings. For example, it's your first day in a new job and you're invited to a team meeting. Should you question decisions that are being made? In some settings this would be seen as a way of demonstrating your commitment, intelligence and engagement. Yet the same behaviour in another setting might be read as inappropriate, disrespectful and even career-limiting.

Over time, we become socialised into our organizational settings such that we no longer need to think about the nuances of acceptable behaviour. It is for this reason that Ed Hall argues that "culture hides much more than it reveals, and strangely enough what it hides, it hides most effectively from its own participants" (1959, p. 53). A major problem for those inside the organization is becoming so steeped in the culture that even subjective judgements of whether things are normal, acceptable, helpful or limiting are difficult. Organizational culture gradually recedes from the view of those most familiar with it, yet culture can drive decision making, change and strategy in significant ways. For this reason, Cohen describes cultures as "collections of solutions 'looking for' problems" (1968) in that the most comfortable, reassuring thing to do is to repeat tried, tested and familiar processes. The Cultural Web (Johnson, 1988) offers one way of capturing a rudimentary description of an organization's culture.

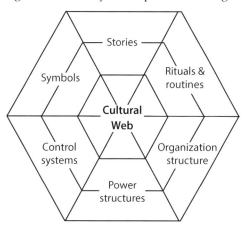

Figure 6.4: The Cultural Web (adapted from Johnson, 1988)

The cultural web attempts to summarise organizational culture by capturing observations about the physical, symbolic and social/organizational aspects of a specific setting. The model uses six overlapping but separate dimensions as a means of establishing a sense of the otherwise illusive culture of an organization. The six aspects of the model interlock, reinforcing each other to form a cultural web. It is then argued that this is why change is difficult because, in order to change culture it is necessary to address all six dimensions almost simultaneously. Individual changes may not be enough to break the web of interconnections currently in place.

For Johnson, culture tends to persist and is responsible for a tendency toward incremental change. First, organizations develop ways of doing business which quickly become embedded as **routines**. How firms recruit staff, develop products, manage suppliers, etc. might be conceptualised as routines and these routines characterize and form part of the organization's culture as the routine is repeated again and again over time. Some routines represent commonplace and everyday activity whilst others carry more significance. Johnson's early training as an anthropologist sensitized him to the importance of **rituals**, which he would describe as special events which highlight or reaffirm aspects of the organization's culture. In his most recent work he has examined the rituals associated with strategy away-days (Johnson et a. 2010) and there have been related studies of the effectiveness of away days as a means of effecting change

(MacIntosh et al., 2010). Rituals of this type are also repeated, perhaps less frequently than routines, and may be associated with rites of passage, celebration or reprimand. Other examples of organizational rituals might include the wrap party that follows the completion of a movie, graduation ceremonies that mark the conclusion of a period of study, retirement or long-service celebrations, the way that failure or rule-breaking is dealt with, etc.

These routines and rituals often form important aspects of the **stories** which circulate within the organization. Story telling in organizations is an established area of research and scholars argue that stories need to be succinct enough to be retold, have some memorable point or moral and be engaging or entertaining. Larger complex narratives are summarised down into snippets to facilitate story-telling (Sims et al., 2009) and the most powerful stories are viral. You don't need to have been there to interpret the story of a young entrepreneur striking a deal with a global firm and redrawing the map of an entire industry. Only a handful of individuals were actually involved in the interactions between a young Bill Gates and IBM, but many of us have subsequently heard snippets of the story where he convinced IBM to allow Microsoft to provide the operating system for personal computers. The story is short, has heroes and villains who may be interchangeable depending upon the point of view from which the story is told and the story itself tells you something about the ambition, vision and entrepreneurial drive that many see as characterising Microsoft.

Next, Johnson's model draws our attention to the symbolic aspects of the organization. These **symbols** are likely to be artefacts or events that hold meaning beyond their functional purpose. A named parking space is intended to ensure that you can always get parked outside the office, but it also symbolises importance and status. Company credit cards, frequent flyer lounges, numbers of direct reports, the use of first names or nicknames and jargon all operate at a symbolic level. Hence many other aspects of the cultural web, such as organizational structure, also operate symbolically to reinforce the culture and paradigm of the organization.

These first three parts of the cultural web (Rituals and Routines, Stories and Symbols) are common to all members of the organization. In many ways, these three aspects of organizational culture pervade organizational life. However, the next three (Power Structures, Organizational Structures and Control Systems) tend to be more prominent in the minds of those in managerial positions. **Power Structures** say something about the extent to which individuals, teams or groups can exert influence on others within the organization. This influence could be formal and directive (e.g. I am giving you an order) or informal and coercive (e.g. I am persuading you that this is the right thing to do). Power structures are therefore related to but distinct from organizational structures.

Someone further up the organizational hierarchy may have formal power over a more junior group of staff whilst in reality being unable to use that power.

Organizational structure then relates to the formal organograms that set out which groups and individuals report to each other as a means of capturing roles, responsibilities and authority. Organizational structure also says something about the number and frequency of meetings, who attends those meetings, etc. Again, it may be that in formal terms, key decisions are taken a monthly management meetings but informally everyone acknowledges that these formal proceedings simply rubber stamp outcomes agreed in some other forum.

Hence, the sixth and final category in the cultural web is that of **control systems.** These are the mechanisms which formally and informally monitor behaviours and outcomes throughout the organization. Examples might include performance indicators, bonus systems, promotion procedures, etc. For example, the way that people are rewarded encourages certain types of behaviour and also expressed the values of the organisation. In financial services, the reward system is likely to be highly individualised and increased rewards that are accrued by individuals who are able to act in an entrepreneurial way to attract new clients and earn commission. This reveals the underlying assumption that people are motivated by money and work best when focused on their own performance. In other settings where team work is important, for example to bring different skills together to achieve a creative product that could not have been produced by any of the individuals working on their own, team-based bonuses or rewards that accrue to the whole team on the basis of outcomes encourage a different kind of behaviour and reveal different assumptions about how people are motivated – in this case by the ability to make a contribution to an outcome that is valued and to be a professional who is highly regarded by his/her peers. Such arrangements exist, for example, in parts of the creative industries such as some music productions where groups agree to share rewards on the basis of joint effort going into the product.

Using the cultural web, it is possible to make some aspects of organizational culture explicit. This is not to say that the model offers a complete or necessarily accurate representation of culture. For example, different sub-groups within an organization might produce completely different cultural webs if a differentiated or fragmented culture is in place. Many scholars are critical of overt attempts to manage culture on the basis of over-simplified models. Alvesson (2002) suggests a number of ways in which culture is over-simplified, including a tendency to reify culture as something which exists and is amenable to intervention because our mode of explaining it is superficial. Taking such reservations on board, the cultural web can form a useful basis for further discussion, if it is simply taken as one account, at a point in time, of how culture is read by those involved in the analysis.

Learning and change

A related body of work considers learning processes in an organizational context. One of the most influential scholars in this field is Chris Argyris. As a species, a large part of our success in evolutionary terms is because of our capacity to learn. From early childhood we learn new tasks, internalise these and can recall stored solutions on future occasions. Argyris defines learning as a circumstance where "the use of the programme necessary to perform the requisite action is so much under control that the control over the performance does not have to be conscious or explicit" (Argyris, 1977). That is to say, we have truly learned something when we can execute tasks without giving it too much thought. A simple example such as learning to walk, ride a bicycle or drive a car, reinforces this sense that the activity sinks below our conscious awareness. We may drive a car, changing gears, lanes or speed without "thinking" about it. We may even be able to hold a conversation, think about our destination or admire the scenery whilst driving. However, to achieve mastery of the task such that it can be recalled in this way involves the ruthless generalisation and storage of routines (Sussman, 1973). Notably, routines also form part of our sense of culture and the very familiarity that they introduce is a double-edged sword.

Argyris and Schön's explanation of what happens as we learn something for the first time is simple. The experience of learning a complex task such as driving, playing a musical instrument or learning a language often involves failure, errors and disappointment (Argyris & Schon, 1978). That is the essence of what is called learning by 'trial and error'. Argyris and Schön recognise two different modes or models of learning, which they labelled double loop and single loop. Double loop learning is learning from first principles. As described in Figure 6.5, the learner considers what Argyris and Schön call the governing values of the problem. Imagine trying to strike a golf ball for the first time. One must conceptualise how to hold the golf club, how far away from the ball to stand, how fast to move, etc. These various 'governing values' form part of our initial attempt to strike the ball. As we execute the task for the first time we may well make a mistake in one or more aspect of the problem. Perhaps we stood too close to the ball and missed altogether. Perhaps we were also trying to hit the ball too quickly and lost balance. The disappointment of missing the target would, in the terms of Argyris and Schön's model, be seen as a mismatch or error in relation to expectations.

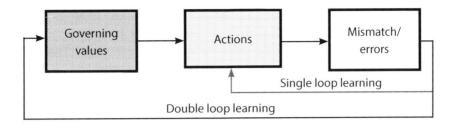

Figure 6.5: Single and double loop learning

Our learning process would take us back to reconsider the governing values of the problem, conceive a new plan for action, try this out and judge whether the results are acceptable. As we proceed we hope to reduce the mismatch or error that we experience to a point where results meet our expectations even though the outcome may not be perfect. For example, we may eventually develop a method of striking the ball which means that it travels fairly straight but perhaps not as far as we had hoped. Once, the mismatch or error reduces to a level that we can tolerate, Argyris and Schön suggest that we switch to a fundamentally different mode of learning. Single loop learning may continue to involve modest adjustments to the actions taken but no longer revisits the governing values of the problem. For example, our stance when striking the ball begins to become fixed and is no longer subject to revision. This is the ruthless generalisation and storage process that Sussman refers to since we need standardisation in order to memorise and categorise with any efficiency. A useful diagnostic test is to consider how much spare mental capacity you have when executing a particular task. If the task demands all of your attention it is likely that you are engaged in double loop learning. If the task can be executed whilst you think of other things, engage in conversation or other activities, it is likely that you have transitioned from double to single loop learning.

Argyris and Schön apply the same distinction between single and double loop learning when they consider organizations. When an organization begins to grow and eventually undertakes its first acquisition or foreign venture, it is likely that double learning will occur. If the organization continues to undertake a series of acquisitions over time, a single loop routine will develop such that the task is not learnt from first principles every time. The routines from a cultural web would simply be single loop learning activities which the organization has at its disposal. These routines would represent the 'way we do things round here' but as the environment in which the routines are used changes, some routines become obsolete and strategic drift can occur. By definition, we are not consciously thinking about the single loop routines that we use and when they become inappropriate we therefore struggle to notice. Hence a third category of learning is introduced to signify those sub-conscious routines which are actually unhelpful or inappropriate. Argyris suggests that we invoke so-called **defensive routines** when the social consequences of double or single loop learning are unpalatable. Defensive routines are described as those single loop routines that have become unhelpful in the way that many sub-conscious habits can (Beech and MacIntosh, 2012). As such, defensive routines offer a good explanation of the difficulties many organizations experience when trying to change organizational culture. Historical, embedded and habitualised patterns reassert themselves despite overt attempts to move beyond them.

The proposition we are making here is that organizational life tends to involve a life cycle. First, there is double loop learning when new circumstances or problems are encountered. Next we engage in single loop learning as we master these new problems and develop reliable, repeatable, routinised solutions. Finally, we invoke defensive routines where we are unaware that our single loop routines are no longer appropriate. Each stage in the cycle is driven by a strong evolutionary tendency to codify, "to ruthlessly generalise and store." All defensive routines were at some prior stage, highly functional single loop routines and were therefore probably associated with past success, or at the least with the lack of failure. To get some sense of the level of comfort and reassurance that a routine can provoke try this simple exercise. Sit with your arms in front of you, then cross your arms. After a few moments, place them in front of you again then cross them the other way around. The second time around there is usually some hesitation and sense of awkwardness about the simple process of folding your arms. Argyris's argument is that for more complex, organizational tasks a similar phenomenon occurs and we struggle to move beyond established patterns or habits.

Creativity and change

Having examined both culture and learning, it is clear that individuals and organizations accumulate ways of doing things which become habitualised. Once embedded, these ways of responding become difficult to change and this begs the question: how does creativity occur in organizations? To explore this question, MacLean and MacIntosh (2012) use the example of the world heavyweight boxing championship contest between George Foreman and Muhammad Ali to study the emergence of novelty. They draw on the work of a German social theorist, (Joas, 1996) to suggest that creativity flows from three interacting themes. First, the embodied biography of the individuals involved; second, the emerging intention of those in the circumstance; and third, interaction and relationships with others embedded in the same situation. From these three themes, creative action flows in ways which would be seen as unplanned by those describing the situation from a rational perspective (MacLean et al., 2015). Ali famously won the fight but did so through a series of key strategic changes and innovations which emerged *during* the fight. In their analysis of the fight, MacLean and MacIntosh (2012) suggest that this is a more compelling explanation of what actually happened than any other accounts of pre-planned or pre-determined strategic change.

In a similar vein, the American scholar Karl Weick notes that "there is not a transition from imagination, through intention, into execution. Instead, there is an imaginative interpretation of execution that imputes sufficient coherence to the execution that it could easily be mistaken for [prior] intention." (Weick, 1993, p. 351).

Conclusions

Managing change is a complex, demanding yet essential skill for the modern manager. Whether one agrees that we are living through a period of unprecedented change, or that change is either the norm or a temporary interruption to the normal state of affairs in organizations, it is a feature of modern organizational life. Change itself can be characterised using a number of different dimensions and not all change challenges are alike. Managers faced with change may draw on processual or prescriptive advice about how to approach their task but they will almost inevitably be faced with issues which relate to both culture and learned behaviours. Some basic analytical frameworks can help to engender conversations with those involved in the situation about how they are involved in (re)creating the organization. At some point however, change implies the development of a new way of operating (or perhaps a return to an older, long forgotten way of operating). As this occurs, it may be helpful to draw on more than linear, logical, rational accounts of the sources of novelty.

References

Alvesson, M. (2002) *Understanding Organizational Culture*, London: SAGE.

Argyris, C. (1977). Organizational learning and management information systems. *Accounting, Organizations & Society*, **2**(2), 113-123.

Argyris, C., & Schon, D. (1978). *Organizational Learning: A theory of Action Perspective*. Reading: Maddison- Wesley

Beech, N., & MacIntosh, R. (2012). *Managing Change: Enquiry and action*. Cambridge, UK: Cambridge University Press.

Drennan, D. (1992). *Transforming Company Culture*. London: McGraw-Hill.

Hall, E. T. (1959) *The Silent Language*, New York, Anchor Books

Hall, E. T. (1976). *Beyond Culture*. Garden City, NY: Anchor Press.

Joas, H. (1996). *The Creativity of Action*. Cambridge, UK: Polity Press.

Johnson, G. (1988). Rethinking incrementalism. *Strategic Management Journal,* **9**(1), 75-91.

Johnson, G., Prashantham, S., Floyd, S. W. and Bourque, N. (2010). The ritualization of strategy workshops. *Organization Studies,* **31**(12), 1589-1618. doi: 10.1177/0170840610376146

Kotter, J P (1996) *Leading Change*, Harvard Business School Press

MacLean, D. and MacIntosh, R, (2012) Strategic change as creative action, *International Journal of Strategic Change Management,* **4**(1): 80-97.

MacLean, D., MacIntosh, R. and Seidl, D, (2015) Rethinking dynamic capabilities from a creative action perspective, *Strategic Organization*, forthcoming (November Issue)

MacIntosh, R. (2003). BPR: alive and well in the public sector. *International Journal of Operations & Production Management,* **23**(3/4), 327-344.

MacIntosh, R., MacLean, D. and Seidl, D. (2010). Unpacking the effectivity paradox of strategy workshops: do strategy workshops produce strategic change? In D. Golsorkhi, L. Rouleau, D.Seidl, E. Vaara (Eds), *Cambridge Handbook of Strategy as Practice*. Cambridge, UK: Cambridge University Press.

Nazar, J. (2014). 14 Famous Business Pivots. *Forbes Magazine*. [online] Available at: http://www.forbes.com/sites/jasonnazar/2013/10/08/14-famous-business-pivots/ [Accessed 22nd of June, 2015].

Prindle, G. (2003). *No Competition: How Radio Consolidation has Diminished Diversity and Sacrificed Localism*. Fordham Intell. Prop. Media and Entertainment.

Robertson, B.J. (2015) *Holocracy: The Revolutionary Management System that Abolishes Hierarchy*, London: Penguin

Sims, D, Huxham, C. and Beech, N. (2009) On telling stories but hearing snippets: sense-taking from presentations of practice, *Organization,* **16**(3): 371-388.

Sussman, G. J. (1973). *A Computational Model of Skill Acquisition*: Massachusetts Institute of Technology. Available at http://hdl.handle.net/1721.1/6894

Tsoukas, H. Chia, R. (2002) On organizational becoming: Rethinking organizational change. *Organization Science* **13**(5):567-582

Weick, K.E. (1993) Organizational redesign as improvisation. In G.P. Huber & W.H. Glick (Eds), *Organizational Change and Redesign*. New York: Oxford University Press

7 Entrepreneurship and Business Growth

Laura Galloway and Rebecca Stirzaker

Entrepreneurship is a concept many people think they understand. Upon closer scrutiny though, entrepreneurship is a very difficult thing to pin down. Does it refer to the creation of firms? If so, then is all business creation entrepreneurship and are all business owners entrepreneurs, from window-cleaners to shop owners, from bakeries to high-tech manufacture? What defines a firm or a firm owner as entrepreneurial? Is it ambition, growth orientation, level of innovation? So does that apply differently in different firms, depending on industry – for example, a technology firm is likely to be highly innovative while a new restaurant may not be; yet that technology firm may have little or no growth while the restaurant may develop to the point where it can become a franchised chain. Which firm is the entrepreneurial one – the innovative one or the growth one or both? And does this mean that a lack of innovation and growth in a firm render it un-entrepreneurial and the individual who created it not an entrepreneur?

Additionally, does entrepreneurship apply where no new firm is created, such as where an existing organization develops and grows, particularly through innovation? If this does not involve entrepreneurship then Apple and BP and Nando's are not entrepreneurial firms. These firms reply on the ability of the people who lead and work in them to act entrepreneurially, and this is referred to sometimes as intrapreneurship. But does intrapreneurship refer to the workers, the management team, both, or does it refer to the organization as an entity in itself? And what do we mean by growth anyway? Are we referring to financial growth and profit? If so, then entrepreneurship cannot exist in social enterprises, charities or the public sector as profit is not possible in these types of organizations. Yet we know some highly innovative developmental activities are undertaken in these sectors, sometimes on a global scale; just think about the value generated by the ice-bucket challenge.

These are just some of the issues and challenges we are faced with when we try to capture what we mean by 'an entrepreneur' and 'entrepreneurship.' Despite these, while we may not be able to pinpoint it, there is definitely still something out there that is entrepreneurship. This introductory article will explore some of the ways that we understand entrepreneurship, what we need it for, and why it is important.

Theory and entrepreneurship

There are two main approaches to entrepreneurship theory. The first is the approach often associated with 'the entrepreneur' as an individual. The second is associated with established businesses and their development, 'entrepreneurial organizations'.

■   The entrepreneur

Classic approaches to understanding the concept of the entrepreneur include the Austrian or Economic School. Notably, Knight, Schumpeter and Kirzner are most often referred to as modern entrepreneurship theorists from this economic discipline. These theorists regarded uncertainty and risk as important features of the economic system, and this is what affords entrepreneurs the opportunity to make profit. Other approaches refer to the 'entrepreneurial personality' and the influence of the environment. Each of these will be discussed in turn below.

The economic approach
(e.g., Knight, 1921; Schumpeter, 1939; 1942; 1949; Kirzner, 1973; 1979)

Knight's (1921) *Risk, Uncertainty and Profit* has come to be known as the first work to make substantive contributions to the understanding of entrepreneurship (Carter and Evans, 2012). Knight argued that a market must be in a constant state of uncertainty, referred to as 'disequilibrium', and it is this uncertainty that entrepreneurs exploit. For Knight, the entrepreneur is prepared to undertake risk and the reward is profit.

Joseph Schumpeter understood the key feature of entrepreneurship to be innovation, where innovation created new products, services, and processes. Within capitalist economic structures, social and technological life develop as a consequence of 'creative destruction', the consistent and dynamic process of replacing old methods, products, technologies, etc with new ones. Schumpeter (1942, p. 82-83) defined it thus:

"the process of industrial mutation that incessantly revolutionizes the economic structure from within, incessantly destroying the old one, incessantly creating a new one"

Schumpeter considered innovation and perpetual creative destruction as the key drivers of economic growth. Entrepreneurship is described not as an ordinary event or process, instead, Schumpeter (1942) described economic development borne of creative destruction as special and extraordinary. He also argued though that competition among market participants leads to continual development and improvement of technology, services, and of ways of doing business, so these extraordinary events are enabled and encouraged by market competition.

Schumpeter is often cited as if approaching entrepreneurship from an individualist perspective. In fact though, entrepreneurship is presented as a function of large companies instead of the 'heroic' creative labour of a single entrepreneur (Schumpeter, 1949).

For Kirzner, the entrepreneur is associated with those who are alert to errors or gaps in a markets and can identify where fixing the errors or filling the gaps might generate profit. Thus, it is alertness to opportunity that is key to defining the entrepreneur:

"that element of alertness to possible newly worthwhile goals and to possible newly available resources ... the entrepreneurial element in human decision-making. It is this entrepreneurial element that is responsible for our understanding of human action as active, creative, and human rather than as passive, automatic, and mechanical." (Kirzner, 1973, p. 35).

While Kirzner focuses on opportunities and the ability to identify and leverage profit from them, by referring to alertness and perception as qualities of the entrepreneur, he implies there is a set of personal characteristics or a psychology that contributes to entrepreneurship. This points to a personality-based approach to understanding the entrepreneur and it is to this that we now turn.

The entrepreneurial personality
(e.g., McClelland, 1961; Meredith et al. 1982; Timmons and Spinelli, 2007)

The entrepreneurial personality school identifies entrepreneurship as associated with specific personality or psychological types. For example, Meredith, Nelson & Neck (1982) assert that the entrepreneur possesses five key traits: self-confidence, risk-taking, flexibility, need for achievement, and a strong desire to be independent. Timmons and Spinelli (2007) assert similar, citing high energy but emotional stability, creativity, conceptual ability, vision, and an ability to inspire as amongst the features of an entrepreneur.

On their own, personality-based approaches to understanding entre-preneurship are weak: no study has identified a core 'set' of entrepreneurial characteristics, and no study has definitively separated the qualities of a good manager from a good entrepreneur. Nevertheless, studies have found robust correlation of some traits and qualities with entrepreneurship. One of the most famous empirical studies of the entrepreneurial personality was by McClelland (1961). McClelland studied the needs of various individuals, classifying them as achievement-, power- or affiliation-oriented. He found entrepreneurs to score highest in the need for achievement category. Need for achievement describes a strong desire to excel; achievers seek neither power nor approval, but rather, their focus is on success. They assume responsibility for solving problems and they set challenging targets for themselves and bear deliberate risk to achieve them. Such individuals look for innovative ways of performing, and they perceive achievement of goals as the reward. McClelland argued that the need for achievement is the key psychological characteristic of an entrepreneur. He also noted though that need for achievement may not be innate, but may be acquired, and culture is a particular influence.

Timmons and Spinelli (2007) also note that many skills can be acquired. They extend this beyond the cultural to include the formal development of skills and abilities that can be useful to acting entrepreneurially. This points to the influ-ence of the socio-economic world on behaviour, discussed in the next section.

Socio-economic environment approach
(e.g., Global Entrepreneurship Monitor)

Rates of entrepreneurship vary region by region and some demographic fea-tures, such as race and gender, seem to have an effect on them. If entrepreneur-ship was about personality alone, this could not happen. The socio-economic environment, including structure, economic system, culture and conditions affect entrepreneurship. The Global Entrepreneurship Monitor (GEM) is a multi-country study of the rates of business creation throughout the world and it shows that different conditions have a large effect on both the rates and the types of entrepreneurship found in a country (global and national reports available at www.gemconsortium.org). GEM looks closely at structural, policy and cultural conditions in a country to see the extent to which entrepreneur-ship is affected. Some conditions are obvious; for example, in the absence of availability of state welfare, rates of self-employment are very high. In this case, entrepreneurship is not a positive feature; in response to poverty and lack of economic alternatives entrepreneurship is not correlated with innovation and opportunity. Entrepreneurship rates and quality are affected by other structural conditions such as policy, legislative infrastructure, access to finance, communications and physical transport infrastructure, and education in a country. National conditions can have substantial influence on different sections of the population, for example, between men and women, in-migrants and indigenous people. National culture, defined as the set of shared values, perspectives and formal and informal rules, can similarly influence entrepreneurship. For example, in the USA with its 'American dream' culture, entrepreneurship and private ownership are celebrated. Similarly, in countries like India or Pakistan or Bangladesh, owning a business is very highly respected, though this tends to be restricted in many cases to refer only to men.

Other socio-economic environment influences include social and human capital. Human capital is the skills, traits and experiences that an individual has, including personality characteristics, formal education, talents. Social capital is access to capital that will develop abilities or create links to people with appropriate skills and experience. Networks and trust are important aspects of social capital within a community. A person's human and social capital might also include their access to role models, which increases their perception of entrepreneurship as a feasible and attractive prospect; various research has found that having family or friends in business increases the chances of an individual doing the same (eg. Baron, 2007). The way that structural and cultural conditions can affect social and human capital, and the way social and human capital can in turn affect the propensity of a person to act entrepreneurially and perceive entrepreneurship to be an attractive and feasible prospect, brings us round once again to examining the personality of the entrepreneur.

Thus when it comes to theories of entrepreneurship that we might use to apply to the concept 'the entrepreneur', each approach, the Economic, the Personality, and the Socio-economic Environment, helps us to understand. As noted though, entrepreneurship is not always associated with individuals who start firms. Sometimes entrepreneurship is understood in terms of established firms' orientation and business development, and it is to this that we now turn.

Entrepreneurial orientation theory
(Miller, 1983; Lumpkin and Dess, 1996)

Entrepreneurial orientation theory (EO) is a commonly cited theoretical means by which entrepreneurship is enacted in firms.

Miller (1983, p.771) introduced the idea of entrepreneurial orientation, detailing that an entrepreneurial firm is one that "engages in product market innovation, undertakes somewhat risky ventures, and is first to come up with 'proactive' innovations, beating competitors to the punch". Thus, innovativeness, risk-taking and proactivity are three basic criteria that are required within firms for entrepreneurial activity. Lumpkin and Dess (1996) added to these three criteria a further two: competitive aggressiveness and autonomy. These five component parts of entrepreneurial orientation are described as follows:

- *Innovation* was first introduced as a feature of entrepreneurial firms by Miller (1983), and Lumpkin and Dess (1996) later divided it into two types; technological or product-market. Technological innovation comprises technological advance through R&D, while product-market innovation comprises market application of products. In technology firms there is much overlap of the two types of innovation, as new technologies and applications are refined and developed to market orientation.

- *Risk-taking* refers to the classic Knightian proposition: the pursuit of business development and business opportunity with finite resources where the outcome is uncertain, with profit being the potential reward for bearing such risk (Knight, 1921).

- *Proactivity* involves pioneering in the market. Proactivity is seeking business growth "derived from being the first mover" (Casillas and Moreno, 2010 p.270).

- *Competitive aggressiveness* is how firms address the established market, including market demand and how they respond to competition.

- *Autonomy* is the extent to which individuals and teams can act independently in organisations to pursue ideas and opportunities. Lumpkin and Dess (1996, p.142) identify that entrepreneurship in the form of new ideas and opportunities are made available in a firm by people who have the freedom to generate them: "creating market interest…scavenging for resources, going outside the usual lines of authority and promoting risk taking".

To act entrepreneurially, a firm does not have to engage in each type of activity described above. Instead, organizations that are known to be entrepreneurial – in that they innovate and grow – have been found to feature at least some of these five types of activity. Like theoretical approaches to 'the entrepreneur', therefore, the entrepreneurial organization cannot be definitively described. In the attempt to explain some of the features of 'the entrepreneur' and 'entrepreneurial organizations', much overlap is evident though.

■ So what is entrepreneurship?

Notably, entrepreneurship seems to be associated with value. This is often expressed as financial value, though this is a consequence of being inspected in the context of commercial organizations most often. This can be expressed in terms of the creation of commercial organizations; in fact Bygrave and

Zacharakis (2004, p.2) define entrepreneurship as such:

> "An *entrepreneur* is someone who perceives an opportunity and creates an organization to pursue it.... The *entrepreneurial process* involves all the functions, activities, and actions associated with perceiving opportunities and creating organizations to pursue them".

Elsewhere, entrepreneurship is associated with value creation in terms of financial (or other) growth in existing firms (eg. Mintzberg, et al., 1998; Karlsson, et al., 2005). Other recurring themes are the idea of innovation, as per Schumpeter above (Drucker, 1986; Florida, 2003). But conceptually, entrepreneurship is hard to pin down. As Moroz and Hindle (2011) note, even in the business world there is nothing that is *distinctly* entrepreneurial, nor is there anything *always* entrepreneurial.

With this in mind, we must tread carefully when we consider entrepreneurship and be clear in terms of what we are seeking to explore. At its most basic, entrepreneurship is about adding value, and most often we think of entrepreneurship as a business activity. The reasons why this is important and interesting are discussed in the next few sections.

The extent and importance of entrepreneurship

Taking entrepreneurship to mean business creation, the Global Entrepreneurship Monitor (GEM) has statistics for many countries showing how many people are starting firms, what types of firms, and the value and quality of new firms in different countries. GEM also finds that business creation and self-employment do contribute to economic growth and prosperity, but that there are different types of these and the extent to which they contribute varies. Most marked is the distinction made in GEM between 'opportunity entrepreneurship'– business creation in response to the pursuit of opportunities; and 'necessity entrepreneurship' – business creation in response to few or no economic alternatives (for instance a lack of jobs in the labour market, lack of welfare state). This way of looking at types of entrepreneurship is very similar to the idea first introduced in Storey (1991) that referred to 'pull' motivations for entrepreneurship – ie. pursuit of opportunities; as opposed to 'push' motivations – ie. entrepreneurship in the absence of reasonable alternative employment. Opportunity-based entrepreneurship adds value to an economy, as does necessity entrepreneurship, but while necessity entrepreneurship can be found in all countries, where it is the most common type of entrepreneurship its contribution is most likely to be about survival and sustainability, rather than innovation, development and 'creative destruction'. Thus, the type of economy can have an effect on the quality of entrepreneurship in a country and its contribution. In all contexts, GEM defines entrepreneurship exclusively in terms of business start-up and self-employment, and we will review the contribution of the small private business sector later on in this chapter. But as noted already, there are other interpretations of entrepreneurship, and these can be seen to be of critical economic importance also.

When defined as innovative behaviour and growth orientation in existing businesses and other types of organizations, entrepreneurship is also vital. With an increasing global focus on knowledge and innovation, and a highly competitive environment, organizations require entrepreneurship amongst their workforces. As a result, this is impacting on the skills and competencies required in workforces, particularly amongst graduates. Consider how quickly industries such as IT, energy, and engineering would collapse without entrepreneurial opportunity exploitation and innovation. In turn, to support entrepreneurship in private business, sectors such as law, public policy and education also have to understand and engage entrepreneurially. As Roberston and Collins, 2003, p.307) describe it, national competitiveness is developed by:

> "a workforce which will express itself in an innovative and creative
> manner irrespective of its current function – large firm, local authority,
> *small firm or community-based organization"

Thus entrepreneurship is important in all sectors. At the same time, modern economies are increasingly based on small firms and, as noted, one of the most common interpretations of entrepreneurship synonymises it with small business creation and ownership. It is to this sector therefore that we now turn.

The small firms sector

According to GEM, around 7 percent of individuals in the UK are in the process of starting a firm or becoming self-employed, and this rate is reasonably typical of European countries. Elsewhere, in countries such as USA and Canada the rate is a bit higher at around 12 percent. In countries such as in subSaharan Africa or Latin America it may be twice that, but in these cases entrepreneurship is often based on necessity rather than opportunity.

In terms of volume of firms, in most countries the vast majority of private businesses are defined as small or medium, abbreviated to SME (small and medium enterprises). SMEs are defined differently in different regions of the world, and often there are several different definitions available, for example, based on number of employees, turnover, and sometimes profit. Most often, employee numbers are used to describe the size of a firm. The definition provided here is the one used throughout Europe (see http://ec.europa.eu/ enterprise/policies/sme/facts-figures-analysis/sme-definition/index_en.htm).

Number of employees	Definition
0-9	Micro firm
10-49	Small firm
50-249	Medium firm
250+	Large firm

Deakins and Freel (2012) separate firms into two types: growth or entrepreneurial firms; and lifestyle firms. Broadly these describe the orientation of a firm, though growth and lifestyle are poles on a continuum rather than discrete business types. While the academic and policy specialists focus most often on growth and entrepreneurship, because of the inferred economic contribution, in fact the vast majority of firms are small and even micro. Most of these will be lifestyle firms – they have been created to provide employment and lifestyle to the owners and are not created with the intention of spectacular growth.

The cumulative economic contribution of the SME sector is impressive. Using UK data to illustrate, the Department for Business Innovation and Skills (BIS, 2013) reports that SMEs comprise 99.9 percent of all private firms and they employ around 15 million people (this represents nearly 60 percent of private sector employment). According to the Federation of Small Businesses (FSB, 2014), the vast majority of these firms are classified as small (ie. with fewer than 50 employees). In fact, the most common type of business is a sole trader – or self-employed person. Levie and Lichtenstein (2010) estimate that in the USA for example, more than 70 percent of businesses have no employees other than the owner, while in the UK this is even higher at 75 percent (BIS, 2013). Within the SME sector there will be lifestyle firms and growth firms and everything in between. In fact, many firms change their orientation over time, sometimes as a result of change in circumstances of the owner, where to begin with perhaps they considered starting a business for lifestyle reasons and then saw opportunities to expand and had the time and resources to do this. This can even happen inter-generationally; many family firms change their orientation from one leader to the next, for example, both Wal-Mart and Michelin started small and grew over several generations. Elsewhere, small firms – including sole proprietorships – are started with highly entrepreneurial ambitions from the outset. Firms such as Microsoft, Amazon and EasyJet were started with large amounts of investment and the ambition always was to establish, grow and 'harvest' into a stock exchange potential.

7

Most firms are not growth-oriented though (Morris, et al., 2006; Levie and Lichtenstein, 2010). But that does not mean entrepreneurship is not enacted in these firms, and indeed, the importance of small firms is represented in several ways other than their direct contribution to regional economic growth.

With their vast cumulative volume, SMEs are important in terms of their ability to create employment – including through self-employment; with their preponderance, they make a significant employment contribution. Small firms also afford diversification in an economy. They often are small enough to specialize in niches, providing products or services larger firms will not trade in as they are insufficient in scale. SMEs also can be started in any sector, they provide support and services in sectors dominated by larger firms, they form parts of supply chains, and are often the seedbed of ideas and creativity that large firms do not have scope for. In addition, SMEs can contribute in terms of revitalization. For example, in regions of industrial or commercial decline, a burgeoning SME sector can revitalize local economies. This is the underpinning premise of some government interventions, for example, lots of city authorities will use incentives to create restaurant or entertainment clusters, for instance, in areas of retail decline. Elsewhere, workshop and small scale manufacture might be encouraged in an area experiencing industrial contraction, for example, following the withdrawal or cessation of a large industrial firm or sector. Other contributions made by the SME sector relate us, full circle, back to entrepreneurship associated with innovation and opportunity. Most firms start small, sometime started with little or no capital. SMEs are the commercial means by which ideas can take shape and in some cases and in some industries this is where exploration and opportunity are most appropriate. Smaller scale equates to smaller, more manageable risk in many cases. A very famous example of this is the small firm Tokyo Tsushin Kenkyujo, which started as a communications firm in post-war Japan in the 1940s. As the patent expired for the American-invented semiconductor, this firm spotted an opportunity to use it to mass produce small radios. To go global required a name easily pronounced in any language, and thereby Sony was born.

Conclusion

Entrepreneurship is many things to many people. Primarily it is viewed as a means of adding value, be that by creating a new organisation or by developing an existing one. Most often it is associated with innovation and with growth and development. It has clear links to profit and capitalism, but this does not represent entrepreneurship entirely. There are many ways in which adding value and acting entrepreneurially can be applied without the requirement of profit.

Social enterprises in particular exist to add social value, not profit, as all surplus created is reinvested back into the social enterprise or the community it serves. Dees (2001) describes entrepreneurship as associated with change, whereby the component features of problem solving, opportunity identification and adding value can be applied socially just as well as financially. Charities also often operate on this basis, and while they are not businesses in that they do not exist to sell a product or service and are often supported by donation and other non-sales-based fund-raising, some very entrepreneurial strategies and behaviours are observed there. Even when a business is created in the traditional profit-oriented manner, social and other objectives are not necessarily precluded. For example, Muhammad Yunus created Grameen Bank in Bangladesh as a means by which poverty might be alleviated. It provides small loans to people without requiring collateral, a system of lending known as microfinance. The most poor cannot use regular banks for lending purposes as they have no collateral. Grameen Bank now trades all over the developing world, including throughout Asia, in Africa and in South America and Muhammas Yunus has received a Nobel Peace Prize for his contribution to the alleviation of poverty. From a business perspective he points out:

> "Business is about problem-solving, but it does not always have to be about maximizing profit. When I went into business, my interest was to figure out how to solve problems I see in front of me. That's why I looked at the poverty issue... You can also have social objectives. Ask yourself these questions: Who are you? What kind of world do you want?"

Fundamentally, entrepreneurship is about positive action to generate change based on improvement and opportunity. The contribution it might make at an individual person or firm level may be enormous or may be merely about creating employment for oneself. Thus, however it is defined, the cumulative economic and social effects of entrepreneurship are unequivocally associated with the inexorable development of technologies, products, services and values.

Next steps

The Galloway et al. paper listed below supports this chapter refers to the impact of small businesses to local rural economies. It explores the challenges of remoteness and isolation from extended markets and other businesses and supply chains. In particular, the paper investigates the extent to which the internet has mitigated some of these challenges by giving firms access to supply chains and global markets. Where in theory this might facilitate growth through affording access to networks with other business and support, and especially through extending market reach, the paper finds the opposite. Instead of using internet technologies to grow markets, small rural firms were more likely to use internet technologies to augment local sales and sustainability. The contribution of small local firms in rural areas is highly important to the rural economy in terms of employment and turnover. This is most often experienced as the cumulative contribution of the local sustainable sector, rather than attributable to spectacular growth amongst individual firms though. While entrepreneurial growth was certainly observable in a few firms, the paper concludes that the most common type of entrepreneurship in rural areas is not definable in growth terms. The contribution made is no less significant for that, and our understanding of what entrepreneurship is and how it contributes to economies is challenged and developed.

Further reading

Deakins, D. & Freel, M. (2012) *Entrepreneurship and Small Firms*, 6th edition, McGraw-Hill.

Global Entrepreneurship Monitor, Global Reports and National Reports (various), available at www.gemconsortium.org.

Galloway, L., Sanders, J. & Deakins, D. (2011) Rural small firms use of the internet: from global to local, *Journal of Rural Studies*, **27**, 254-262.

References

Baron, R.A. (2007). Entrepreneurship: A process perspective. In Baum, J.R., Frese, M. and Baron, R.A. (eds) *The Psychology of Entrepreneurship*. New York: Society for Industrial and Organisational Psychology.

BIS (2013) Busines Population Estimates for the UK and Regions 2013, available at https://www.gov.uk/government/uploads/system/uploads/attachment_data/file/254552/13-92-business-population-estimates-2013-stats-release-4.pdf

Bygrave, W. & Zacharakis, A. (2004) *The Portable MBA in Entrepreneurship*, John Wiley & Sons, New Jersey

Carter, S. and Jones-Evans, D. (2012) *Enterprise and Small Business*, London: Prentice Hall, London: Prentice Hall.

Casillas, J. C., & Moreno, A. M. (2010). The relationship between entrepreneurial orientation and growth: The moderating role of family involvement. *Entrepreneurship and Regional Development*, **22**(3-4), 265-291.

Deakins, D., & Freel, M. (2012). *Entrepreneurship and Small Firms*: McGraw-Hill Education.

Dees, J. G (2001) 'The Meaning of Social Entrepreneurship', online paper available at http://www.fuqua.duke.edu/centers/case/documents/dees_SE.pdf.

Drucker, P. (1986) *Innovation and Entrepreneurship* HarperCollins Publishers: New York.

Florida, R. (2003) 'Entrepreneurship, Creativity and Regional Economic Growth' in D.M. Hart (ed) *The Emergence of Entrepreneurship Policy: Governance, Start-ups and Growth in the US Knowledge Economy*, Cambridge, Cambridge University Press.

FSB (2014) Small Business Statistics, available at www.fsb.org.uk/stats

Karlsson, C., Friis, C., and Paulsson, T. (2005), Relating entrepreneurship to economic growth, in B. Johansson, C. Karlsson, and R.R. Stough, (Eds), *The Emerging Digital Economy: Entrepreneurship, Clusters and Policy*, Springer-Verlag, Berlin.

Kirzner, I. M. 1973.*Competition and Entrepreneurship.*Chicago and London: University of Chicago Press.

Kirzner, I. M. 1979. *Perception Opportunity and Profit: Studies in the Theory of Entrepreneurship.* Chicago and London: University of Chicago Press.

Knight, F. (1921) Risk, *Uncertainty and Profit.* Boston: Houghton-Mifflin.

Levie, J., & Lichtenstein, B. B. (2010). A terminal assessment of stages theory: Introducing a dynamic states approach to entrepreneurship.*Entrepreneurship Theory and Practice*, **34**(2), 317-350.

Lumpkin, G.T. and Dess, G.G. (1996) Clarifying the entrepreneurial orientation construct and linking it to performance, *Academy of Management Review*, **21** (1) 135-172.

McClelland, D. (1961) *The Achieving Society.* Princeton, NJ: Van Nostrand Publishing

Meredith, G. G., Nelson, R.E. and Neck, P.A. (1982). *The Practice of Entrepreneurship.* International Labour Office, Geneva.

Miller, D. (1983) The correlates of entrepreneurship in three types of firms, *Management Science*, **29**, 770-791.

Mintzberg, H., Ahlstrand, B. & Lampel, J. (1998). *Strategy Safari*, Prentice Hall.

Morris, M.H., Nola, M.N., Craig, W.E. and Coombes, S.M. (2006) The dilemma of growth: understanding venture size choices of women entrepreneurs, *Journal of Small Business Management*, **44**(2): 221-244.

Moroz, P. W. & Hindle, K. (2012). Entrepreneurship as a process: Toward harmonizing multiple perspectives. *Entrepreneurship Theory and Practice* **36**(4), 781-818.

Robertson, M., & Collins, A. (2003). Developing entrepreneurship in West Yorkshire: West Yorkshire universities' partnership and business Start-Up@ Leeds met. *Education+ Training*, **45**(6), 303-307.

7

Schumpeter, J.A. (1939) *Business Cycles*. Porcupine Press: Philadelphia.

Schumpeter, J.A. (1942) *Capitalism, Socialism and Democracy*, New York: Harper & Brothers.

Schumpeter, J.A. (1949) *Economic Theory and Entrepreneurial History- Change and the Entrepreneur, Postulates and Patterns for Entrepreneurial History*. Harvard University Press: Cambridge, MA.

Storey, D. (1991) 'The birth of new firms – does unemployment matter', *Small Business Economics*, **3**, 21-25.

Timmons, J.A. and Spinelli, S. (2007), *New Venture Creation: Entrepreneurship for the 21st Century*, New York: McGraw-Hill.

8 Economics and Regional Development

Mike Danson and Christopher Kerry

The macroeconomic environment and how this is managed has a direct influence on our daily lives. The performance, structure, behaviour, and decision-making of an economy as a whole have long held the attention of both policymakers and academia. Casual familiarity with daily newspapers, websites or other media suggests that we have not yet developed a clear understanding of how best to secure stable and prosperous economies. Nevertheless over time terminology, theories and indicators have been developed in an effort to explain what is happening within any given macroeconomic environment. Additionally, policymakers have developed tools and strategies in an effort to ensure stability and economic growth at national, regional, and even local levels. Trade is a vital component of any macroeconomic policy, with governments displaying various different attitudes towards its management.

This chapter will explain some the most important theories and concepts regarding the macroeconomic environment. It will also look at the different economic systems and the complex nature of trade, noting its impact on economies.

What is the macroeconomic environment?

When attempting to explain **macro**economics it is imperative to distinguish it from **micro**economics, as they are two commonly confused concepts. **Micro**economics is the study of decisions that individuals and businesses make regarding the allocation of resources and the prices of goods and services. It is concerned with the study of markets (e.g. food markets, financial markets) and specific segments and sectors of the economy. It focuses on supply and demand in these individual markets and analyses forces that help determine prices in the economy. These forces include individual labour markets, looking at areas such as the demand for labour as well as how wages are determined. It is also concerned with both positive and negative externalities of production and consumption. For example, the pollution caused from cars and motorbikes, or the impact of research and development, which often leads to new technologies that other firms can benefit from.

Macroeconomics looks at the bigger picture (aggregate economy), focusing on the movement and trends of the 'economy as a whole', rather than on individual markets. These can be national, regional, and global economies. Macroeconomics examines economy-wide phenomena such as output and income, inflation and deflation, and unemployment, using aggregated indicators to measure and understand how the economy functions. It usually involves the development of models that analyse and explain the relationship between major economic factors including: national income, output, consumption, unemployment, inflation, savings, investment, international trade and international finance. Such models help governments and corporations formulate economic policies and strategies. The study of macroeconomics also covers the analysis of the role of these fiscal and monetary policies, along with issues surrounding economic growth, the determination of consumption and investment levels, and to do with foreign trade and its economic relationships with other countries.

■ The circular flow of income

The concept of the circular flow of income allows us to better understand the 'economy as a whole' along with the role that individuals and households, businesses and governments play in the flow of money, goods and services. Understanding the circular flow process is key to explaining how national income, output and expenditure are created over time. It can be shown in its most basic form as a simple economy consisting solely of businesses and individuals, to more complex iterations that include financial and factor markets as well as incorporating the rest of the world. Figure 8.1 provides a suitable overview of the interdependence of the 'flows', or activities, that occur in the economy, such as the production of goods and services (or the 'output' of the economy) and the income generated from that production.

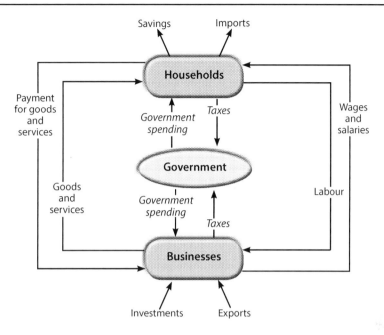

Figure 8.1: The circular flow of income model

■ **Households:** Provide labour to businesses in return for wages and salaries. Make payments for goods and services provided by businesses in an attempt to satisfy their unlimited needs and wants. Receive support from the government in return for paying taxes. Make savings and make purchases from other economies.

■ **Businesses:** Provide wages and salaries in return for labour. Provide goods and services in return for payment. Receive support from the government in return for paying taxes. Purchase capital goods from other firms, replacing worn out machinery or increasing their capacity to produce. Receive payment for exports made to other economies.

■ **Governments:** Provide support to businesses and individuals by spending on public and merit goods like defence and policing, education, and healthcare, and also on support for the poor and those unable to work. Levy taxes in order to fund their activities.

■ **Injections** come from investment, government spending and export sales, and flow into the economy, increasing the demand for domestically produced goods and services. Conversely, **leakages** are when demand for domestically produced goods and services is reduced due to money being diverted or lost into savings, taxes or imports. So long as leakages are equal to injections the circular flow of income continues indefinitely. This is known as being in equilibrium.

Savings (S) + Taxes (T) + Imports (M) = Investment (I) + Government Spending (G) + Exports (X)

However, due to the dynamism of any given economy, it is often in varying states of disequilibrium. Economies suffer from inherent instability. If $(S + T + M) > (I + G + X)$, levels of income, output, expenditure and employment will fall causing a recession or contraction in overall economic activity. But if $(S + T + M) < (I + G + X)$, levels of income, output, expenditure and employment will rise causing a boom or expansion in economic activity.

In each case, changes to expenditure and output lead to equilibrium being regained. For example, if $(S + T + M) > (I + G + X)$, households will save less, pay less in taxation, and with a lower income spend less on imports. Alternatively, if $(S + T + M) < (I + G + X)$, households will have the opportunity to save more, the levels of tax they pay will rise and they will be able to spend more on imports. National income can increase and decrease as a result of the changes in the various flows.

When there is a new injection of spending, the resulting increase in final income is called the **multiplier effect**. The size of the **multiplier** depends upon households' marginal decisions to spend, called the marginal propensity to consume (MPC), or to save, called the marginal propensity to save (MPS).

Gross Domestic Product (GDP) measures the total value of economic activity in a country (including both domestic and foreign producers) over a 12-month period and is commonly used as an indicator of the economic health and standard of living. However, when making year-on-year comparisons it is important to take into account inflation. **Inflation** is the increase in the general level of prices for goods and services. Therefore, it is important to distinguish between **nominal GDP**, which measures GDP at current prices, and **real GDP**, which measures GDP taking into account inflation. This allows us to make comparisons with a base year, enabling us to see how much real GDP had changed from one year to another.

Gross National Income (GNI) is the total income from products and services produced by a national economy (including residents' foreign investments). It is another indicator used to measure national income. Some of the incomes earned in an economy from wages, interest, profit or rents will be repatriated abroad by foreign residents. Conversely, some of the incomes earned by domestic residents will come from abroad. GNI takes this 'net income from abroad' into account. GDP, however, is only concerned with incomes generated within the country, irrespective of ownership. Hence it can be said that GDP is based on location, while GNI is based on ownership. GNI is quite similar to **Gross National Product (GNP),** which measures output from the citizens and companies of a particular nation, regardless of where they are located.

Economic growth

Economic growth is a country's increase in national income over time, conventionally measured as the percentage rate of increase in real gross domestic product (real GDP). Governments try to achieve both long term (growth sustained over a number of years) and stable economic growth (avoiding recessions and excessive short-term growth that cannot be sustained). It is important to recognise the difference between **Actual growth** – the percentage increase in national output – is different from **Potential growth** – the percentage increase in the economy's capacity to produce. Increases in resources and increases in the efficiency with which these resources are used lead to an increase in potential economic growth. When statistics on growth rates are published they are referring to *actual* growth.

Economic growth provides a number of benefits for both developing and developed countries.

Exercise 8.1: What might the benefits of economic growth be? Write a short description for both developing and developed countries

Provided it is higher than population growth, economic growth leads to higher real income per capita, resulting in increased levels of consumption through spending on goods and services. This is important as people aspire to higher living standards. However, without growth in productive potential, households' demand for higher wages is likely to lead to inflation, the purchase of more imports and industrial disputes. Also, some resources are likely to be working beyond their normal capacity, e.g. making extra use of shift work and overtime. This is known as a **positive output gap.** A positive output gap is associated with countries where an economy is over-heating because of fast and rising demand.

Exercise 8.2: Name some examples of countries running positive output gaps. Why are they good examples? How can governments manage this?

Economic growth can make it easier to redistribute wealth. Extra tax revenues can be spent on programmes reducing poverty without increasing the burden or tax levels of the rich. Additionally, as people become more affluent their attitude to the preservation of the environment may change. But, it is not guaranteed that income is distributed more equally and that the environment better protected. Increased economic growth leads to increased output and often, therefore, to increased pollution and congestion, causing an increase in health problems and reduction in the quality of life. Additionally, the financing of growth must come from savings, profits or taxes, leading to a reduction in short-term consumption. Changes in production made to accommodate growth can result in redundant skills in the labour market and skills shortages in new and developing industries.

Exercise 8.3: What other negative effects of economic growth might there be?

Long-term growth (increase in potential output) has two main determinants: increases in the quantity of resources available (capital, labour, land and raw materials) and increases in the productivity of resources.

Short-term growth tends to be cyclical and can fluctuate rapidly. Countries can experience high rates of economic growth in some years, known as a boom, and often associated with inflation. This is then often followed by lower or sometimes negative growth, known as a recession. Booms and recessions can be short-lived, lasting only a few months. They can also be much longer, over multiple years. The magnitude of these phases can also vary.

■ Inflation

Inflation is a sustained increase in the general price level of goods and services in an economy over a period of time. Usually it is done by looking at a selection of consumer prices, monitoring their changes and measuring them. In the UK this done through a consumer price index (CPI), with the rate of inflation being the percentage change over the previous 12 months. Items included in the index include around 700 separate representative items (Office for National Statistics, 2015).

One major cause of inflation is a rise in aggregate demand known as **demand-pull inflation**. Aggregate demand is the total amount of goods and services demanded in the economy at a given overall price level and in a given time period. It is represented by this formula:

$$\text{Aggregate Demand (AD)} = C + I + G + (X\text{-}M)$$

C = Consumers' expenditures on goods and services.
 I = Investment spending by companies on capital goods.
G = Government expenditures on publicly provided goods and services.
X = Exports of goods and services.
M = Imports of goods and services.

It is represented by the aggregate-demand curve, which describes the relationship between price levels the total quantity of goods and services demanded by an economy. Typically associated with a booming economy, firms will respond to a rise in demand partly by raising prices (P1 to P2) and partly by increasing output (Q1 to Q2).

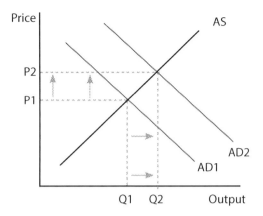

Figure 8.2: Demand-pull inflation

Figure 8.2 illustrates a single increase in demand, otherwise known as a demand shock. This could be due to an increase in government spending or a reduction in income tax rates, giving households more disposable income. The effect is to give a single rise in the price level of goods and services. However, once the effect has taken place inflation will return to zero. In order for inflation to persist there must be continual rightward shifts in the demand curve

The other major cause of inflation is **cost-push inflation,** which is associated with, rises in costs and therefore leftward shifts in the aggregate supply curve (independently of aggregate demand). Aggregate supply measures the volume of goods and services produced each year. It represents the ability of an economy to deliver goods and services to meet demand. In the short run, the short run aggregate supply (SRAS) curve is assumed to be upward sloping (i.e. it is responsive to a change in aggregate demand reflected in a change in the general price level). Shifts in the position of the SRAS curve in the price level / output space may be caused by, e.g., rising employment costs (wages, employment taxes), or raw materials and commodity prices may rise, with the exchange range often being a major factor.

Take Figure 8.3 for example, a rise in the oil price has increased the costs of production. Firms, facing a rise in costs will respond by putting up prices (P0 to P1) and by reducing output by cutting production. This is illustrated by the leftward shift is the SRAS curve to SRAS1.

High inflation can be extremely detrimental to an economy as a country's goods become less competitive in global markets, the country looks unattractive to investors, and the resulting high interest rates can depress demand. Governments therefore use a number of anti-inflation policies in order to tackle inflation. These will be discussed later in the chapter (See monetary policy and fiscal policy).

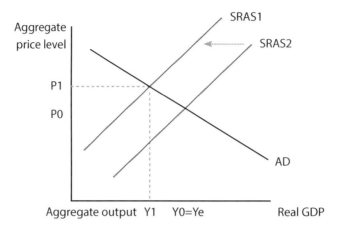

Figure 8.3: Cost-pull inflation

Unemployment

Unemployment is the percentage of people in the country willing to work but without jobs. It can be expressed either as a number or a percentage. There are two common measures of unemployment: the number of people who are claiming unemployment-related benefits (In the UK, jobseekers allowance), or a form of a **standardised unemployment rate, e.g.** the number of people of working age who are out of work, able to start work within two weeks and actively seeking employment (Sloman, 2006).

There are a number of different types and causes of unemployment. **Structural unemployment** happens when there is a long-term decline in demand in an industry. **Cyclical unemployment**, also known as Keynesian unemployment or demand-deficient unemployment, is when there is involuntary unemployment due to a lack of demand for goods and services. **Technological unemployment** occurs when productivity-enhancing innovation displaces workers and creates periods of higher unemployment.

Exercise 8.4: What are some examples of the causes of unemployment for each of the different types of employment?

High levels of unemployment not only hurt households but also have consequences for the economy as a whole ,as lower employment levels lead to a fall in tax revenues and to higher spending on welfare payments for those out of work. These reduce the ability of governments to invest in infrastructure and education, etc. If individuals choose to leave the labour market permanently because they have lost the motivation to search for work, this can have a negative effect on long run aggregate supply, damaging the economy's growth potential.

There can also be huge social costs, including increased levels of inequality and rises in crime and social dislocation. Long-term unemployment is very much a concern of governments.

■ The balance of payments

The balance of payments (BOP) is a statement that summarises the credit and debit transactions between a country's residents and other countries. It includes all transactions involving goods, services and income; any financial claims and liabilities to the rest of the world; and transfers such as gifts. The balance of payments classifies these transactions in two accounts – the current account and the capital account. The **current account** focuses on trade in goods and services, income from investment and employment and transfer payments (transfers) arising from gifts between residents of different countries, donations to charities abroad, and overseas aid. There are several possible causes of a persistent current account deficit. These include:

1 Excessive growth, meaning aggregate output (AO) cannot keep up with aggregate demand (AD);

2 High export prices as a result of inflation or foreign exchange rates, reducing a countries price competitiveness;

3 Lack of export markets for goods produced within an economy;

4 Poor productivity levels as a result of a lack of R&D investment or excessive interest rates; and

5 A lack of investment in real and human capital resulting in high levels of unemployment or underutilisation of capital.

The **capital account** mainly includes transactions in financial instruments. It records flows of real foreign direct investment (FDI), portfolio investment, financial derivatives and reserve assets. When all components of the BOP accounts are included, by definition **they must sum to zero** with no overall surplus or deficit. Imbalances in the capital account can result in surplus countries accumulating wealth, while deficit nations become increasingly indebted. The financing of a deficit can only be achieved by selling gold or holdings of foreign exchange, or by borrowing from other Central Banks or the International Monetary Fund (IMF).

Governments implement policies in an attempt to manage the balance of payments, as they do with economic growth, inflation and unemployment.

8

Managing the macroeconomic environment

Monetary policy involves using interest rates and other monetary tools to influence the levels of consumer spending and aggregate demand (AD). This includes altering the supply of money in an economy, usually done by changing the amount of money banks need to keep in the vault (bank reserves). For example, governments or central banks can reduce AD by reducing the money supply, making less money available for spending. Or, they can put up interest rates making borrowing more expensive and reducing spending levels. On the other hand, if governments are looking to stimulate AD they can cut interest rates, decreasing the cost of borrowing and encouraging people to spend and invest. This not only increases AD but should also help to increase GDP (economic growth) and reduce demand deficient unemployment. However, doing so is likely to lead to an increase in inflation as the demand for goods and services increases, resulting in price rises.

Monetary policy also influences the exchange rate. By engaging in open market operations (e.g. purchasing of government bonds) nations often attempt to devalue their currency in the hope of reducing the cost of exports and thus bolstering their economies. Additionally, changes in interest rates can make a nation's currency more or less desirable and thereby reducing or increasing the exchange rate and impacting imports and exports.

It is impossible to use monetary policy as a precise means of controlling aggregate demand. If authorities operate a tight enough monetary policy it is possible eventually be able to reduce lending and aggregate demand. However, when trying to stimulate AD monetary policy can be extremely unreliable, particularly if people are averse to borrowing even with low interest rates. Perhaps the most important aspect of monetary policy is the message it sends to the public. That inflation will be kept under control. Or, that the government is committed to stimulating demand in an economy.

The central goal of monetary policy in the UK is to manage **inflation.** In the UK this is done mainly through adjusting interest rates with the target of monetary policy being to keep inflation within a target of CPI 2% +/-1. However, when making decisions on interest rates, the Bank of England (responsible for the UK's monetary policy) also considers other macroeconomic variables such as economic growth and unemployment.

■ Fiscal policy

Fiscal policy is the means by which a government adjusts its spending levels and tax rates to monitor and influence a nation's economy. Fiscal policy works in tandem with monetary policy in attempt to manage an economy and influence the key macroeconomic objectives. Governments try to find a balance between effective tax rates and appropriate levels of public spending. Money from taxes can come from direct taxation, such as income tax and corporation tax, and from indirect taxation, (e.g. VAT and consumption tax) and from social contributions (e.g. national insurance or social security payments). Central and local governments (the public sector) need to spend money for a variety of reasons and most particularly because of market failures. For example, the private sector often fails to supply public goods (e.g. defence, roads and bridges) as well as merit goods (e.g. hospitals and schools, welfare payments, and benefits) so governments step in to supply these. Additionally, governments tend to inject extra spending into the macro-economy to achieve increases in aggregate demand and economic activity. Also, there may be a need for supply-side improvements in the macro-economy, resulting in spending on education and training to improve labour productivity. Finally, governments often attempt to redistribute income and reduce inequality through benefit schemes and supporting organisations dealing with social issues.

There are two types of fiscal policy, discretionary and automatic. **Discretionary policy** refers to policies that are decided, and implemented, by one-off policy changes **Automatic stabilisation** is where the economy is stabilised by processes called fiscal drag and fiscal boost. Fiscal drag means that as incomes rise, the impact of rising incomes for the better off is reduced as they pay proportionately higher taxes, and the impact of rising incomes on the poor and unemployed is reduced as they come off benefits, and start to pay tax. On the contrary, a fiscal boost is when incomes fall in a recession and households then pay proportionately lower taxes, and retain proportionately more post-tax income. This then stabilises national income, with bigger changes in income resulting in bigger changes in tax rates and spending.

Use of fiscal policy instruments incurs costs. An expansionary fiscal policy will involve raising government expenditure and/or lowering taxes. This will either increase the budget deficit or reduce the budget surplus. A **budget deficit** is when central government's spending is in excess of its tax receipts. A **budget surplus** is when central government's tax receipts are in excess of spending. If a government runs persistent deficits over a number of years then these accumulate, which is known as the **national debt**. The national **budget balance** is the extent to which public spending is balanced by receipts in any given year.

A government's fiscal stance can be an **expansionary fiscal policy** of increasing spending and/or reducing taxes, or a **contractionary fiscal policy** of reducing spending and/or increasing taxes.

Governments often try to achieve structural balance, structural deficits and structural surpluses. The public sector deficit (or surplus) is what would occur of the economy were operating at a sustainable level of national income. If an economy is producing above or below this level then there will be a cyclical component to the public-sector surplus or deficit. Under such circumstances governments are often willing to accept a deficit or surplus knowing that it is likely to reverse due to natural changes in the economy.

Economic systems

An **economic system** is a system of production and exchange of goods and services as well as allocation of resources in a society. All societies have to deal with the problem of scarcity and different societies deal with the problem in different ways, creating different broad economic approaches to manage their resources. A key difference is the degree of control a government has on the economy. It can be said that these lie on a spectrum: from a **planned** or **command economies,** where a government makes all economic decisions, along to **free-market economies**, where there is no government intervention at all. As the vast majority of economies are a mixture of the two they operate at various points across the spectrum. An economic system has numerous subcategories such as planning, coordination, and reform; international trade, finance, investment; and the political economy (e.g. institutions, property rights). In reality the degree of control a government exerts across them tends to vary, resulting in often quite different types of government intervention.

North Korea and Cuba are prominent examples of economies that are skewed towards planned or command economies. Whereas the economies of the US and Hong Kong have over the years had a considerably more free-market orientation.

■ Planned economies

In a **command economic system** or **planned economy**, the government controls the economy and decides how to use and distribute resources. It is usually associated with socialist or communist economic systems. In a command economy the state plans the allocation of resources at three levels. It plans the allocation of resources between current consumption and investment for the future. At a microeconomic level, it plans the output of each industry and firm, the techniques used, and the labour and resources required. The state also plans how output is distributed between households.

Under central planning a government can direct the nation's resources in alignment with appropriate national goals. Supporters of centrally planned economies argue that when economic decisions are left to the free market monopolies emerge, exploiting consumers. Furthermore capitalists extract profit from the labour of national citizens, draining a country's resources. High growth rates can be achieved through directing resources into investment, planning the allocation of resources in line with production requirements and labour skills, as well as, taking into consideration the social costs of production and consumption. However, in reality a command economy can only achieve these goals at great economic and social cost.

Exercise 8.5: What might the problems be in running a planned economy?

■ Market economies

In **free market economies**, individuals are free to make their own economic decisions. They are free to decide what to buy and firms are free to choose what they sell. These demand and supply decisions are transmitted to each other through the **price mechanism.** The price mechanism works as follows:

- **Demand-side mechanism:** A rise in demand is signalled by a rise in price. This then incentivises supply to rise as it becomes more profitable to produce. Price rises then moderates demand, discouraging consumers from buying so much. A fall in demand is signalled by a fall in price, an incentive for supply to fall, as goods are less profitable to produce. It will also encourage consumers to purchase more.

- **Supply-side mechanism:** Prices also respond to changes in supply. A rise in supply is signalled by a fall in price, acting as an incentive for demand to rise. Whereas a fall in supply is signalled by a rise in price, acting as an incentive for demand to fall.

A key part of the price mechanism is how it impacts on **interdependent markets**. Changes in goods markets also cause changes in factor markets (i.e. inputs of production) and vice versa. Additionally, there are interdependencies between different goods markets; a rise in the price of one good will encourage consumers to buy alternatives. Therefore, whilst households are looking to their own self-interest in the free-market economy, they are in fact responding to the wishes of others as a direct result of the price mechanism.

The price mechanism therefore has a moderating influence on an economy as no individual wields ultimate power, keeping prices down and acting as an incentive for firms to become more efficient. Indeed this mechanism is one

8

of the free-market's major advantages. Not only does it moderate an economy but it also reduces the need for costly bureaucratic systems to co-ordinate economic decisions. The economy can respond quickly to changes in supply and demand, minimising the problem of scarcity, and encouraging the efficient use of resources.

However, there are a number of problems associated with free markets. Large firms can often dominate an industry, resulting in reduced levels of competition. Rather than responding to consumers' needs, firms will invest in advertising in an attempt to persuade them to change their purchasing habits. A lack of competition can also reduce the need for firms to be efficient and result in socially undesirable outcomes (e.g. pollution). Free markets may result in power and property being unequally distributed, so that those who wield it gain at the expense of those without. They may lead to market failure, as some goods would simply not be produced by private enterprises. They can also lead to macroeconomic instability.

Exercise 8.6: What are the problems in leaving the market to decide all economic activities and flows?

The social market model introduces the social justice dimension, including social welfare programmes. This model promotes extensive state ownership, resulting in often high human development rankings, but at high costs for business.

We have also seen an **East Asian model**, where the government invests in certain sectors of the economy in order to stimulate the growth of new (or specific) industries in the private sector. Governments such as Japan, Korea and Taiwan have displayed high levels of state control over finance, have directly support state-owned enterprises in 'strategic sectors' and/or the creation of privately owned 'national champions', have placed a high level of dependence on the export market for growth, and encouraged high rates of savings (Kuznets, 1988).

Recently many governments have been erring towards **regionalisation**. Regionalisation potentially extends beyond trade and FDI to political and institutional integration. A prominent example is that of the European Union (EU). What was envisaged from its birth (in the 1950s) as a political union (helping governments deal with security concerns and promoting both peace and stability) has quickly become a monetary union (the euro). It is also an increasingly large set of economies cooperating on a whole range of economic issues in an attempt to deal with the rise of globalisation. Today's globalized economy challenges states' capacity and their manoeuvre room. Therefore, by entering into regional organisations they hope to regain some control over flows of capital, enhancing their bargaining power against transnational economic actors such as investor groups, multinational enterprises and so on. Domestic companies also benefit from belonging to a regional market big enough to allow them scale economies while still being protected from global competition.

International trade and global competition

International trade is the exchange of goods and services across national borders. It has tripled since the Second World War, growing at consistently higher rates than GDP. Over 40% of the world's trade is made up of goods that are used by a business in the production of goods or services (intermediate goods); dominated by trade between plants of multinational enterprises, this shows the importance of the rise of globalized supply chains. International trade has grown because countries have different endowments of factors of production (e.g. labour skills, climate, raw materials and capital equipment). Therefore, the ability to supply certain goods differs between countries, as the cost of producing the good also varies.

Adam Smith back in 1776 was the first to highlight the positive interactions between economic growth and international trade, coining the concept of **absolute advantage** in *The Wealth of Nations*. Absolute advantage is when one country can produce a good with fewer resources than another country. For example, the UK can produce whisky using fewer resources than Italy, but Italy can produce wine using fewer resources than the UK; each has an absolute advantage – in whisky and wine, respectively. Production of both whisky and wine would be maximised by each country specialising and trading with the other.

But David Ricardo (1817) has had the biggest impact on our understanding of trade, developing what has since become known as the theory of **comparative advantage** in his book *On the Principles of Political Economy and Taxation*. In a famous example, Ricardo considered a world economy consisting of two countries, Portugal and England. At the time, it was possible for Portugal to produce wine and cloth with less labour than it would take to produce the same quantities in England. However, the relative cost between the two countries differed.

Country	Cloth	Wine
England	100	120
Portugal	90	80

Table 8.1: Hours of work necessary to produce one unit

Despite Portugal having an absolute advantage in both cloth and wine, England had a comparative advantage in producing cloth. This is because England could commit 100 hours of labour to produce one unit of cloth, or produce 5/6 units of wine. Meanwhile, in comparison, if Portugal had committed 90 hours of labour to produce one unit of cloth, they would have produced 9/8 units of wine. In other words, the **opportunity cost** of producing 1 unit of cloth for England was 5/6 of wine, whereas for Portugal it was 9/8. If each country specialised in the good for which it had a comparative advantage, then the global production of both goods would increase. England can spend 220 labour hours to produce 2.2 units of cloth (instead of 1 unit of cloth and 1 unit of wine) while Portugal can spend 170 hours to produce 2.125 units of wine. Furthermore, if England then trades a unit of its cloth for 5/6 to 9/8 units of Portugal's wine, both countries can consume at least a unit each of cloth and wine, with 0 to 0.2 units of cloth and 0 to 0.125 units of wine remaining in each respective country. This could then be consumed or exported.

Therefore, a country is said to have a **comparative advantage** in those goods that can be produced at a lower **opportunity cost** than in other countries. If countries are to gain from trade then they should export goods in which they have a comparative advantage and import goods where they have a disadvantage.

Exercise 8.7: There are other important theories of international trade. Take a look at the product life cycle theory by Raymond Vernon (1966) and Krugman's discussion of globalised production and its impact on the location of manufacturing and gains on trade (Krugman, & Venables, 1995).

Recently, countries with low costs and abundant labour have seen economic growth due to export-oriented manufacturing. But, comparative advantages are not necessarily permanent. Trade involving such countries will tend to lead to greater equality in factor prices. For example, over recent years wage costs have risen substantially in China, threatening their low-cost manufacturing advantage (Rochan, 2014). Increased demand for labour pushes up wage rates. Consequently, countries are increasingly seeking to diversify their manufacturing base in order to mitigate against risks associated with international trade, moving into e.g. knowledge-intensive industries where countries are more likely to have long-term comparative advantages. These may be based on exploiting **first-mover advantages**, where a firm (or nation) enters the market first, has a production cost advantage over any rivals who may want to enter the market later. The already established firm has cost advantages – perhaps based on economies of scale, and other **barriers to entry** – which can make it very difficult for the other firms to sell enough products or services to reach the level of these economies.

Porter, in *The Competitive Advantage of Nations* (Porter, 1990), attempted to modernise comparative advantage theory, suggesting that some nations are more successful than others because they have advantages in one or more of four broad attributes that shape the national competitive environment. These are factor conditions, demand conditions, related and supporting industries, and firm strategy, structure and rivalry. Perhaps most importantly, Porter also addresses the role of chance and government policies in the development of trade competitiveness.

The role of government in international trade

Trade theories are claimed to show free trade can benefit all countries, with countries risking falling behind if they isolate themselves from global markets; however, many governments tend to try and protect national industries, as citizens demand security and independence. When they do so, this is known as **protectionism**. They are trading off protecting national employment and allowing national industries to compete globally, once they are ready, against the gains of free trade now. Industrialisation can be promoted by restricting imported products (import substitution), which helps to protect domestic jobs but can lead to loss of competitiveness in the long term. National culture can be promoted by restricting the import of cultural products and availability of foreign media content. For example, France has a number of policies that protect its art, its big film industry, its music industry – and, not least, its fledgling internet players (Carnegy, 2013). Yet, countries do not ban trade altogether. Instead they weigh up the marginal benefits against the marginal costs of altering restrictions, utilising various methods to restrict trade when necessary. The main methods include:

- **Tariffs:** taxes on imports or exports – a direct trade barrier. They are usually set as a percentage of the price of the import or export and can vary from good to good. Import tariffs are often used to protect domestic producers from 'unfair' external competition.

- **Import and export quotas:** limits on the quantity of a good that can be imported or exported, including **voluntary export restraint**.

- **Embargoes:** complete bans on certain imports or exports to certain countries. For example, the US embargo against Cuba.

- **Subsidies:** These can be given to domestic producers to help them compete against low-priced imports.

- **Procurement policies:** This is where governments favour domestic producers when purchasing equipment.

Exercise 8.8: Read these two articles on solar panels (Cardwell, 2014) and UK codes (gov.uk, 2015) and see how they apply to both imports and exports.

■ The nature of international trade

Today, trade is very much international. Most of the trade of European countries is with other European countries, and similarly in Asia, trade is also largely intra-regional, though North America is a major destination of Asian exports. Meanwhile African countries are not nearly as integrated in intra-regional trade as other world regions, but Asian exports to Africa are increasing rapidly, particularly to sub-Saharan Africa (Drummond, & Liu, 2013).

In the late 1940s after the protectionism of the previous decade, there was a desire to reduce trade restrictions resulting in the creation of General Agreement on Tariffs and Trade (GATT). Over the years this has developed into what we know as the World Trade Organisation (WTO). GATT and the WTO aim to liberalise trade. The WTO now has 148 members accounting for 97% of trade and has the power to impose sanctions on countries breaking trade agreements. Although WTO members have to follow a number of rules, many have **preferential trading agreements** often based upon regional groupings of countries known as **regional trade agreements** (RTAs): a European region centred on the European Union, a North American region based on the US, and a Latin American region.

Exercise 8.9: There are three types of preferential trading agreement: a free trade area, a customs union, and a common market. Write a 300 word description of each, highlighting the effects they have on trade creation and trade diversion.

In Europe, the EU single market aimed to dismantle internal barriers by 1992, but many still exist. North American Free Trade Agreement (Nafta) is the free trade area including the US, Mexico and Canada. In Asia, there is the Association of South East Asian Nations (Asean) – a political and economic organisation of ten Southeast Asian countries. There is also the Asia-Pacific Economic Co-operation Group (Apec) – a forum for 21 Pacific Rim member economies that promotes free trade throughout the Asia-Pacific region. In Africa, despite less regional integration than in other world regions there is the Economic Community of West African States (Ecowas) – a customs union. There is also the East African Community (EAC) – a common market.

Economic development is linked to integration in the world economy. However, the proliferation of bilateral and regional trade agreements is now overshadowing multilateralism in world trade, with discriminatory trade policies. This is particularly concerning as the increasingly global strategies of multinational enterprises have been a driver of increasing trade flows.

Conclusions

This chapter highlights the link between four key macroeconomic objectives and government policy, the variety of different economic systems available to authorities, and the role and magnitude of international trade. In doing so it addresses a multitude of concepts. The circular flow of income, economic growth, economic systems and international trade have been used to introduce some basic building blocks for understanding the economic environment of which government and global businesses are parts. The next chapter will look at how firms manage quality.

References

Cardwell, D., (2014). U.S. Imposes Steep Tariffs on Chinese Solar Panels. *New York Times*. Available at: http://www.nytimes.com/2014/12/17/business/energy-environment/-us-imposes-steep-tariffs-on-chinese-solar-panels.html?_r=0 [Accessed June 26, 2015].

Carnegy, H., (2013). France defends cultural barricades in digital era. *Financial Times*. Available at: http://www.ft.com/cms/s/0/b60f4182-bbea-11e2-a4b4-00144feab7de.html?ft_site=falcon [Accessed June 26, 2015].

Drummond, P. & Liu, E.X., (2013). Africa's Rising Exposure to China: How Large are Spillovers Through Trade? *IMF Working Paper*. Available at: http://www.imf.org/external/pubs/ft/wp/2013/wp13250.pdf.

gov.uk, (2015). Classify imports and exports using the UK Trade Tariff. Available at: https://www.gov.uk/classification-of-goods#classifying-your-goods [Accessed June 26, 2015].

Krugman, P. & Venables, A.J., (1995). *Globalization and the Inequality of Nations*, National Bureau of Economic Research.

Kuznets, P.W., (1988). An East Asian Model of Economic Development: Japan, Taiwan, and South Korea. *Economic Development and Cultural Change*, pp.S11–S43.

Office for National Statistics, (2015). Consumer Price Indices. Available at: http://www.ons.gov.uk/ons/guide-method/method-quality/specific/economy/consumer-price-indices/index.html [Accessed June 26, 2015].

Porter, M.E., (1990). The Competitive Advantage of Mations. *Harvard Business Review*, **68**(2), 73–93.

Rochan, M., (2014). Rising Wages May Erode China's Low-Cost Manufacturing Advantage. *International Business Times*. Available at: http://www.ibtimes.co.uk/rising-wages-may-erode-chinas-low-cost-manufacturing-advantage-1431142 [Accessed June 26, 2015].

Sloman, J., (2006). *Economics*, 6th Edition, Financial Times Prentice Hall: London.

Vernon, R. (1966). International investment and international trade in the product cycle. *The Quarterly Journal of Economics*, 190-207.

9 Managing Quality

Jiju Antony

Quality is an elusive concept, and in everyday language describing something as 'high quality' tends to imply that it is better than expected. In managerial terms, the definition of quality has evolved over the years as people have tried to move away from a subjective view that might vary from industry to industry. Take, for instance, a low cost item such as a disposable pen. As defined by the Oxford Dictionary, where quality is seen as the degree of excellence, a disposable pen may be seen as having a more inferior quality than a more expensive, luxurious or brand name equivalent. Yet, looked at from a different perspective, quality may be defined as the extent to which a product adheres to the expectations or specifications demanded by customers. Defined in this way, the disposable pen may be seen as a quality product that matches expectations. Indeed it may match or exceed expectations better than a far more expensive pen since the expectations of the latter may be far higher. Similarly with two types of cars; is a Mini or a Rolls-Royce the higher quality car? For the lay observer or someone operating with the Oxford dictionary, we might conclude Rolls-Royce is a higher quality mode of road transport than Mini. Yet both may satisfy the purpose for which they were purchased by their customers and both could therefore be argued to be quality cars. Over the years, a variety of management thinkers have tried to define the concept of quality:

- Quality is defined as fitness for purpose – **Joseph M Juran**

- Quality is conformance to requirements – **Philip Crosby**

- Quality should be aimed at the needs of the consumer, present and future – **William E Deming**

- The total composite product and service characteristics of marketing, engineering, manufacture and maintenance through which the product and service will meet the expectations of the customer – **Armand V Feigenbaum**

- The minimum loss imparted by the product to a society from the time the product is shipped to consumers – **Genichi Taguchi**

Organizations such as the International Standards Organization (ISO) have also offered definitions:

- Quality is the totality of features and characteristics of a product or service that bear on its ability to satisfy stated or implied needs – **ISO 8402**

- Quality is a system of means to economically produce goods or services which satisfy customers' requirements – **Japanese Industrial Standards Committee**

And commercial organizations have also tried to develop their own definitions:

- Quality is to satisfy the ever-changing needs of our customers, vendors and employees, with value added products and services emphasizing a continuous commitment to satisfaction through an ongoing process of education, communication, evaluation and constant improvement – **Nokia**

- Quality is defined as "providing our customers, internal and external, with products and services that fully satisfy their negotiated requirements"– **Xerox**

It is clear from these definitions that quality is both something that we each experience in our interaction with products or services and yet, an unusually slippery concept. In terms of a working definition for our purposes:

Quality means that a product or service has exceeded standards of what is expected in an industry; accepted/acceptable by the customer. A reputation for quality sets a standard for what is expected. Quality results from tested processes of research and development. Quality sets you apart from your competitors, has appeal, is durable, and meets standards set by industries.

Why quality matters?

Think about something that you have bought recently. It may be a meal, an item of clothing or something more expensive such as a computer or car. In almost every product category there are many more providers of a product or service than there are consumers. There may be dozens of places to eat but you will only pay for one meal. Quality then, is a crucial way of differentiating one organization from its competitors. Managing quality is crucial for all types of businesses today: manufacturing, service and public sector organisations. Quality products and world class services help to maintain customer satisfaction and loyalty and reduce the risk and cost of replacing faulty goods and poor services. Quality helps determine a firm's success in a number of ways:

■ Quality builds up the brand and makes the product more profitable. Think of your perception of various airlines and ask whether their price point is matched by your expectations in terms of service.

■ Quality, and of course the lack of it, influences your company's reputation. A strong reputation for quality can be an important differentiator in markets that are very competitive. Equally, poor quality or a product failure that results in a product recall campaign can create negative publicity and damage your reputation.

■ Superior quality products or services lead to positive customer experience and these tend to produce both repeat sales and sales based on recommendations. It may also be easier to attract and retain highly motivated staff if customer expectations are regularly being met or exceeded since few people enjoy dealing with complaints on a recurring basis.

In the long run, quality experts argue that inferior quality costs more money. If defective products reach the customers, you will have to pay for returns and replacements and, in serious cases, you could incur legal costs for failure to comply with customer or industry standards.

Evolution of quality

Systems for improving and managing quality have evolved in significant phases. During the last three decades or so, simple inspection activities have been replaced or supplemented by Quality Control (QC), Quality Assurance (QA), Total Quality management (TQM) to Lean Six Sigma (LSS). This section charts the evolution, from inspection through to the present day concepts of Lean Six Sigma.

■ Inspection

Under a simple inspection-based system, one or more characteristics of a product or service are examined, measured, tested or assessed and compared with specified requirements to assess conformity with a specification (ISO 8402). Materials, components, products, goods/services which do not conform to specification may either be scrapped or reworked; and those products/services which conform to specification can be shipped to customers. However, there are some fundamental problems with this approach to assure quality from a modern quality management perspective.

■ Inspection system is an after-the-event screening process with no prevention built into the process.

- There is an emphasis on reactive quick-fix corrective actions and the thinking is department-based.

- There is very little or no room for continuous improvement within the inspection system.

- Expensive and fallible. There is no guarantee associated with the final quality of the product or service. Good products/services can still be rejected by the inspector and bad products/services can still be accepted by the customer.

- Focus is on products or services and not on processes. Dr Deming calls this as 'burning the toast and then scraping it'!

- For some single use products (e.g. matches) 100% inspection is problematic

Quality Control

Quality Control (QC) is the operational techniques and activities that are used to fulfil requirements for quality (ISO 8402). Under a system of QC, one might expect to find in place detailed product and performance specifications, paperwork and procedures control system, logging of process performance data and feedback of process information to appropriate personnel and suppliers. Generally, Quality Control measures lead to greater process control and a lower incidence of non-conformance. Organisations whose approach to the management of quality is based on inspection and QC are operating in a detection-type mode (that is finding and fixing mistakes). The focus tends to be on switching the blame to others, people not being prepared to accept responsibility and ownership and taking disciplinary action against people who make mistakes. Companies operating in this mode are often preoccupied with the survival of their business and little concerned with making improvements.

Quality Assurance

ISO 8402 defines Quality Assurance (QA) as all those planned and systematic actions necessary to provide adequate confidence that a product or service will satisfy given requirements for quality. Examples of additional features acquired when progressing from quality control to quality assurance are a comprehensive quality management system to increase uniformity and conformity, use of seven tools of quality improvement (histogram, check sheet, Pareto analysis, cause and effect analysis, scatter plot, control chart and stratification), and the use of quality costs to evaluate the cost of not getting things right first time. When organisations move from QC to QA, one would expect to see a shift in emphasis from mere detection of non-conformances to prevention of non-conformances. In QA, the emphasis is given on advanced quality planning, critical problem solving methods, improving the design of the products and services and increased involvement of people with greater sense of accountability and ownership. In other words, one would see a clear change of emphasis from downstream to the upstream processes and from product to process. Changing from detection to prevention requires not just the use of a set of tools and techniques, but the development of a new operating philosophy and approach which requires a change in management style and way of thinking.

■ Total Quality Management (TQM)

TQM is a philosophy for continuous improvement by involving everyone in the organisation. According to Dale et al. (2007), TQM is a broad management philosophy embracing all activities through which the needs and expectations of the customer and the objectives of the organisation are satisfied in the most efficient and effective manner by maximising the potential of all employees in a continuing drive for improvement. For the success of a TQM initiative, the above definition emphasises three core and basic principles which include: total involvement of employees, customer focus and a drive for continual improvement. The following eight principles are well explained in BS EN ISO 9000(2000). They are essential for the successful implementation of TQM.

- *Leadership:* Leaders in the organisation should establish an environment in which people can become fully involved in the development and implementation of TQM.

- *Engagement of workforce:* People are the essence of an organisation and their full involvement enables their abilities to be used for the organisation's benefit.

- *Process management approach:* All work activities in the business should be viewed as a series of processes. Process efficiency and effectiveness should then be looked into for all critical processes using process management tools and techniques.

- *Customer focus:* Everything begins with the voice of the customer and it is imperative that organisations should understand the needs of their customers today and tomorrow and strive to delight them in the best possible way.

- *System approach to management:* identifying, understanding and managing interrelated processes as a system contributes to the organisation's effectiveness and efficiency in achieving its objective.

- *Decisions based on facts:* Decisions should be made based on facts and data. In God we trust, the rest will have to bring data! (Hastie et. al., 2009)

- *Mutually beneficial supplier relationships:* The principles of TQM have been extended to the supply chain for over two decades and the idea is to create value for both manufacturers and their associated suppliers.

- *Continual improvement:* This is not limited to quality initiatives. Continual improvement includes improvement in business results, employee and supplier relationships, customer satisfaction, etc. Continual improvement should focus on enablers such as communication, leadership, people and processes, resources and organisational architecture – in other words, everything in the organisation, in all functions, at all levels.

Lean Six Sigma (LSS)

LSS is a continuous improvement methodology that aims to reduce the costs of poor quality, improve the bottom-line results and create value for both customers and shareholders. The first integration of Lean and Six Sigma was in the US in the George Group in 1996 (Salah *et al.*, 2010). However, the term LSS was first introduced into literature around 2000 (Timans *et al.*, 2012). LSS teaching was established in 2003 as part of the evolution of Six Sigma (Kubiak, 2011).

Fitzpatrick and Looney (2004) argue that the combination of Lean and Six Sigma works well because Lean on its own does not typically bring statistical control and capability to operational processes. Equally, Six Sigma cannot dramatically improve the speed of processes. These methods both complement and reinforce each other to help impact the bottom line. Bringing both together creates a powerful vehicle for value creation. A review of several case studies in the literature has identified many drivers for organizations implementing an LSS strategy in the new millennium: for example, to improve their business performance and operational efficiency, especially in the growth of global markets, to improve product quality (Vinodh *et al.*, 2012), reduce production costs and enhance customer satisfaction (Chen and Lyu, 2009).

Why quality initiatives fail in organisations?

This section presents some of the common reasons for the failure of many quality initiatives we have witnessed in the past. The list below summarizes some references to quality improvement or continuous improvement initiative failures reported in the literature:

- Many quality improvement programs had very promising starts and encouraging initial results, but died down after two to three years (Shih and Gurnani, 1997).

- Failure rate for the initiated TQM programs is 95% (Burrows (1992) cited in Choi and Eboch (1998)).

- Two-thirds of the TQM programs are terminated, because they did not lead to expected results (*Economist* (1992) cited in Choi and Eboch (1998)).

- Putting together all the independent research, shows that only one-fifth or, at its best, one-third of TQM programs in the United States and Europe have achieved success (Harari, 1993).

- Specifically, in relation to Continuous Improvement (CI) implementation, Angel and Pritchard (2008) state that 60% of Six Sigma initiatives fail to achieve the desired results.

- Bhasin (2012) indicates that less than 10% of UK organisations are in fact successful in their Lean implementation efforts, whilst the rate of failure of TQM implementations is similar to other strategies (Candido and Santos, 2011), with success levels reported to be between 10-30% in Europe (Oakland and Tanner, 2007).

A recent study of quality improvement project failures indicated eight possible themes which are set out below. In 'Failure of Continuous Improvement (CI) initiatives in manufacturing environments: A systematic review of the evidence', McLean *et al.* (2015) argue that failure can flow from:

Theme1: Motives and expectations

The reason for introducing and continuing the initiative is critical. The motivation should be based on individual company needs, and not simply adopting an initiative because other firms have already done so. Responding to external pressures rather than the needs of the organization, or being driven by inadequate quality performance rather than the customer, are believed to be misguided motives. An absence of pressure or the presence of urgency will be problematic. Zbaracki (1998) identifies that some organisations will hold unrealistic expectations. Setting unrealistic targets is likely to lead to disappointment and overall failure can result when these expectations are not met. The motivations and expectations of employees are also important, as issues can arise if differing perceptions exist amongst managers and operatives (Bhasin, 2012). Snee (2010) believes a lack of incentive to individuals can be problematic, whilst Sterman et al. (1997) state that inconsistent incentives are more likely to lead to failure.

Theme2: Organisational culture and environment

A failure to change the organizational culture or environment (Yeung et al., 2006) can be problematic; as the existing culture of an organization could impair performance and stifle change. Some organizations will make unrealistic assumptions about their ability to transform their beliefs and create a new culture (Powell, 1995). The environment in which the organization operates can also influence the implementation. Whilst the organization may not have as much control over these factors, it is important that they are considered and planned for. Timing may not be ideal for implementation where failure can result, for instance, if a tight economic environment exists (Cudney and Elrod, 2011).

Theme 3: The management leadership

An organizational change program will demand intense leadership commitment and consume large amounts of management time (Powell, 1995). A lack of senior management commitment will lead to failure (Snee, 2010). This lack of commitment could be evident through the management shifting attention from the initiative, having strategic priorities elsewhere, providing poor management support (Jeyaraman and Teo, 2010) and poor involvement or delegating responsibility to others. Soltani et al. (2005) highlight a lack of knowledge and training amongst senior managers as a potential cause. This lack of commitment will in turn cause a lack of commitment amongst the workforce. Initiatives also fail when abandoned due to management frustration with teething problems. This behaviour could result from complacency and an underestimation of the effort required to achieve desired results.

Theme 4: Implementation approach

Implementation is regularly referred to by scholars as a reason for failure of a continuous improvement initiative. Poor implementation, deployment, or execution are given as holistic, over-arching reasons (Snee, 2010; Jeyaraman and Teo, 2010). These, however, provide little guidance on the specifics of an implementation, which warrant consideration.

The mechanics of implementation also requires consideration, as organizations have been guilty of employing related strategies in isolation (Ahire et al., 1996), potentially understanding the individual techniques involved but struggling with how these fit together. The efforts will suffer where a weak implementation structure exists in terms of roles, planning and organising, or where the organization is not planning to involve everyone. This issue could, in part, be due to the organization not having a roadmap to follow during the implementation process (Snee, 2010).

Theme 5: Training

A lack of training and education (Al-Najem et al., 2013; Bhasin, 2012) is identified as a major issue. It would be wrong to focus on training everyone rather than achieving delivery of improvement (Snee, 2010; Breyfogle, 2005). Some organizations will provide training programmes that are not capable of developing the necessary skills, that are delivered using inappropriate methods (Cudney and Elrod, 2011), or that provide diluted training content (Gijo, 2011). The varied standard of training and certification offered by consultants (Gijo, 2011) is highlighted, yet it is argued that internal resource delivering training removes focus from delivering improvements and risks the quality of material delivered (Breyfogle, 2005).

Even if the training is delivered to the required standard, the benefits will not be realized if the support received afterwards is inadequate (Sterman et al., 1997). The application of the training, typically through projects, can lead to issues. The initiative will struggle if employees use the approach less frequently, consistently or assiduously than required. Frustration can also develop if there is a perceived lag between the training and results (Snee, 2010).

Theme 6: Project management

Projects are typically the mechanisms employed to achieve results. Poor selection (Gijo, 2011) and resourcing (Snee, 2010) of projects can contribute to failure of the initiative. Specifically, an issue exists when project selection is not aligned to strategy (Kornfeld and Kara, 2013). In terms of project selection, there are many areas in which the organisation can fail. Projects may have the wrong focus (Cudney and Elrod, 2011), which could mean they are not tied to business goals (Snee, 2010); not focus where the business will benefit most (Breyfogle, 2005), or focus on cost reduction rather than the customer. Projects may also be too large in scope (Hariharan, 2006) or selected using inappropriate methods (Kornfeld and Kara, 2013). It is also wrong to target a number of project completions as a measure of success, as this leads to incomplete or abandoned ones from selecting insignificant projects (Hariharan, 2006). In terms of resources, project failure can stem from assigning the wrong people to the project, not getting enough time to work on the project, or conversely having too large a project team (Snee, 2010).

Theme 7: Employee involvement levels

Sterman et al. (1997) note that improvement efforts may take too much time away from the primary responsibilities of employees. This can result in a feeling of role conflict, with tension between work demands and the problem-solving methods. The necessary resource must be allocated to the initiative, as a lack of, or limited, resource (Azis and Osada, 2010) will lead to failure. Allowing non-participation and therefore a lack of employee involvement (Cudney and Elrod, 2011) is identified as a possible cause for failure. On the other hand, forcing people to be involved or lead efforts is also detrimental (Hariharan, 2006). Failure to invest in human resource or not using top talent for the initiative (Snee, 2010) will increase the risk of failure.

Theme 8: Feedback and results

Issues will arise if the feedback is distorted or the metrics being used are misleading (Sterman et al., 1997). During the initial period of implementation, issues such as excess capacity, financial stress and pressure for layoffs can result and lead to significant costs being incurred in the short term (Sterman et al., 1997). In fact, initiatives rarely produce short-term results (Powell, 1995), as the costs are immediate and the benefits arise in the longer term (Hahn and Doganaksoy, 2011). Implementations will therefore suffer where the business only focuses on hard savings (Breyfogle, 2005).

What is the role of quality professionals in the twenty-first century?

What sort of skills must be acquired by quality engineers and managers in the future? Many organisations do have a dedicated quality department. In my experience with a large number of local companies, many of our quality managers and engineers received training in the quality area only *after* they started a career in industry. Engineers and managers should receive their education on quality related topics at universities and colleges. What proportion of quality engineers and managers working in UK companies have taken university or college level quality-related courses? I would be very surprised if it is more than 25%. I have also noticed that very few quality engineers and managers are dealing with Lean and Six Sigma topics (Antony, 2013). Their view is that process efficiency and effectiveness problems in organisations must be tackled by Lean practitioners or Six Sigma Black belts or Green Belts.

It would be a great achievement to get our future Quality Professionals to be trained based on the Statistical Engineering (SE) principles that have been discussed in the literature for more than 60 years. SE encompasses the appropriate selection and use of statistical tools, integrated with other relevant tools from other disciplines (operations management, operations research, finance, marketing, etc.) into a comprehensive and disciplined approach to tackling complex problems. However, in order to make this a reality, I argue that academic institutions have a crucial role to play, especially in providing the right education on such statistical tools and techniques with practical exercises, case studies and fun, interactive games.

Quality in the last century was defined by control and improvement; however, it is clear they are not sufficient for the twenty-first century. Change and transformation are the emerging tools of quality and we need to invest more time and energy to obtain skills related to them. So what sorts of attributes are essential for the future quality professionals in organisations of the twenty-first century? Well, I would like to share my personal thoughts on this – some of which present quite a challenge.

- *Customer Advocates* – Customer advocacy is a specialized form of customer service in which companies focus on what is best for the customer. It is a change in a company's culture that is supported by customer-focused customer service and marketing techniques.

- *Process Excellence Experts* – Quality professionals of the future should be able to apply Lean and Six Sigma tools and techniques in a confident manner to reduce the waste and process variation that leads to defects. Both Lean and Six Sigma methodologies should be used on a routine basis to achieve and sustain process excellence.

- *Investors in sustainable long term results* – Quality professionals of the future must be pursuing continuous improvement projects, which should deliver not only short term quick wins but also long-term sustainable results. This requires a paradigm shift in the mindset of these professionals. Quality should be viewed as a journey and not as a destination. This is a serious mistake made by many Quality professionals in organisations today.

- *Innovation Leaders* – Quality professionals of the future should be the innovation leaders of tomorrow. Innovation starts with customers whose unfulfilled needs are the trigger for innovation.

- *Statistical Thinkers* – Quality professionals of the future are expected to be good statistical thinkers. This implies they should view everything as processes, that all processes exhibit variation, and it is essential to collect data from the business processes which exhibit variation.

Ten Commandments of Quality

In this section, I offer my personal thoughts and views, highlighting the key ingredients for achieving and sustaining quality in organisations of the twenty-first century. These ingredients can act as a practical guide for developing best-in-class practices of quality management (QM). However, I argue that the following commandments can be very useful for organisations who want to sustain quality for establishing a competitive advantage (Antony, 2015).

Commandment 1: Leadership for quality

Bigliazzi et al. (1995) stated that, "attaining quality leadership requires that senior managers personally take charge of the quality initiative." The best example of this is explicitly demonstrated by the former CEO of Motorola, Robert Galvin, who has made a habit of making quality the very first item on the agenda of executive staff meetings. Perhaps the leadership style that most relates to quality leadership is transformational leadership, which "searches for ways to help motivate followers by satisfying higher order needs and more fully engaging them in the process of the work" (Horner, 1997). Moreover, transformational leaders encourage quality improvement by creating a culture of trust, creating an inspirational vision focusing on quality, developing a culture that supports a paradigm shift in quality, etc.

Commandment 2: Customer advocacy

The underlying premise of customer advocacy is that if a company serves the best interests of its customers, then the customers will reciprocate with their trust and enduring loyalty, transforming the relationship between the company and its customers. One of the core principles of QM is to create a customer-focused organisation. This means organisations should fully understand the current and future customer needs and strive continuously to not only meet customer expectations but also to delight customers.

Commandment 3: Emphasis on teaching applied statistical methods to quality professionals

Most companies rely unnecessarily upon mean-based performance for critical-to-quality characteristics, with very little attention paid to variance-based performance. Customers today feel the variance performance and not the mean performance. It is essential that our quality professionals are taught the importance of applied and practical statistical methods to reduce variation in business processes, followed by bringing the process mean on target performance.

Commandment 4: Creating a culture of CI or incremental innovation (II)

Boer and Gertsen (2003) provide a meaningful definition of CI as "the planned, organised and systematic process of ongoing, incremental and companywide change of existing practices aimed at improving company performance." A senior management team should convey the message that CI is not just a cost-cutting exercise; rather it is about changing the culture of the organisation. In order to weave CI into their DNA, organisations should focus on some key principles of CI such as: leadership, employee engagement, process improvement metrics for CI, a data-driven approach to improvement, and robust governance. Many senior managers often demand a quick-fix solution to their problems, which can deliver short-term results. Moreover, to successfully build a culture for CI and other change initiatives, people in the organisation need to be engaged as part of the change process.

Commandment 5: Employee empowerment, ownership and engagement

Empowerment refers to making people feel valued by involving them in decisions, asking them to participate in the CI and quality improvement activities across the organisation, praising them, and continually providing adequate training and support. Employee ownership, on the other hand, is more about psychological ownership and feeling part of the organisation. The employee sees a link between what they do on a daily basis and helping the company to achieve its goals. Employee engagement is the extent to which employees feel passionate about their jobs, are committed to the organisation, and put discretionary effort into their work. Truly engaged employees are attracted to and inspired by their work, committed and fascinated. Engaged employees care about the future of the company and are willing to invest their effort to see that the organisation succeeds. For organisations to deliver quality, it is essential to create a culture of ownership and empowerment, and to make sure that employees are engaged across the various business functions for quality and process-related activities.

Commandment 6: Training and education for quality

Education is a learning process that deals with unknown outcomes and circumstances. This requires a complex synthesis of knowledge, skills and experience to solve problems. The concept of training, on the other hand, may be applied when there is some identifiable performance and/or skill that has to be mastered, and practice is required to master it. It is important to recognise that we need both education and training for the implementation of any quality or CI initiative.

Commandment 7: Extending quality into the supply chain

Supply chains compete based upon cost, quality, time and responsiveness. Moreover, quality improvements in reducing process variation and waste directly impact upon several supply chain performance measures, such as consistency in the supply chain, on-time delivery times and so on. Organisations of the twenty-first century should foster a quality culture, in which employees and managers take the responsibility to work together with each other, and with their suppliers and customers.

Commandment 8: Quality and the environment

The implementation of a quality management system (QMS) and an environmental management system (EMS) within an organisation is likely to be an important strategy towards sustainable business. ISO 9001 and ISO 14001 fulfil the requirement of QMS and EMS, respectively. Even if some of the requirements of ISO 9001 and ISO 14001 standards are somewhat different and specific to each management practice, they are not mutually exclusive and can fit into the integrated management system to achieve both quality and environmental performance.

Commandment 9: Learning Organisation (LO)

An LO is defined as an organisation skilled at creating, acquiring and transferring knowledge, and at modifying its behaviour to reflect new knowledge and insights (Garvin, 1993). Organisational research over the last two decades has shown that three broad factors are essential for LO and adaptability. These factors include a supportive learning environment, concrete learning processes and practices, and leadership behaviour that reinforces learning (Garvin *et al.*, 2008). It has been observed that very few organisations today are integrating QM and LO for creating and enhancing competitive capabilities for tomorrow. Perhaps the building blocks of LO must be considered more seriously by all organisations for sustaining a CI initiative.

Commandment 10: Sustainability issues of quality

Sustaining a competitive advantage in quality requires sustaining a high level of quality relative to competition. Sustaining a high level of quality entails meeting and exceeding customers' expectations over time. A recent study has shown that companies who practice effective change management are 71% more likely to achieve and sustain their objectives than those that minimise the people side of change. This is in addition to the fact that those same companies are 55% more likely to be on or ahead of schedule in their efforts to accomplish their business goals (Barnhart, 2011). In my view, organisations that advocate a dynamic capability approach will likely stay ahead in the race for quality in the coming years.

Summary

This chapter provided an insight into what quality is about, followed by a quick overview on the evolution of quality. It also outlined the fundamental reasons why many quality initiatives in organisations fail today. The chapter then explained the role of quality professionals in twenty-first century organisations, and finally focused on the Ten Commandments of quality management from the author's perspective. The Ten Commandments are based on the 20 year experience of the author as an academic, researcher, consultant and a practitioner in the field of Quality Management.

References

Ahire, S. L., Golhar, D. Y. and Waller, M. A. (1996), Development and validation of TQM implementation constructs, *Decision Sciences*, **27**(1), 23-56.

Al-Najem, M., Dhakal, H., Labib, A. and Bennett, N. (2013), Lean readiness level within Kuwaiti manufacturing industries, *International Journal of Lean Six Sigma*, **4**(3), pp. 280-320.

Angel, D.C. and Pritchard, C. (2008), Where 'Six Sigma' went wrong, *Transport Topics*, June, p. 5

Antony, J. (2013),What does the future hold for quality professionals in organisations of the twenty-first century?, *The TQM Journal*, **25**(6), 677-685

Antony, J. (2015),The ten commandments of quality: a performance perspective, *International Journal of Productivity and Performance Management*, **64**(5), 723-735

Azis, Y. and Osada, H. (2010), Innovation in management system by Six Sigma: an empirical study of world-class companies, *International Journal of Lean Six Sigma*, **1**(3), 172-190.

Barnhart, S. (2011), Why organizations struggle to sustain a continuous improvement culture, available at: www.peoriamagazines.com(accessed June 2015).

Bhasin, S. (2012). An appropriate change strategy for lean success, *Management Decision*, **50**(3), 439-458.

Bigliazzi, M., Spaans, C., Dunuad, M and Juran, J.M. (1995), A history of managing for quality, *Quality Progress*, **28**(8), 125-129.

Boer, H. and Gertsen, F. (2003), From continuous improvement to continuous innovation, a retro-perspective, *International Journal of Technology Management*, **26**(8), 805-827.

Breyfogle, F. III. (2005), 21 common problems (and what to do about them), *ASQ Six Sigma Forum Magazine*, **4**(4), 35-37.

BSI(1995), *Quality Management and Quality Assurance – Vocabulary*, BSI, London, UK

BSI (2000), *Quality Management Systems: Fundamentals and Vocabulary*, BSI, London, UK

Candido, C.J.F. and Santos, S.P. (2011). Is TQM more difficult to implement than other transformational strategies? *Total Quality Management and Business Excellence*, **22**(12), 1139-1164.

Chen, M. and Lyu, J. (2009), A Lean Six-Sigma approach to touch panel quality improvement, *Production Planning & Control*, **20**(5), 445-454.

Choi, T.Y. and Eboch, K. (1998), The TQM paradox: relations among TQM practices, plant performance, and customer satisfaction, *Journal of Operations Management*, **17**(1), 59-75.

Cudney, E. and Elrod, C. (2011), A comparative analysis of integrating lean concepts into supply chain management in manufacturing and service industries, *International Journal of Lean Six Sigma*, **2**(1), 5-22.

Dale, B., Van der Wiele, T. and Iwaaarden, J. (eds), (2007), *Managing Quality*, Blackwell Publishing Ltd., Oxford, UK

Fitzpatrick, D. and Looney, M. (2004), A roadmap to greater efficiency in aerospace operations through Six Sigma and Lean, available at: http://docserver. emeraldinsight.com (accessed 10 June 2015).

Garvin, D. (1993), Building a learning organisation, *Harvard Business Review*, July-August, 78-91.

Garvin, D.A., Edmondson, A.C. and Gino, F. (2008), Is yours a learning organisation?, *Harvard Business Review*, March, 109-116.

Gijo, E. V. (2011), 11 ways to sink your Six Sigma project, *ASQ Six Sigma Forum Magazine*, **11**(1), 27-29.

Hahn, G. J. and Doganaksoy, N. (2011), The challenge to long-term improvement, *ASQ Six Sigma Forum Magazine*, **10**(4), 4-5.

Harari, O. (1993), Ten reasons why TQM does not work, *Management Review*, **82**(1,) 33-38.

Hariharan, A. (2006), CEO's guide to Six Sigma success, *ASQ Six Sigma Forum Magazine*, **5**(3), 16-25.

Hastie, T., Tibshirani, R., Friedman, J. (2009). *The Elements of Statistical Learning* (2nd ed.), Springer.

Horner, M. (1997). Leadership theory: past, present and future. *Team Performance Management: An International Journal*, **3**(4), 270-287. doi: doi:10.1108/13527599710195402

Jeyaraman, K. and Teo, L. K. (2010), A conceptual framework for critical success factors of lean Six Sigma, *International Journal of Lean Six Sigma*, **1**(3), 191-215.

Kornfeld, B. and Kara, S. (2013), Selection of Lean and Six Sigma projects in industry, *International Journal of Lean Six Sigma*, **4**(1), 4-16.

Kubiak T M. (2011), Six Sigma in the 21st century, *ASQ Six Sigma Forum Magazine*, **11**(1), 7-7.

McLean, R., Antony, J. and Dahlgaard, J. (2015), Failure of continuous improvement initiatives in manufacturing environments: A systematic review of the evidence, *Total Quality Management and Business Excellence* (to be published online in July 2015).

Oakland, J.S. and Tanner, S.J. (2007). A new framework for managing change, *TQM Journal,* **19**(6), 572-588.

Powell, T. C. (1995), Total quality management as competitive advantage: A review and empirical study, *Strategic Management Journal,* **16**, 15-37.

Salah S, Rahim A, and Carretero J. (2010) The integration of Six Sigma and Lean Management, *International Journal of Lean Six Sigma,* **1**(3), 249-274.

Shih, L.C. and Gurnani, H. (1997), Global quality management programmes: how to make their implementation more effective and less culture dependent, *Total Quality Management and Business Excellence,* **8**(1), 15-31.

Snee, R. D. (2010), Lean Six Sigma – getting better all the time, *International Journal of Lean Six Sigma,* **1**(1), 9-29.

Soltani, E., Pei-Chun, L. and Gharneh, N. S. (2005), Breaking through barriers to TQM effectiveness: Lack of commitment of upper-level management, *Total Quality Management and Business Excellence,* **16**(8-9), 1009-1021.

Sterman, J. D., Repenning, N. P. and Kofman, F. (1997), Unanticipated side effects of successful quality programs, *Management Science,* 43(4), 503-520.

Timans W., Antony J., Ahaus K. and Solingen R. (2012), Implementation of Lean Six Sigma in small and medium-sized manufacturing enterprises in the Netherlands, *Journal of Operational Research Society,* **63,** 339-353.

Vinodh, S., Kumar, S.V. and Vimal, K.E.K. (2012), Implementing Lean Sigma in an Indian rotary switches manufacturing organisation, *Production Planning & Control,* **25**(4), 1-15.

Yeung, A. C. L., Cheng, T. C. E. and Lai, K. (2006), An operational and institutional perspective on total quality management, *Production and Operations Management,* **15**(1), 156-170.

Zbaracki, M. J. (1998). The rhetoric and reality of total quality management. *Administrative Science Quarterly,* **43**(3), 602-636.

9

10 Business Ethics in a Global Context

Gordon Jack, Steven Glasgow, Tom Farrington and Kevin O'Gorman

The title of this chapter is a bit of a misnomer: there is not, nor has there been, a global business ethics; moral relativism is prevalent. Moral relativism holds that ethical opinions are true or false only relative to some particular viewpoint, i.e. culture, religion, or a historical period, and that no standpoint is uniquely privileged over all others. Even this is not universally accepted and is continually debated. There is disagreement about what is ethical, and because morality cannot be objectively right or wrong, so we ought to tolerate the behaviour of others even when we disagree about the morality of it.

Today there are many philosophical positions that underpin moral and ethical judgments across different people and cultures, and some of these are explored later in the chapter. Diversity is nothing new and there has never been a universal business ethic. For example, the Jaina Anekantavada principle of Mahavira (c. 599–527 BC) holds that truth and reality are perceived differently from diverse points of view, and that no single point of view is the complete truth. Since long before Herodotus (c. 484–420 BC), the Greek historian, recorded it, societies have always regarded their own ethical systems as superior to all others.

Ethics and personal morality influence our everyday social interactions and decision-making, even when we're not aware of it. When we read words such as *ethical* or *ethically*, thinking tends to veer towards matters of right and wrong, yet this is to oversimplify. It is often down to personal opinion as to what people interpret to be ethical and unethical, but this is to confuse ethics with morality. Although ethics and morality were once synonymous, it is now largely accepted that morality extends to those one knows, while ethics may be applied to those not known. As such, we tend to think of morality as personal, and ethics as political or professional. The example of reckless lending by bankers and financiers prior to the 2008 UK recession is a relatively closed case in clearly delineated unethical business practice. You will soon appreciate that ethical actions are contextual and harmony between the individual and society is not necessarily always apparent or the appropriate goal. Debates over ethics allow people to voice their opinions and beliefs, in an attempt to change business practice for what they see is for the eventual good.

Ethics in business

There is no single agreed definition of ethics. Christie et al. (2003, p. 266) define ethics as "a systematic approach to moral judgments based on reason, analysis, synthesis, and reflection," with business ethics being "the study of what constitutes right or wrong, good or bad human conduct in a business environment." The company may be held responsible for both its conduct and that of individuals affiliated with the organization, which can be difficult to manage. For example, in a multinational corporation that relies heavily on outsourcing to specialist companies, how can that one company facilitate the monitoring process of all these firms, ensuring they adhere to their rules and regulations, and conform to what they believe is ethical and acceptable behaviour?

Individual beliefs, prejudices, values and tendencies inform interpretations of a given situation. Mediation or balancing is required in order to integrate these differences into an organisation. Personal bias must also be accounted for in decisions being made on behalf of an organisation, ensuring that the final outcome is aligned to the ethical principles of the organisation. How can a company ensure that a Human Resources role in their Dubai office is identically fulfilled in the Edinburgh office? The simple answer is this isn't possible. As a result of the diverse range of political, cultural, and religious issues, not to mention the sheer distances involved, it is almost impossible to implement a 'one size fits all' ethical framework. The relative stage of a nation's industrial development may also prove influential on ethical policy, e.g. an organisation in a developing country may find implementing Corporate Social Responsibility (CSR) policies more difficult than one in a developed country. An organisation needs to develop an ethical framework with sufficient diversity and inclusivity so as to be applicable throughout its potentially worldwide operation.

What may be ethical in one social setting may not be acceptable in another. As a result of this ambiguity and the aforementioned geographical and sociocultural differences, businesses must determine the extent of their ethical responsibility. The following section discusses the origins and development of business ethics, alongside shifting ethical perceptions, before a section that explores ethical expectations in several geographical, cultural and religious contexts. The final section discusses the value of ethics to businesses and the ways in which business ethics are operationalised through CSR policies.'

Many argue that capitalism is incompatible with ethical, socially responsible behaviour. Friedman (1970) writes that the sole duty of a company is to maximise profits for its shareholders. Businesses are not people, and have no ethical obligations to wider society, therefore using company resources to benefit society is unethical towards the shareholders. Friedman claims that responsibility for society instead lies with the government and the legal system, and a business should only implement ethical practices insofar as this helps the business achieve its overall objectives. Friedman's business-centric stance is countered by those arguing that businesses have both the duty and the resources to help society. The debate as to whether businesses have an obligation to be ethical has no distinct or unique answer, with views coming from a person's own morality. Corporate Social Responsibility policies are ubiquitous in global businesses and are a way to verbalise their ethicality.

Evolution of business ethics

It is important to realise that the perception of what is ethical in business is not a constant. Business practices deemed appropriate only a few decades ago may be entirely unacceptable by contemporary standards. The following examples attest to the contextual relativity of ethical standards.

■ American slavery – African slaves

Cotton farming was at the centre of business in the southern United States during the 17th, 18th and 19th centuries. Workers were expensive to pay due to the intensive nature of the extraction of cotton, and so plantation owners forced slaves (taken captive from Africa) to work under incomprehensibly cruel and dehumanising conditions. Slavery is now rightly condemned and illegal (almost) globally, but at the time was justified by interpreting the Bible to demonstrate that Africans were 'naturally' inferior to white Euramericans. The slaves were seen as machinery to be bought, sold, and destroyed at the whim of their owners, and thus not worthy of ethical treatment.

■ Industrial Revolution – Child labour

The late 18th century was a time of rapid manufacturing transformation in Great Britain. The use of machinery allowed for a substantial increase in production efficiency and therefore a reduction in costs. Due to their cheaper labour cost and small frames, children were the choice of many to work in the factories, indeed machinery was made specifically to accommodate their smaller hands. Poor working conditions led to children developing various cancers and dying prematurely. Children as young as five and six years old worked in these hot, poorly-lit, and overcrowded factories for twelve to sixteen hours a day, six days a week, without breaks or meals. Child labour in the US was less controversial, being an integral part of the agricultural economy. Children not only worked on the family farm but were often hired out to other farmers. Boys customarily began their apprenticeship in a trade between ages ten and fourteen. This declined in the early nineteenth century, but factory employment provided a new opportunity to employ children. In the textile industry young women and immigrants replaced the children. The use of child labour in developed nations has largely been outlawed since the beginning of the 20th century. Subjecting children to these conditions is typically seen as unethical in the modern, developed world, yet it is only until fairly recently that child labour was considered ethically justifiable. Indeed, child labour remains prevalent in developing countries with a large manufacturing base.

■ Tobacco marketing

A combination of the carcinogenic and addictive properties of tobacco led to marketing restrictions being put in place in 1964 (WHO, 2005). Prior to this, tobacco companies could market their products in any way and to anyone they chose. Key target markets for tobacco companies were (and still are) children and teenagers, due to the decreased life expectancy of smokers. A younger addict will be less well-informed about the risks of smoking, and provide a few more years of loyal brand consumption. The 1960s saw marketing campaigns utilising cartoons (such as the Flintstones) and celebrities, all aimed at children. Despite their claims of innocence, it is now accepted that tobacco companies were aware that smoking cigarettes caused disease as early as the 1950s (Cummings, Brown, & O'Connor, 2007), and as such this behaviour was and remains entirely unethical. Yet these unethical practices continued in the developed world up until 1997, with the Joe Camel brand using a child-friendly cartoon camel in an attempt to entice a younger customer. The effectiveness of the brand was evident, with 90% of 6 year olds recognising the Joe Camel brand, a figure similar to the number who identified Disney's Mickey Mouse character (Markland, 2012). Recent evidence suggests that tobacco companies continue to work to prevent the implementation of global public health policy (Fooks, Gilmore, Collin, Holden, & Lee, 2013). This serves to illustrate that legislation does not lead simply to ethical behaviour.

■ Brazil 2014 World Cup

The Brazilian government's decision to apply to host the 2014 FIFA Football World Cup serves as a reminder that ethically questionable decisions are not limited to commercial organisations. In 2007, Brazil was successful in bidding for the tournament that would eventually cost $11.63 billion (Rapoza, 2014). The role of a Government is to serve its people, but in hosting the tournament, questions begin to arise as to whether this decision was made in the best interests of the people of Brazil. The decision to host the FIFA World cup was taken in spite of ailing education, health and transport provisions throughout the country (Hilton, 2013). Construction of new stadiums led to eight deaths (Watts, 2014), whilst the renovation of the 72,000 seat capacity Mané Garrincha stadium, the second most expensive stadium in the world at $900 million, is now used as a bus depot and for conferences (Banerjee, 2015). The 41,000 seat Arena da Amazônia that was specially built for the tournament and sits in Manaus, a city in the middle of the Amazon rainforest, has no permanent use (Manfred, 2015).

The decision to host the tournament had little economic benefit for Brazil as FIFA agreed a deal for exemption on all levels of tax and kept all revenue directly coming from the tournament (Sinnott, 2013). Despite these controversies, on the field, the tournament was heralded as a "roaring success" in terms of the entertainment of the fans (Moore, 2014). Yet it is difficult to frame the decision to incur these financial and societal costs for a month of entertainment as ethical, particulary in light of subsequent allegations relating to the bidding process used by FIFA.

Looking at business ethics over time serves to illustrate the fluidity of ethics. The development of ethics from the American slave trade to modern day corruption suggests the likelihood that present conceptualisations of ethical practice are subject to change.

Exercises: Evolution of business ethics

1   The examples detailed above have had radical impacts on both the way societies view ethical practices, and the way in which contemporary policies and procedures are introduced and maintained in an organisation.

   a)   Describe and justify a modern day equivalent of these historical, yet major, revolutions affecting ethics.

   b)   Are organisations able to mitigate against ethical issues becoming problematic for their organisation, or with proper planning, can they turn such eventualities to their advantage?

    c)   Reflect upon the historical examples above. How would you have felt during these times and why? You had to earn a living, but perhaps under horrendous working conditions. Does a lack of awareness on the part of the oppressed excuse the actions of the oppressor?

2   Imagine you are the most influential and powerful figure in a country – Prime Minister or President for example. You have been given an opportunity similar to the bid made by Brazil for the 2014 FIFA World Cup, however, your country is in crisis. You have a failing education system, a healthcare system which does not provide basic care and a transport infrastructure that cannot cope with demand. As such, tourists will not visit. What would you do if you were given the opportunity of hosting a worldwide event, such as the Olympics, FIFA World Cup or similar? Detail reasons for your answer.

Helpful hint:

☐   Think of this from a business point of view. You have an incredible opportunity to take on an extensive new contract, which will require capital outlay to be fulfilled. However, there are severe failings throughout your company, which require your urgent attention.

Geography, religion and cultural expectations

Intercontinental and intercultural business transactions can run into difficulty due to the simple fact that different cultures adhere to different norms, depending on factors such as their location, history, and religious orientations. It is therefore imperative that all parties, both assessing the potentiality of such business interactions and those entering the transactional phase of business, appreciate these differences, and work to modify their business practices to suit their new business partners' needs. At the same time, the host country needs to ensure they are conforming to the accepted practices of their own company and that of other partners, who may be influenced by working with another country, not to mention the regulations that govern them.

Despite the relative proximity of the two countries, India and China have very different business ethics. Business ethics have commonly been influenced by the dominant religious ethical beliefs of the countries that the businesses operate in. These ethics guide all aspects of business including the attitudes to profit maximisation, employee welfare and competing organisations. The following insights into business ethics from around the world attests to the necessity of adapting ethical policy to cultural context.

African Philosophy of Ubuntu

Marlene Muller

Ubuntu is a Nguni term used throughout sub-Saharan Africa which encapsulates the African way of social and business life. It is referred to as Batho, Avandu, Watu, Botho, or Hunhu by other regional tribes. It means 'humanity' or 'humanness', recognising the interdependence of humankind. The starting point of explaining the principle of Ubuntu is encapsulated in the saying *'umuntu ngumuntu ngabantu* which translates to 'a person is a person through other persons or 'I am because we are.' It is a communitarian approach to life, and highlights that no man is an island. Within the principles of Ubuntu, there is an obligation to live harmoniously, within and between generations. In all decision-making the community comes first, and there is an emphasis on leadership by consensus. Ubuntu recognises the interconnectedness of human beings, thus strives to be inclusive and promote 'solidarity and sacrifice'. However, within its conceptualisation, Ubuntu defines expectations of society regarding good behaviour and integrity; and those who do not exemplify these characteristics are deemed unfit to be classified as human beings.

Ubuntu falls under the normative branch of ethics, which focuses on classifying what is right or wrong and attempts to govern human behaviour. Although the practice of Ubuntu is about embracing people, the literature does not elaborate on the opposite of Ubuntu. In most traditional circles there are many things or behaviours that are considered to be abominable or taboo. The key tenets of *ubuntu* comprise helpfulness, trust, respect, unselfishness, sharing, community, social justice, reciprocity, dignity, harmony and caring for others. These are elaborated below in Table 10.1:

Humanness	Warmth, tolerance, understanding, peace, humanity
Caring	Empathy, sympathy, helpfulness, charitable, friendliness
Sharing	Giving (unconditionally), redistribution, openhandedness
Respect	Commitment, dignity, obedience, order and humility
Compassion	Love, cohesion, informality, forgiveness, spontaneity

Table 10.1: Key tenets of Ubuntu

From an Ubuntu perspective, organisations should also exhibit these attributes, particularly in management. However, as a management concept Ubuntu still lacks a clear set of rules and regulations, and is yet to be articulated globally. From a strategic point of view, Ubuntu suggests that organisations consider all their stakeholders when making business decisions. This could be related to CSR projects carried out by organisations. It also calls for servant leadership, implying that whoever occupies an office serves others. Ubuntu's influence also exists at a more operational level, where recruitment and selection should place specific emphasis on integrity (Metz, 2010). However, some of the drawbacks of Ubuntu are that it condones affirmative action, and it is indifferent to nepotism due to the spirit of extended family. In terms of the relationship between managers and employees, Ubuntu calls for mutual respect. There is a strong belief that respect is earned rather than automatic, and therefore reciprocal. The practices are compatible with Theory Y in traditional management. By virtue of communal orientation, Ubuntu values teamwork and collective responsibility for success, preferring group bonus schemes rather than individualised schemes. Non-performing employees are subjected to peer or clan control, while being nurtured or assisted. Under Ubuntu, it is important that labour is not reduced to a series of discrete, repetitive tasks undertaken in isolation, but is meaningful, with multitasking encouraged. Furthermore, the underlying values of Ubuntu provide guiding principles for individuals and organisations to organise and behave, resulting in strong organisational cultures.

Further Reading

West, A. (2013). Ubuntu and business ethics: Problems, perspectives and prospects. *Journal of Business Ethics* **121**(1):47–61.

Islam: The Qur'an and the Hadith
Marlene Muller and Helen Verhoeven

Islam is the world's fastest growing religion, with around 50 countries having a Muslim majority population. The Arab word 'islam' literally means "peace that can be achieved through the submission to the will of God in all aspects of life". Islam is founded upon five pillars:

1 Testimony of faith where followers dedicate their life to God: Allah;
2 Five daily prayers;
3 Giving of obligatory and voluntary charity to the poor;
4 Fasting from dawn to dusk during the holy month of Ramadan;
5 Duty to undertake the pilgrimage to Mecca.

The Islamic tradition is encapsulated in Shari'ah, which comprises of two main sources, namely the Qur'an (the Holy book) and the Hadith (examples set by the Prophet Mohammed –PBUH*) as contained in the Sunnah). Additionally, Islam also adheres to (1) the consensus of scholars on what is right/acceptable (halal), or wrong / unacceptable (haram); (2) analogy (deducting new rules based on the Qur'an and the Sunnah).

---

* As a sign of respect when mentioning the Prophet. PBHU means Peace Be Upon Him (or SAW, abbreviated in Arabic)

Islam's meta values are clearly encapsulated by the Qur'an and the Hadith and form the basis for anything Muslims should adhere to in all aspects of their personal and professional life. Figure 10.1 provides examples of how Islam influences and informs business practice.

Figure 10.1: Islam and business practice.

Further Reading

Quddus, M., Bailey III, H., & White, L. R. (2009). Business ethics: perspectives from Judaic, Christian, and Islamic scriptures. *Journal of Management, Spirituality and Religion*, **6**(4), 323-334

China and *Qiye Lunli*
Michelle Min-Hsiu Liao

Business ethics, often translated into *Qiye Lunli* in Chinese, literally as "enterprise *lunli*". The word *Lunli* is composed of *lun*, meaning the relationship between people, and *li*, the principles one should follow. The two concepts under Chinese business ethics most widely discussed by Western scholars are *mianzi* (face) and *guanxi* (relationship).

Mianzi, or face, in China refers to how one is viewed by others in terms of his/her status in the societal hierarchy. One of the most common ways to address others in China is by surname + job title, for example Manager Chen, even though Chen is not your manager but your neighbour. This is to recognize your addressee's societal role. In the management of face, two important behaviours are *losing face* and *giving face*. An example of losing face is if you point out the mistakes of your manager in front of your colleagues, you cause your manager to lose face. An example of giving face is buying gifts for your business partners – the more valuable the gifts, the higher you place their faces in the societal

10

hierarchy. Face in China is often collective rather than individual. An employee, for example, may lose the face of the company for his personal behaviour.

Guanxi is now an entry in most English dictionaries, and defined, for example, by the Oxford dictionary as "the system of social networks and influential relationships which facilitate business and other dealings." *Guanxi* is not the same as professional networking in Western countries, but involves a more private interaction, such as recommending a reliable doctor for your business partner's family. For this reason, online networking websites such as LinkedIn have encountered difficulties in China, because in China business is not done through 'professional' networking.

An example of clashes over the understanding of *face* and *guanxi* can be seen in a business meeting between British and Chinese delegates, as reported by Spencer-Oatey and Xing (2008, p. 262-263):

> After the British chairperson gave a welcome speech, he asked the Chinese delegates to each introduce themselves. The head of the Chinese delegates understood it as his turn to give a return speech, and then was interrupted by the interpreter that the British company wanted *each* Chinese member to introduce themselves. The Chinese delegates felt uncomfortable about the situation, as it is conventional for the head to speak on behalf of the team, as a *group*. In an interview later, the British chair head explained that since they have worked with this Chinese company before, these kind of "formalities" can be skipped, and this may allow a closer personal relationship with each members, as *individual*.

> On the other hand, the Chinese delegates felt insulted. As the Chinese understood relationship in terms of societal hierarchy, they see the British company's rejection to allow them to give a return speech as not giving them an equal opportunity, and therefore treating Chinese delegates as inferior. The meeting then continued with more misunderstandings, so two of the Chinese delegates asked the British company to allow them to talk with a sales manager who has visited the Chinese company before, and therefore be regarded as a *friend* by the Chinese team. However, Tim was on leave with his family and made no contact with the Chinese team. The Chinese delegates were annoyed, and demanded to be given Tim's home telephone number. Later on the Chinese delegates expressed their disappointment that Tim failed to act as a *genuine friend*.

Along with guanxi and face, the long traditions of Confucian principles continue to influence the current business culture in China, but not without challenges. Derived from the teachings of the ancient Chinese philosopher Confucius, it harnesses a set of norms and practices that promote the living of a 'good life'

(Yao, 2000). The focus of this branch of ethics is looking beyond individual actions as being 'right' or 'wrong' and instead abiding by the fundamentals of Confucianism, of which paternalism and collectivism are two facets (Ip, 2009). Paternalism relates to respect for hierarchy, with those in the highest of positions being considered as the most moral to an unquestionable degree, but they must be benevolent. Loyalty to one's family, organisation or society is imperative to this belief. Collectivism is a cultural expectation that actions should be for the social harmony of the collective, rather than for the benefit of the individual, including 'playing one's role' whereby occupying any position in society is only valued if it maintains harmony.

As China plays a more important role in the global market, it faces new challenges such as criticisms on corruption and environmental pollution. Whether the traditional business ethics rooted in Confucian principles should be abandoned or can be adapted to face the new challenges continues to inspire debate. Chinese business practices such as child labour, low wages and lack of human rights may deemed unethical by Judeo-Christian standards, but these individual actions are widely accepted throughout China as they have helped turn the nation into an economic superpower, and thus benefited the collective. Workers subjected to these conditions are simply abiding by paternalism by abiding to the system put in place by those with authority.

Further Reading

Buckley, P. J., Clegg, J., & Tan, H. (2006). Cultural awareness in knowledge transfer to China—The role of guanxi and mianzi. *Journal of world business,***41**(3), 275-288.

Indian philosophical thought and business ethics
Praveen Balakrishnan Nair and *Jaydeep Pancholi*

10

Although Indian ethical perspectives appear to be quite similar to developed countries and Judeo-Christian societies of the West, the thought processes and moral values which underpin these perspectives are very different. In India, ethical viewpoints are heavily influenced by religious tenets, especially Hinduism, which is the major religion practised in India. Other major contributors to Indian ethics include Buddhism and Jainism, which are offshoots of Hindu philosophical thought, and the values of many other religions and cultures absorbed by India through international trade, foreign invasions and colonisations. The texts of these religious philosophies provide an elaborate account of moral values which govern the well-being of mankind, and provide a prescriptive mode for conscious living within those boundaries. The major Hindu religious texts include *Bhagavat Gita, Upanishads and Vedas.* The texts talk at length about *Dharma* (which can be loosely equated to ethical behaviour) and *Adharma* (unethical behaviour), and work towards an ethical society through individual virtue. In an organisational context, focused works like *Arthashastra* written by Kautilya in the 4th century BC, highlight the importance of ethics in business and government. This work discusses the importance of *Nyaya* (Justice) and *Dharma* (ethics) in the process of governance. The influence of these philosophical thoughts is evident in the way in which many Indian business conglomerates are managed, even at present. The organisations are expected to have their own dharma, which is a moral way of life of the organisation, and this defines the ethical orientation of the organisation.

In India, the concept of ethics is ambiguous and historically has been classed as unimportant for business owners. Where inter-state competition is high due to the dense population of India, it is deemed necessary to speed processes and cut costs resulting in unethical practices, such as bribery which is widespread and considered to be part of everyday business (Fernando, 2009). The country's weak regulatory body has therefore neglected unfair business actions, bringing much publicity on corruption. For instance, business managers utilise power to make their business successful, even if it meant befriending government officials. Businesses prefer to maintain vagueness on ethics for personal credit. For example during a factory inspection, a business would pay the inspector a bribe to gain clearance. This means that the business save procedural time, efforts and costs and the inspector gains an extra income (so much that the inspector's lifestyle could become dependent upon the bribes).

It is important to recognise the development of these attitudes through the history of India. Ideologies coming from religions such as Hinduism, Buddhism and Jainism have condemned unethical actions, where many would feel giving to charity or places of worship would bring good luck to their business. However, post-colonialism and World War 2 left a poor economy and rise of 'Black Money' – unaccounted for income – developing into an unofficial currency in the 1960s and is still a significant problem today (Hock, 2007; Kumar, 2002). A weak governing body, 70 years of tax evasion and corrupt practices has installed unethical actions as normal business operations. Nevertheless the country has a foundation in spiritual and religious values, ingraining truth, non-violence and sincerity at childhood. These values are the hope for reforming the country's private sector. With the rise of globalisation, competing in international markets and stronger government infrastructure, Indian businesses in the 21st century are being forced to change their attitudes and uphold an ethical reputation.

Further Reading

Chakraborty, S. K. (1997). Business ethics in India. *Journal of Business Ethics*, **16**(14), 1529-1538.

Malaysia and complex business etiquette

Ros Haniffa

Malaysia is comprised of many ethnic groups with the largest being Malays, followed by Chinese and Indians. Given the diverse cultural make-up, it is important to recognise that each ethnic group has different attitudes towards aspects of life, including business.

The Malays are predominantly Muslims, and so are influenced by Islamic values. When engaging in business, it is important to be aware of which as to avoid unethical actions. They tend to have Islamic names and the word 'bin' or 'binti' which means 'son of' or 'daughter of' appear after the first name followed by the father's name e.g. Mohammad Danial bin Abdullah and Maria binti Abdullah. The majority of Malay females wear headscarves or 'hijab' and some Malay males wear the skull cap. Physical touch between sexes is deemed inappropriate and so shaking hands with a Malay female should be avoided unless she initiates. A slight bow with a hand placed over the position of your heart demonstrates respect. A married Malay woman does not take on the husband's name and hence should be addressed by her own name. Also be aware of the special circumstances of Muslims with regards to prayer, diet and fasting. Muslims pray five times a day: dawn, noon, evening, dusk and night which can be performed anywhere but for Friday, when males will have to perform their noon prayer in the mosque. Given that Friday is a special day for Muslims, some states in Malaysia, e.g. Kedah, Perlis, Kelantan and Terengganu, have their weekend holiday on Friday and Saturday instead of Saturday and Sunday. Hence, if you are scheduling meetings, take into consideration timing for prayers and the state weekend holiday. With regards to diet, it is considered offensive to serve food which is not 'halal' (allowed) including alcohol or pork, and also some forms of entertainment. Similarly, pay attention to the choice of gifts to Muslims which should be Islamically permissible. Muslims fast for a month during the Islamic month of Ramadhan, hence it is courteous not to eat or drink in their presence during the meetings.

The Chinese Malay have other practices and principles which must be remembered in business. It is the norm to have three names, with the first being the family name, and it is common to find English names attached even if they are not Christian e.g. Alex Lee Chew San (Lee is the surname). Similarly, some Indians will also have English names but only if they are Christians, e.g. Paul Rajaratnam. It is appropriate to shake hands lightly with Chinese and Indian females. It is appropriate to address them by their Christian or family name in the first instance. Most Chinese and Indians do not have strict diet requirements but some Indians are strictly vegetarian.

10

Malaysians also share some common business attitudes. Malaysian culture is hierarchical, thus senior ranks and elders are treated with respect. Some Malaysians have been conferred with titles such as 'Tun', 'Tan Sri', 'Datuk' and 'Dato', hence the title and the full name should be used when addressing them for the first time and simply by their title for the rest of the meeting. If there is more than one of them at the meeting, then address them by their title and first name. This also applies for academic titles such as Professor, Associate Professor or Doctor. Arrive in time for a meeting but expect to wait as they tend to have a relaxed attitude to time. Dress appropriately for formal meetings. Females should avoid revealing clothes. Initially, meetings are usually used to build rapport, and always start with small talk on general issues such as interest, hobbies, travels, etc. It is inappropriate to ask very personal questions, although questions related to family are fine. Avoid talking on sensitive issues such as politics, religion and culture. Malaysians are group-oriented, so it is important to take into account the circumstances of different people in the group rather than singling out an individual when praising or giving reward. Politeness and diplomacy are important and directness is often misconstrued as rudeness. Do not expect decisions to be made on the first meeting. A 'yes' does not necessarily mean agreement but may simply be an affirmation of understanding. Business relationships are built on familiarity and trust, therefore paying attention to the various aspects discussed here will help in fostering business deals. More information on the general principles for business ethics in Malaysia can be found on the Malaysian Ministry of Domestic Trade, Co-Operatives and Consumerism website.

Further Reading

Othman, Z., & Rahman, R. A. (2010). Ethics in Malaysian corporate governance practices. *International Journal of Business and Social Science,***1**(3).

Japan, the Numen and Concentric Circles
Steven Glasgow

Japanese ethics combines Confucianist belief with Buddhist principles and societal expectations to form tacit rules that govern society and business. Central to these ethics is the idea of the *numen*. The *numen*, meaning soul or spirit, is present in each individual phenomenon including people, families, businesses and nations (Taka, 1994). The *numen* is connected to the 'great life force of the universe'. In Japan, work is seen to have its own *numen* and therefore working is a way of connecting with the 'great life force'. Although not all Japanese people hold these religious beliefs, it has come to shape the nation's attitude towards work as imperative to life.

These Japanese ethics are evident in business operations. Whilst businesses exist primarily for the benefit of its shareholders in capitalist societies, Japanese businesses exist for their employees. It is this idea of facilitating employment that is central to Japanese business ethics. When firms are in difficult financial positions, the first step companies take is to reduce the benefits and salaries of their executives. Only as a last resort do companies lay off their workers, but even in this case, executives often find their employees new positions at other businesses (Taka, 1994).

Lifetime employment in Japan is an assumed norm which results from Japanese business ethics and strict labour laws. This makes employee redundancies extremely difficult to perform in Japan and is deemed a highly unethical practice. Therefore, faced with the need to reduce workforces due to external financial pressures, firms have been known to implement 'banishment/boredom' rooms. These are rooms where undesired workers are sent to perform remedial tasks for their workdays in an effort to make them unhappy and leave of their own accord (Tabuchi, 2013). The benefit of this is that companies can reduce their workforce without appearing to be unethical, although the ethicality of it in the context of Japan can be debated. It is a practice that is not officially recognised as employees are technically given a role to fulfil, but it has been known to be used by global Japanese firms such as Sony, Hitachi and Toshiba (Torres, 2013).

Reflecting the collectivist beliefs of Confucianism, Japanese ethics also emphasise social harmony and treating those close to you most ethically. This is placed above any absolute values and so ethical behaviour is that of maintaining social harmony in certain *numens*; ethical actions are therefore contextual or 'situational' (Ardichvili, Jondle & Kowske, 2010). Taka (1994) helps illustrate this through what is described as concentric circles of corporations. As shown in Figure 10.2, Businesses operate in four circles, and each has its own ethical principles.

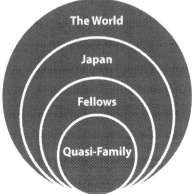

Figure 10.2: Concentric circles of Japanese corporations.

Each organisation has a Quasi-Family circle. Within this circle are close business partners such as suppliers, partners and affiliated companies. For example, engine company Honda has Formula 1 team McLaren in its Quasi-Family as it supplies them with engines for the 2015 season. This is the principle circle and so must be treated with the upmost ethicality. Quasi-Family businesses are expected to aid each other in times of crisis and show loyalty.

In the second circle, Fellows are the organisations with which businesses conduct regular exchanges. These can be banks, regular customers or distant affiliated companies. As businesses in this circle interact often they can accrue debts amongst each other. Ethically, a business must make sure to service debt so as to prevent any negative impacts on its Fellows. However, any actions that could potentially disrupt the social harmony in the Quasi-Family are avoided.

The Japan circle refers to all the other businesses in Japan. There is a principle of free competition but businesses are ethically bound to sustainable operation and so aggressive corporate strategies that could put other firms at risk are unethical.

The world circle is every business outside of Japan. Businesses can partake in free competition but practices that are unethical in Japan such as market share domination and undercutting competitors are allowed. Global Japanese businesses such as Nissan, Sony and Toyota are therefore not subject to ethical boundaries when operating outside of Japan, but will be subject to the ethical norms of the countries they operate in.

Further Reading

Dunfee, T. W., & Nagayasu, Y. (Eds.). (2013). *Business ethics: Japan and the global economy* (Vol. 5).Springer Science & Business Media.

Māori and the concept of *Tikanga*
Geraldine McKay

Originally from Polynesia, Māori people were the earliest settlers in New Zealand and make up around 10% of the present day population. Māori values permeate all aspects of life. *Tikanga* means doing the appropriate, right thing and guides every activity, even in the commercial world. *Tikanga* sets Māori organisations aside from those guided by Western business principles. Māori self-interest is very closely identified with the interest of the collective community, and relationship, inter-connectivity and belongingness are identified as the reasons for existence. Businesses led by Māori principles generally strive to achieve multiple, long term objectives, not driven by profit alone, although profit is seen as an important aspect of the process required to achieve goals.

Māori principles include

- *Whanaungatanga* – kinship and belonging where a sense of obligation to family and the wider community is acknowledged. Relationships that are maintained and developed lead to collective gains for all in the partnership.

- Protecting natural resources. *Kaitiakitanga* is custodianship and the strong belief that there is an obligation to conserve, foster and keep watch over the natural environment, even if this means that short term gains are forgone to ensure sustainability.

- *Wairuatanga* or spirituality requires Māori to observe spiritual protocols to ensure spiritual wellbeing of the individual and society.

- *Manaakitanga* considers the social wellbeing of the business, with the understanding that looking after each other, providing hospitality and kindness mutually increases both the receiver's and giver's *mana* or power. Service is therefore a gift.

Search 'Wakatu' on the internet. It is a very successful Māori enterprise with over 3000 owners, which owns and manages sea and land resources to produce a range of seafood, fruit and wine brands under the umbrella name of Kono. Can you identify what are the main Māori principles in action?

Jamaica and the Caribbean
Dudley Peter Barrett

Located in the sunny Caribbean, Jamaica gained its independence in 1962 after 300 years of British rule. Because of that long history, the prevailing ethical standards in the United Kingdom are commonplace locally – in fact, several of the institutions that shape ethical behaviour in businesses (e.g. the Institute of Chartered Accountants of Jamaica) can trace their origins to the UK. The impact of history on ethical practices has been most telling in the role played by Judeo-Christian practices in business life. It is common to have a religious leader on the leadership board of organisations; spiritual guidance is often sought before major decisions are made; and several firms (especially in the MSME sector) place a premium on building their work policies around religious practices. For example, it is the norm to base opening hours on religious rules, rather than business needs.

Despite this, ethical standards in organisations vary widely. The geographical location of Jamaica (90 miles from the coast of the US) has meant that there is a high level of exposure to negative cultural influences, such as the 'get rich quick' attitude and the belief that 'the end justified the means.' When these attitudes are mixed in with weak controls, the result is a relatively high level

10

of white-collar crime and ethical lapses. In general, the larger the organisation and the more formal the corporate governance, accountability and performance management system, the higher the ethical standard.

Corporate Social Responsibility

For Bowen (1953), CSR referred to the responsibility of business leaders to make decisions and pursue goals which furthered the aims and values of wider society. Bowen's initial concerns with the place of business in society have since been subject to such widespread debate and interpretation that there is now no universally accepted definition of CSR, nor agreement as to what constitutes successful CSR policy and practice. Each company may have its own interpretation of social responsibility, and different aspects of CSR will be more prominent in some industries than in others. This problem is exacerbated by globalization. Again, as firms expand into different countries, so needs, standards, and regulations are likely to differ from the country of the company's origin. That the current field of CSR scholarship is dominated by Anglo-American perspectives further hinders cross-cultural understanding.

As a general principle, businesses should act in a way so as to benefit society, contribute to economic development, and have a positive and engaging relationship with the firm's workforce. Yet many companies will attempt to claim that these good and fair business practices (e.g. paying employees a living wage) are examples of their CSR policies in action. Despite these definitional and operational discrepancies, common themes emerge from each permutation and understanding of CSR across industries and firms. In an analysis of 37 definitions, Dahlsrud (2008) found five key dimensions to CSR policies, which often do not occur or manifest in isolation and are generally found to overlap or interact. These are:

- **Environmental:** Associated with *sustainability*, this facet sees firms strive to limit the harm they inflict on the natural environment, compensating equally or excessively for damage caused. If their industry necessitates damage to the environment (e.g. oil companies, tree felling, power stations) then interested parties will want to see what they are doing to reduce the amount of collateral damage caused, and to research alternative sources and methods.

- **Social:** A firm needs to be seen as having a positive impact not only on its workers, but also upon society as a whole, which in turn is made up of organisations, groups and individuals. The fact that a company employs local people is a relatively facile example of how to define a low level interaction between a business and society, however, there needs to be equal weighting placed upon strategic objectives for a firm to be able to contribute as a whole, and not on just an operational level, to global society. Relatively small population centres throughout the world sometimes rely upon one or perhaps two main local employers, without which the town or village would most likely cease to exist, e.g. a local coalmine would have been a majority employer in small villages. Once shut down, it is unlikely that people would be able to afford to stay and would have to move to find work.

- **Economic:** The fundamental reason for a business being in operation is to make a profit, and this inevitably contributes to not only the growth of a company, but also the economic stability and subsequent development of a nation. A firm needs to make a profit in order to remain viable. Without it there would undoubtedly be job losses, cutbacks and potential dissolution of the company, thus having a detrimental effect on society.

- **Stakeholders:** There are a number of parties who will have a vested interest in a company, for example employees, shareholders, suppliers and customers. These are termed as business stakeholders and the firm must act appropriately in order to maximise shareholder return and in their best interest. Different stakeholders are interested in different outputs and actions of a company, summarised below in Table 10.2.

Stakeholder	Areas of interest
Employee	Job security Potential for promotion and furthering of career Trust, transparency and honesty
Shareholder	Return on investment (ROI) Trust, transparency and honesty Company reputation
Suppliers	Repeat business / loyalty Recommendations Trust, transparency and honesty
Customers	The best product or service provided to them Reliability Trust, transparency and honesty

Table 10.2: Stakeholder areas of interest.

- **Voluntariness:** This concerns voluntary CSR activities that are not governed by law or governmental policy. It encompasses activities that are beyond the regular and routine remit of the organisation, and which exceed industry standards. This non-regulatory engagement can boost a firm's corporate image, particularly if they have had bad publicity in the past or operate in an industry that is controversial amongst the general population.

Despite the seemingly transferrable nature of the dimensions above, applications of CSR are largely based on the ethics of individual companies. The value of CSR policies to the organisation will also vary, as will the value of related publicity. The ideal is surely a genuine, altruistic interest in utilising the considerable resources of the business to identify and help meet the needs of society, yet current research suggests that CSR policies are largely implemented as a highly publicised means to a private, profitable end (Bolton et al. 2011). Alexander et al (2014) argue that the CSR ideal is incompatible with the profit-maximising principles that keep businesses alive, and can therefore only function as a smokescreen, concealing the power structures that uphold social inequality. For instance, certain companies (see *Tobacco Marketing*, p. 166) will flaunt CSR policies to deflect potentially restrictive governmental attention from their otherwise highly unethical and societally detrimental practices (Fooks et al., 2013).

Exercises: Corporate Social Responsibility (CSR)

1   With reference to the five broad dimensions above, contextualise these into an organisation of your choice, and give examples of each of the areas. You should aim to answer the following sub-questions:

   i)   How does your chosen organisation deal appropriately with these main aspects of CSR?

   ii) What aspects of the business, both internal and external, have an impact on the CSR policy of your chosen organisation?

   iii) Is the implementation of CSR done effectively? Justify your answer.

   iv) Reflect upon your answers for (i), (ii) and (iii) and come up with improvements for the way in which your chosen firm implements the above in their organisation.

   v)   Is CSR a necessity for every organisation?

2   There is no universal CSR policy that can be utilised by all organisations across all sectors. However, the fundamental principles are often similar and can be transferrable in some situations. With this in mind, develop a framework, pictorial, or a set of sub-headings, detailing how a new and expanding organisation, with plans to diversify into a global market, might go about creating and developing a CSR policy.

Helpful hint:

☐   Make reference to other areas of the business and utilise some of these to help inform your answer - e.g. market research, customer segments.

Our discussion of CSR brings us neatly back to the central problem of understanding global business ethics: ethics for whom? It is easy to imagine an ethical principle that can be rigorously upheld and yet affects no-one in particular, e.g. eggs must be broken on the small end first. Problems with the practical application of ethics only occur when they begin to affect that most tricky of variables: human beings. Like any form of ethics, at its most basic business ethics separates people and societies into those who we have the resources to look after, and those who we do not. How far beyond the boundaries of our organisation do we wish to extend the usefulness of our resources, if at all? If our principles of right and wrong only function within the business, then how do we anticipate the expectations of the external consumer? Are we working for the short- or long-term good? And who decides what is 'good' anyway? It is crucial that businesses (and students!) remain permanently open to ethical debate, in order to avoid stagnation, and a swift descent into irrelevance in an ever-changing world.

References

Alexander, M.J., Beveridge, E. Maclaren, A.C. and O'Gorman, K.D. (2014) "Responsible drinkers create all the atmosphere of a mortuary": Policy implementation of responsible drinking in Scotland. *International Journal of Contemporary Hospitality Management.* **26** (1): 18-34

Ardichvili, A., Jondle, D., & Kowske, B. (2010). Dimensions of ethical business cultures: comparing data from 13 countries of Europe, Asia, and the Americas. *Human Resource Development International,* **13**(3), 299-315.

Banerjee, R. (2015). Mane Garrincha stadium in Brazil becomes BUS DEPOT less than a year after hosting the World Cup. *Daily Mail.* Retrieved from http://www.dailymail.co.uk/sport/football/article-2984074/Mane-Garrincha-stadium-Brazil-BUS-DEPOT-year-hosting-World-Cup.html

Bolton, S.C., Kim, R.C. and O'Gorman, K.D. (2011). Corporate Social Responsibility as a Dynamic Internal Organisational Process: A Case Study. *Journal of Business Ethics.* **101**(1) pp 189-208.

Bowen, H. R. (1953). *Social Responsibilities of the Businessman.* New York: Harper & Row.

Buckley, P. J., Clegg, J., & Tan, H. (2006). Cultural awareness in knowledge transfer to China—The role of guanxi and mianzi. *Journal of World Business,* **41**(3), 275-288.

Chakraborty, S. (1997). Business ethics in India. *Journal of Business Ethics* **16**(14), 1529–38.

Christie, P. M. J., Kwon, I-W. G., Stoeberl, P. A., & Baumhart, R. (2003). A cross-cultural comparison of ethical attitudes of business managers: India Korea and the United States. *Journal of Business Ethics*, **46**(3), 263-287.

Cummings, K. M., Brown, A., & O'Connor, R. (2007). The Cigarette Controversy. *Cancer Epidemiology Biomarkers & Prevention*, **16**(6), 1070-1076. doi: 10.1158/1055-9965.epi-06-0912

Dahlsrud, A. (2008). How corporate social responsibility is defined: an analysis of 37 definitions. *Corporate Social Responsibility and Environmental Management*, **15**(1), 1-13.

Dunfee, T. W., & Nagayasu, Y. (Eds.). (2013). *Business ethics: Japan and the global economy* (Vol. 5). Springer Science & Business Media.

Fernando, A. C. (2009). *Business Ethics: An Indian Perspective*. Pearson Education India.

Fooks, G., Gilmore, A., Collin, J., Holden, C., & Lee, K. (2013). The limits of corporate social responsibility: techniques of neutralization, stakeholder management and political CSR. *Journal of Business Ethics*, **112**(2), 283-299.

Friedman, M. (1970). The social responsibility of firms is to increase profits. *The New York Times, 13*.

Hilton, I. (2013). Brazil erupts: Football, filthy lucre and fury. *New Statesman*. Retrieved from http://www.newstatesman.com/politics/2013/07/brazil-erupts-football-filthy-lucre-and-fury

Hock, D. K. W. (Ed.). (2007). *Legacies of World War II in South and East Asia*. Institute of Southeast Asian Studies.

Ip, P. K. (2009). Is Confucianism good for business ethics in China? *Journal of Business Ethics*, **88**(3), 463-476.

Kumar, A. (2002). *The Black Economy in India*. Penguin Books India.

Manfred, T. (2015). Brazil's $3 billion World Cup stadiums are turning into white elephants 6 months later. *Business Insider UK*. Retrieved from http://uk.businessinsider.com/brazil-world-cup-stadium-white-elephants-2015-1

Markland, M. E. M. A. (2012). *Advertising for Tobacco Products*: Salem Press.

Moore, G. (2014). World Cup 2014: Why has this World Cup been so good to watch?. *The Independent*. Retrieved from http://www.independent.co.uk/sport/football/international/world-cup-2014-why-has-this-world-cup-been-so-good-to-watch-9546614.html

Othman, Z., & Rahman, R. A. (2010). Ethics in Malaysian corporate governance practices. *International Journal of Business and Social Science*,**1**(3).

Quddus, M., Bailey III, H., & White, L. R. (2009). Business ethics: perspectives from Judaic, Christian, and Islamic scriptures. *Journal of Management, Spirituality and Religion*, **6**(4), 323-334

Rapoza, K. (2014). Bringing FIFA To Brazil Equal To Roughly 61% Of Education Budget. *Forbes*. Retrieved from www.forbes.com/sites/kenrapoza/2014/06/11/bringing-fifa-to-brazil-equal-to-roughly-61-of-education-budget/

Sinnott, J. (2013). A fair World Cup deal for Brazil?. *CNN*. Retrieved from http://edition.cnn.com/2013/06/24/sport/football/brazil-protests-fifa-tax/

Spencer-Oatey, Helen and Xing, Jianyu (2008) Issues of face in a Chinese business visit to Britain. In Spencer-Oatey, Helen (ed.) *Culturally Speaking: Culture, Communication and Politeness Theory*, 2nd edition. London: Continuum. P.p. 258-73.

Tabuchi, H. (2013). Layoffs Taboo, Japan Workers Are Sent to the Boredom Room. New York Times, p. A1. Retrieved from http://www.nytimes.com/2013/08/17/business/global/layoffs-illegal-japan-workers-are-sent-to-the-boredom-room.html

Taka, I. (1994). Business ethics: A Japanese view. *Business Ethics Quarterly*, 53-78.

Torres, I. (2013). Japanese companies using 'banishment rooms' to push employees to resign. *Japanese Daily Press*. Retrieved from http://japandailypress.com/japanese-companies-using-banishment-rooms-to-push-employees-to-resign-3029793/

Watts, J. (2014). World Cup 2014: eighth construction worker killed in Brazil. *The Guardian*. Retrieved from http://www.theguardian.com/football/2014/may/09/world-cup-2014-eighth-construction-worker-killed-in-brazil

West, A. 2013. Ubuntu and business ethics: Problems, perspectives and prospects. *Journal of Business Ethics* **121**(1):47–61.

WHO. (2005). *WHO Framework Convention on Tobacco Control*. Geneva: World Health Organisation.

Yao, X. (2000). *An introduction to Confucianism*: Cambridge University Press.

10

11 Running a Global Organization

Robert MacIntosh, Kevin Krebs and Julian Jones

Some brands seem omnipresent. Today's consumers can board a plane, travel to the other side of the planet and still find the same fast food chains, movies, clothing and perfumes waiting for them at the other end of their journey. Indeed, global organizations are ubiquitous – they probably made your breakfast cereal this morning (Kellogg's), brought you to work (Toyota) took you from the elevator to your office (Kone) and will make your lunch at the canteen (Sodexho). In this chapter we explore the challenges which flow from managing global organizations.

The firms that own these brands face a particular challenge since they must balance the desire to serve local tastes and interests with the consistency needed to maintain a global brand. For those managing a global business issues such as labour regulation, currency fluctuations, political change, transportation costs and any number of other concerns create challenges which must be overcome in a way which balances the requirements of local circumstances with the needs of the wider global organization. Today some businesses are 'born global' (Madsen & Servais, 1997) whilst others have achieved global status over time.

Both McDonald's and Skype are globally recognised brands yet their histories are very different. McDonald's has grown from a single restaurant in the 1950s to serving millions of customers via a network of 36,000 outlets globally today. The process of expansion has been relatively slow and steady when compared to global telecoms firm Skype, which is a good example of a 'born global' firm. Most 'born global' firms share some common features. Their management team has an international orientation, the firms are typically active in international markets at, or at least close to, foundation and they often start life as small, self-financed businesses focusing on a particular niche. Many such firms, like Skype, can achieve global reach through the use of technology. Whilst McDonald's is technologically sophisticated in many ways, the fact that it delivers physical products means that to internationalise it needs a presence in each market that it wishes to serve.

Even looking at one location it is clear that we operate in an increasingly international world. Fast food may seem like a relatively simple product but this would be deceptive. The burgers or pizzas that we find on our high streets may be international because they are provided by a global chain or franchise. However, they are also likely to be international in that they will use ingredients sourced from many countries. Flour from one, onions from another, meat from yet another. Almost nothing that we consume in any volume is exclusively locally sourced. Our challenge then is how best to manage organizations with a global footprint?

A useful starting point might be to revisit some classic ideas about organizations. Ronald Coase's, *The Nature of the Firm* is remarkable in many ways. For one, it was written in 1937 when Coase was just 26 years old but more importantly, it explains the role transaction costs play in the genesis of commercial businesses. Coase argues that "the main reason why it is profitable to establish a firm would seem to be that there is a cost of using the price mechanism" (Coase, 1937, p. 390). For commercial organizations this logic remains largely unchanged even by the vagaries of internationalisation or the internet. Low transaction costs are just one of the reasons that China became, and remains, a noted producer of goods for a range of Western firms. Many of Taiwan's well-known computer companies began in the 1980s as Chinese entrepreneurs in Silicon Valley sought lower cost locations for their ventures (Saxenian, 2002). In the decades since Coase shaped our thinking on commercial firms, a focus has also emerged on public, voluntary and inter-governmental organizations. These are often driven not by the desire to lower transaction costs in isolation, but rather by the desire to fulfil some obligation, offer a service or fulfil political or regulatory purposes. Organizations like the National Health Service, Unicef or the United Nations face the need to be commercially astute and yet mindful of their non-financial missions.

Today we recognise commercial, charitable, public, voluntary, inter-governmental and non-governmental organizations as being capable of global reach. Yet, global organizations differ in many ways from local organizations. Beyond the obvious statement issues of scale, scope and geography, the way in which we interact with global organizations is different. Taxation, for example, is often different for smaller and larger organizations. Take the example of State taxes in the United States; companies only need to collect a sales tax where they have a physical presence – effectively excluding e-commerce firms like Amazon from paying sales tax in many states (Ainsworth & Madzharova, 2013). This crucial legislative glitch probably pre-dates the internet revolution but it gave

Amazon a vital edge during its start up and early expansion. For global brands, office complexes may offer better rates so that they can become 'anchor tenants' for new developments. In the early 1990s, with London in the grip of the last recession, the landmark Canary Wharf office development was offering 10-year free leases to blue-chip companies to become anchor tenants (Ashworth, 2013, p. 303).

It doesn't stop there. The procedures and practices of global businesses become industry standards to follow. Take the example of Toyota's Lean Six Sigma, an efficient production system developed by the Japanese auto manufacturer (Dahlgaard & Mi Dahlgaard-Park, 2006), 'McDonaldization' (Ritzer, 1983) or Amazon's incredible logistics centres (Crandall, Crandall, & Chen, 2014), which the company are planning to augment using same-day drone deliveries (Bensinger, 2013). Global organizations are often the ones pushing boundaries within their industries. Around a third of the world's largest economies are corporations, not nation states. As a result, commercial global organizations often challenge the ability of regulators working at national or international levels to impose external control.

Running a global organization which is larger than many nation states requires the "daily assessment of opportunities, risks and trends. Corporate leaders who ignore economic, political, or social changes will lead their companies towards failure. So too will those who overreact to change and perceived risk" (Schmidheiny, 1992, p. 1). This in turn introduces new challenges such as those faced when McDonald's entered the Indian market and had to introduce non-beef choices for the local market (Kumar & Goel, 2007) or where Google experiences a different form of government regulation in countries like China (Deva, 2007).

Given these challenges, one might wonder why businesses go global at all. The traditional answer has been, "in search of new markets, cheap labour, and unrestricted production sites" or generally, when a company reaches a certain size and the growth trajectory that its revenues initially experienced begin to tail off" (Farazmand, 1999, p. 512). There are a few options to generate growth in those circumstances, for instance undertaking a merger or acquisition or diversifying to launch new products or services. None of these answers is risk free but increasing the scale and scope of the organization can mean that there are diminishing costs and effort required by those organizations which are already present in several markets when they try to enter new ones. The accumulation of experience and resources, sometimes described as 'experiential learning' is claimed by some scholars as part of the explanation of global firms operating in many countries (Zahra, Ireland, & Hitt, 2000).

11

In this chapter we aim to explore the challenges that global businesses face by addressing a set of four interdependent questions with which those leading a global business tend to wrestle. First is the question of the extent to which global organizations need or expect standardization across all geographies or will permit, or perhaps even encourage, elements of local variation. Globalization itself may be driving the convergence of local consumption patterns and culture, in turn enhancing the appetite for global products and services and implying that global organizations can achieve superior performance through the implementation of truly centralized global standards (Fukuyama, 1992). However, other authors present evidence that differences between countries and cultures have not been attenuated globally and local contexts are becoming increasingly important suggesting that global homogenization is neither inevitable nor desirable. Whichever view is taken, local contexts are critical for embedding knowledge and strategies in the wider global organization (Ghemawat, 2007; Rugman, 2003). Some global organizations, such as long established firms from North American and West European experience significant challenges when exploring emerging economics in large countries as China and Russia. Those leading these organizations need to embed established organizational culture in the context of multiple host contexts in a way which is plausible and effective (Narula & Dunning, 2010).

Second is the need to question whether the organization is serving a single global audience or a series of distinct and differentiated local audiences. Clearly, these questions are linked and there is often a complex interplay between global and local contexts such that it can be difficult to conceptualise the primacy of one over the other (Arnett, 2002). In developing countries like China and other Asian countries, for example, global elements of consumption conflict with norms and values defined by local tradition (Zhou & Belk, 2004). Product positioning may need significant adjustment as organizations explore the local cultural meaning of global images and advertisements. Adopting local ethnic identities within global images and advertising is one approach which can help a local audience recognise local culture meaning (Ozsomer, 2012; Steenkamp, Batra, & Alden, 2003).

Third, business leaders must ask how they will deal with talented individuals within the organization and how future leaders will be recruited, trained, promoted and incentivised both within geographies and across the global presence of the organization. Local demand may outstrip supply yet local government policies may constrain a firm's ability to effect labour migration. Global organizations often accumulate technologically advanced knowledge with clusters in specialised economic or geographic zones. This can lead to difficulties in recruiting and maintaining skilled labour (Sheldon, Kim, Li, & Warner, 2011), particularly in terms of managing access to expertise across the organization as a whole. Global organizations may respond by poaching skilled labour from neighbouring businesses as a systematic recruiting strategy (Cooke, 2005). Over time, emerging economics, such as India and China, offer examples of a growing pool of skilled labour that enables global organizations to reach local expertise through global research and development networks (Criscuolo & Narula, 2007; Simonin, 2004). Nevertheless, there remains a tendency for global organizations to assume that technological resources are relatively weaker the further you travel from the country where the organization was founded, producing an inclination towards a network of expatriate experts operating in other countries.

Finally, in answering these questions, one of the challenges is to balance the cultural needs of the organization as a whole and the social, cultural, linguistic and regulatory differences that exist within those countries where the organization operates. Research shows that three out of four global organizations manage twenty or more operations overseas. Managing such a diverse network of social, cultural and linguistic differences is challenging (John, Ietto-Gillies, Cox, & Grimwade, 1997). Cultural differences are recognised as a multinational organizations are often defined as multilingual (Tietze, Cohen, & Musson, 2003). Language barriers are so critical that only those global businesses able to tackle linguistic differences can increase their competitiveness globally (Anne-Wil, Köster, & Ulrike, 2011). Issues such as leadership style and negotiation tactics require careful management from the human resource experts within the organization. The fusion extent between cultural characteristics and management practice is thought to be one of the key determinants of successful global practice (Veiga, Lubatkin, Calori, & Very, 2000).

Standardization versus localization

Once an organization operates in more than one geographic location, managers face questions over whether to standardize the product or service offering or to permit local variations to reflect differences that may occur. The advantage of offering a standard product is that there are conveniences to offering the same thing in all locations. Where products are concerned there can be economies of scale which can be achieved. Industrialist Henry Ford operated in a different competitive climate, but his claim that "you could have any colour you want, as long as it's black" is one famous example of standardisation. Today's automotive industry has headed in precisely the opposite direction with significant opportunities to personalise vehicles. To return to Coase's economic interpretation of events, if you can get away with standardising you eliminate further cost from the transaction. There are other benefits too: customer expectations may be better served by encounters which are consistent. Bear in mind that significantly more people travel now than in previous eras and there may be particular market benefits which are conferred when consumers experience the safety and familiarity of what to expect. In new markets, one of the opportunities you may be looking to exploit is the very fact that your new customers are keen to associate themselves with the values, heritage or imagined lifestyle of your brand. Many established western brands have been entering emerging markets on this basis. Presenting a different product or service in the local market can undermine this sense of connection to a lifestyle or brand caché.

Most global organizations make some effort to localize their offering yet this is a real challenge for management teams (Pudelko & Harzing, 2008). When it comes to organizational practices such as incentive schemes, standardization or localization throw up significant differences such as the relative importance of length of service (which is a common theme in many Japanese firms) versus individual achievement (which is a common feature of many North American firms).

Of course, there may be very strong drivers for local variation. These could be cultural, as with the earlier example of McDonald's focusing on non-beef products for the Indian market. There are also instances of local difference that may have been unanticipated. Products or services which have a history of working well with one demographic in the home market may be adopted, or perhaps abducted, by a very different demographic in new markets. Hence, German automotive firm Volkswagen has one model, the Jetta, which sells to a more mature and family market in some countries but has been adopted as the mode of transport by a different, younger audience of surfers in parts of the United States.

Variation may even be imposed by local regulatory restrictions. Aspects of the product or service which may be seen as 'normal' in one territory may be precluded in another. Issues such as warranties, price points, raw materials and many others can cause difficulty unless local variation is introduced. Beyond these regulatory restrictions, it may simply be impractical to offer the same service in all locations because one cannot access the same resources, support mechanisms, training, personnel or raw materials. Local expectations may also vary enormously. In the hotel industry for example, the inclusion of breakfast, service charges, wi-fi or other services may be the norm or a source of additional income.

Finally, a hybrid position is adopted by many organizations. In essence, customers are offered the illusion of local difference but this masks a largely unchanged offering. John Travolta's character in *Pulp Fiction* famously observes that in Paris they call a quarter pound burger "the Royale with Cheese" because they "have the metric system." Though the name is different, the product is essentially unchanged.

The nature of your market(s)

One of the key factors affecting the decision to standardise or allow local variation of products or services is an assessment of the markets in which you operate. It may be that the ways in which your market is segmented is the same in all locations, either because this is most convenient or perhaps because it chimes with certain key strategic choices that the organization has made. If you are servicing essentially the same market demographic with your product or service, then it is more likely that you will either offer the same product or engage in some modest adjustments as described in the hybrid example above. However, there can be many issues which create noticeable market differences. In developed economies the mobile phone market is a mature market where consumers appear to value innovation and cutting edge technologies. A significant proportion of all handsets are so-called smartphones enabled for web access, gaming, photography and even financial transactions. Competing for market share, the main providers such Apple, Samsung and HTC strive to differentiate themselves with advanced features, larger and higher resolution screens, faster processors and the like. However, these same firms are also keen to find market share in emerging economies. The same products tend not to work well in these environments because the infrastructure is different. Mobile phone usage in rural areas can be high because there are no landline facilities but web usage is not always the priority. Indeed, Nokia had success with handsets which were far less complex but which were robust and worked effectively as a torch. Understanding how customers will use your product is simply good practice, but for global organizations there is a need to pay particular attention to geographic differences. In the example of mobile telephones it could be that some markets may offer a way of extending the life cycle of products by selling older models at lower cost to new markets. Alternatively it may be that it is worth designing a different type of product or service that better serves the needs of individual markets.

Managing organizational talent

Just as products or services can vary across geographies, so too can the people working in global organizations. There are often perceived benefits of working at headquarters, or at least in the geographic home of a global organization.

For Microsoft, Seattle holds a particular caché that other locations may not. In the diplomatic services, some postings are seen as more glamorous, exciting or career enhancing than others. Likewise, there can often be a sense in which future organizational leaders need to 'earn their stripes' by gaining experience in particular territories.

Global organizations often employ tens of thousands of people and we have already observed that some commercial firms are larger than nation states. With scale comes the problem of managing recruitment, training, development and retention of staff. Creating future leaders normally implies the need to be able to identify individuals with high potential and create a career structure which will see them gain the requisite experience and skills. This is a difficult process in its own right but is further complicated when spread across multiple locations and cultures.

There are coordination issues to consider. For the organization as a whole it may make sense to offer a key individual the chance to gain experience in a particular location. For those in that location, it can feel that their territory is being used as a training facility, test laboratory or soft play area as new leaders are parachuted in, then moved on just as they begin to find their feet. In practical terms there are significant domestic challenges for the individuals concerned. Everything from where to live through to relocation of family members can be a source of significant stress. It has been observed that foreign postings as part of a career in a global organization increases the likelihood of divorce (Steers et al., 2013) and there is little doubt that these domestic issues can impact on both the individual and the organization.

Dossani and Kenney (2007) observe that "in less than six years, offshoring of services has evolved from an exotic and risky strategy to a routine business decision". This growth in offshoring (Ernst, 2006) means that a range of organizational activities are being distributed from design, through sales and support for both global and/or domestic provision and this can alter the balance of global and local human resources (Lewin & Peeters, 2006). The increasing complexity of global organizations mean that there is a need for highly mobile, culturally sensitive and talented managers (Manning, Lewin, & Massini, 2008). Factors such as the size and accumulated international experience of the organization may influence the decision to offshore key tasks.

Social, cultural and regulatory differences

One cause of difficulty for global organization can be the need to adapt to different social, cultural, linguistic and regulatory frameworks. In practical terms, not everyone has mastery of languages. In the UK and US it is less typical for individuals to have multiple languages, whereas many continental Europeans leave high school speaking their own native language plus two others to a reasonable standard. English is increasingly becoming the language of international business, in part because it is often the most common second language for employees in global organizations. The pervasiveness of English language films, TV and music means that it is familiar to many people from non-English speaking countries.

Beyond the linguistic challenge there are many other subtle but important social and cultural norms to master. Researchers such as Hofstede (2011) claim that there are discernible national differences which affect the ways in which communication and decision making occur. One such distinction is that between so-called low-context and high-context settings (Steers et al., 2013). In low-context cultures, communication patterns are relatively more direct, to the point and frank. Although it may be a caricature, citizens from countries such as the US or the Netherlands have a reputation for direct forms of communication. Citizens from the UK are often perceived as being more reserved. Think of a practical example such as complaining about a meal. The stereotype would be that some cultures would complain openly, directly and constructively whilst others would say nothing at the time then complain off-line. In a low-context setting, ideas or arguments are put forward clearly and relatively less attention is paid to the mode of communication, body language, setting, etc.

In contrast, when working in a high-context setting non-verbal cues are relatively more important and convey important information about the status of the speaker(s). The middle-East and Asia are both regarded as high-context settings and this is reflected in the ways in which 'good' communication occurs. Skilled leaders in global organizations need to be able to navigate both high and low context settings, moderating their own default preferences in order to resonate with their peers in different locations. In one country it may be that time is pressured, and direct, short conversations are needed. In another, it may be that a certain amount of ritual and process are needed before getting to the important decision making phase of the conversation. Misreading the context can significantly hamper your ability to conduct business effectively.

11

Of course, stereotypes are just that and are never universally true. One can always find counter-examples of reserved individuals from low-context settings and outgoing, direct or plain speaking individuals from high-context settings. Paying attention to attitudes such that you become aware of the balance between individual and collective, the sense of time as either wasted or invested, the tendency toward honesty or guardedness, etc. will help make you a better leader.

Scotland's International University

We close the chapter by applying the ideas set out above, not to a global firm but to a university. Universities have been in existence for centuries and most modern campuses feature a diverse group of international students. In recent decades however, a small number of universities have begun to internationalise by opening campuses in overseas locations. This offers a good opportunity to examine one of our oldest forms of organization, with a long history of welcoming foreign students from distant corners of the globe, and to see how the process of leading such an organization changes when it becomes global.

Heriot-Watt University was founded in Edinburgh, the capital of Scotland. It gained university status in 1966 and can trace its roots back to 1821 when the world's first mechanics institute was created, from which the University was ultimately formed. The University has had international students on the Edinburgh campus since its inception but in more recent times it has created campuses in both the United Arab Emirates and in Malaysia.

The Dubai campus, located in Academic City, was established in 2006 and was the first non-UAE university to have a campus in Dubai. In November 2011, the University won an international tender to establish a new purpose-built University in the Malaysian city of Putrajaya. Heriot-Watt University Malaysia opened its new campus in September 2014, meaning that there are currently campus locations in three different countries. Heriot-Watt also has a network of academic partnerships which enable students to study toward a degree whilst registered with a partner college or institution, in addition to students who study by independent distance learning. These academic partnerships cover the globe, making Heriot-Watt a very geographically dispersed organization with students in 150 countries. Although UK universities are often thought of as public organizations, they are independent bodies, typically registered as charities; in many cases, public funding makes up only a small portion of the revenues of the university.

In Heriot-Watt's case, it is helpful to think of the university as sharing many of the traits and challenges which characterize global organizations. It has sought out new markets and now offers its services (teaching and research) in multiple locations. Internationalisation brings scale but also helps offset the potential threat of reduced government funding for student places and research. Heriot-Watt University has increased its revenue base by moving into two geographies where economies are growing rapidly. Yet, it also faces the same kinds of questions that all global organizations must confront.

First, on the issue of standardization versus local variation, Heriot-Watt has developed a series of policies and procedures that ensure that there are many student experiences which lead to the same degree standard. Students studying at different campus locations, through academic partnerships elsewhere in the world or registered as independent distance learners, are managed in accordance with the same academic procedures and awarded the same degree certificate on successful completion of their studies. This is an important issue for the University since it bears on the academic integrity and credibility of the institution. Significant amounts of time and effort are spent to ensure that academic policies are enforced and that standards are maintained. This approach would not work for all types of global organization but the incentive for Heriot-Watt to standardise its offering is clear.

Having set out to offer the same product in different locations, the University faces a second question which is to ascertain whether it is dealing with a single audience or a series of differentiated audiences. Here, the experience of running campuses in different locations suggests that the University is actually dealing with different audiences. The high school systems vary from one location to another as does the perceived importance of specific subject areas. The newest campus in Malaysia has experienced stronger demand for undergraduate than postgraduate degree programmes. It has also experienced a strong emphasis on engineering and science disciplines, perhaps as a result of the local economy in which Heriot-Watt University Malaysia sits. Understandably, the world-class brewing and distilling research and teaching conducted in Edinburgh has no place in those campus locations where Islamic faith is the norm.

In terms of managing the talent pool across campus locations, the University has adopted a few strategies. First, it has seconded people from one location to another to ensure skills are embedded across the whole organization. Second, it has created HR processes such as annual reviews and promotion rounds which use the same approach regardless of location. Third, leaders and managers in the organization have responsibility for academic disciplines rather than geographic locations. Hence academic staff in a single discipline or School will report through a unified structure.

Finally, the three campus locations are marked by strong cultural and social differences. The business language is English but accommodations have to be made for issues such as religious and other public holidays which differ. In terms of regulation there are multiple layers of complexity. In order for the university to offer a degree programme it must be approved by the Senate (the highest academic body in the university). However, for a degree programme to run in either the United Arab Emirates or Malaysia, it must also be approved by the relevant national qualifications authority. To further complicate matters, many degrees articulate with professional bodies to ensure chartered status for graduates. Academic programmes are therefore subject to multiple, overlap-

11

ping regulatory systems, meaning that any changes to programme content need careful management to ensure compliance. In some specific cases, this has meant local changes have been needed to satisfy one or more of these regulatory bodies.

Heriot-Watt University is a truly global organization. To manage its operations it engages in a highly structured strategic planning process. The university has a strategic plan (covering the period 2013-2018) which is available in the public domain and this strategic plan drives local financial and resource allocation decisions in the campus locations. Planning is integrated in order to help the university deliver its core purpose to be "world-leading within all its specialist areas of science, technology and business", while its mission is to "create and exchange knowledge for the benefit of society" (Heriot-Watt, 2012, p. 1).

It was Coca-Cola, that brought the phrase 'think global, act local' to an international business context. Heriot-Watt University now offers an example of this maxim being played out by a different kind of organization but a global organization nonetheless. Its key academic principles – the principles behind its success – are identical academic standards and diversity of learning experiences.

References

Ainsworth, R. T. & Madzharova, B. (2013). Leveling the international playing field with the Marketplace Fairness Act. *Boston Univ. School of Law, Law and Economics Research Paper, No. 13-25*.

Anne-Wil, H., Köster, K. & Ulrike, M. (2011). Babel in business: The language barrier and its solutions in the HQ-subsidiary relationship, *Journal of World Business*, **46**(43), 279.

Arnett, J. J. (2002). The psychology of globalization, *American Psychologist*, **57**(10), 774–783.

Ashworth, A. (2013). *Cost Studies of Buildings*: Taylor & Francis.

Bensinger, G. (2013). Before the drones come, Amazon lets loose the robots. *Wall Street Journal, 9*.

Coase, R. H. (1937). The nature of the firm. *Economica*, **4**(16), 386-405.

Cooke, F. L. (2005). Vocational and enterprise training in China: Policy, practice and prospect *Journal of the Asia Pacific Economy*, **10**, 26–55.

Crandall, R. E., Crandall, W. R., & Chen, C. C. (2014). *Principles of Supply Chain Management, (2nd Ed.)*. Taylor & Francis.

Criscuolo, P., & Narula, R. (2007). Using multi-hub structures for international R&D: Organisational inertia and the challenges of implementation. *Management International Review*, **47**, 639–660.

Dahlgaard, J. J., & Mi Dahlgaard-Park, S. (2006). Lean production, six sigma quality, TQM and company culture. *The TQM Magazine, 18*(3), 263-281.

Deva, S. (2007). Corporate complicity in internet censorship in China: Who cares for the Global Compact or the Global Online Freedom Act? *George Washington International Law Review, 39*, 255-319.

Dossani, R., & Kenney, M. (2007). The next wave of globalization: Relocating service provision to India. *World Development 35*(35): 772–791.

Ernst, D. (2006). *Innovation offshoring: Asia's emerging role in global innovation networks, East–West Center Special Report Number 10.* Honolulu, US: East–West Center.

Farazmand, A. (1999). Globalization and public administration. *Public Administration Review*, 509-522.

Fukuyama, F. (1992). *The End of History and the Last Man*. New York, US: Free Press.

Ghemawat, P. (2007). *Redefining Global Strategy*. Boston, US: Harvard Business School.

Heriot-Watt, U. (2012). 'Global thinking, worldwide influence' Strategic Plan 2013-18. Edinburgh Campus: Heriot-Watt University.

Hofstede, G. (2011). Dimensionalizing cultures: The Hofstede model in context. *Online Readings in Psychology and Culture, 2*(1)

John, R., Ietto-Gillies, G., Cox, H., & Grimwade, N. (1997). *Global Business Strategy, International* London, UK: Thomson Press.

Kumar, S., & Goel, B. (2007). *Glocalization in food and agribusiness: strategies of adaptation to local needs and demands.* Paper presented at the 17th Annual World Food and Agribusiness Forum and Symposium on Food Culture: Tradition, Innovation and Trust–A Positive Force for Modern Agribusiness, Parma.

Lewin, A. Y., & Peeters, C. (2006). The top-line allure of offshoring. *Harvard Business Review, 84*(83), 22–24.

Madsen, T. K., & Servais, P. (1997). The Internationalization of Born Globals: An Evolutionary Process? *International Business review, 6* (6): 561–583.

Manning, S., Lewin, A. Y. & Massini, S. (2008). The globalization of innovation: A dynamic perspective on offshoring. *Academy of Management Perspectives, 22*(23), 35–54.

Narula, R., & Dunning, J. H. (2010). Multinational enterprises, development and globalisation: some clarifications and a research agenda. *Oxford Development Studies, 38*, 263–287.

Ozsomer, A. (2012). The interplay between global and local brands: A closer look at perceived brand globalness and local iconness *Journal of International Marketing, 20*(22), 72–95.

Pudelko, M. & Harzing, A. W. (2008). Standardization towards headquarters practices, standardization towards global best practices and localization.

11

Organizational Dynamics, **37**(34), 394–404.

Ritzer, G. (1983). The 'McDonaldization' of society. *Journal of American Culture,* **6**(1), 100-107.

Rugman, A. (2003). Regional strategy and the demise of globalization. *Journal of International Management*, **9**, 409–417.

Saxenian, A. (2002). The Silicon Valley connection: Transnational networks and regional development in Taiwan, China and India. *Science Technology & Society,* **7**(1), 117-149.

Schmidheiny, S. (1992). *Changing Course: A Global Business Perspective on Development and the Environment*: MIT Press.

Sheldon, P., Kim, S., Li, Y. & Warner, M. (2011). *China's changing workplace: Dynamism, diversity and disparity*. London, UK Routledge.

Simonin, B. L. (2004). An empirical investigation of the process of knowledge transfer in international strategic alliances. *Journal of International Business Studies*, **35**, 407–427.

Steenkamp, J. E. M., Batra, R. & Alden, D. L. (2003). How perceived brand globalness creates brand value, *Journal of International Business Studies*, **34**(31), 53–65.

Steers, R. M., Nardon, L. and Sanchez-Runde, C. J. (2013) *Management Across Cultures: developing global competencies*, Cambridge: Cambridge University Press

Tietze, S., Cohen, L. & Musson, G. (2003). *Understanding Organizations Through Language*. London, UK: Sage

Veiga, J., Lubatkin, M., Calori, R. & Very, P. (2000). Measuring organizational culture clashes: A two nation post-hoc analysis of a cultural compatibility index, *Human Relations*, **53**(54), 539–557

Zahra, S. A., Ireland, R. D. & Hitt, M. A. (2000). International expansion by new venture firms: International diversity, mode of market entry, technological learning, and performance. *Academy of Management Journal*, **43**(5), 925-950.

Zhou, N., & Belk, R. W. (2004). Chinese consumer readings of global and local advertising appeals *Journal of Advertising*, **33**(33), 63–76.

12 Becoming a Manager

Elaine Collinson and Jane Queenan

In this chapter the role of the manager is discussed in order to investigate the many roles they play and the skillset required to be a successful manager. Witzel's *Dictionary of Business & Management* (1999) defines a 'manager' as:

> *"anyone within a firm who bears responsibility for planning, direction and controlling the work of others "* pp.186

while 'management' is defined as:

> *"a general term for the coordination and direction of resources, capital and labour to ensure the organisation meets its goals"* pp.184

Definitions of both management and manager have changed little over the decades, but from these short descriptions it is clear that the area is both wide and complex, including all areas of the business, both at the operational and the people management levels.

What is a manager?

So what exactly is a manager? A person, acting as a manager, can be in charge of people, processes, budgets, decision-making, manufacturing, recruitment, marketing strategies or the overall running of a business. In any business there are likely to be a range of management duties at junior, middle and senior management levels which require varying skillsets and are either closely or loosely aligned to the functional departments of the business. In addition to the differing skillsets, it is also important to understand the different tasks which managers undertake in specific roles and how progression from junior to senior management takes place.

This chapter investigates the theories surrounding managerial competencies whilst looking at the different contexts within which managers perform their tasks. Being a manager in a large global firm and being a manager in a small firm of five people are very different environments, so the context and the culture of the business will have a direct impact on how managers behave, perform, communicate and ultimately succeed. The manager operating in an international business will also require a level of intercultural awareness when dealing with both international clients and colleagues across the group.

The first section of this chapter discusses the key theoretical managerial studies, while the second looks at the culture and context within which management takes place. A range of quotes are provided by three UK based managers from different sectors who provide an insight into their practical experience of management and the skills learned along the way. These senior level managers range from the small business sector, namely Arran Aromatics, a large emergency public services organisation, the Fire and Rescue Service, and Iberdrola, a large international group based in five countries, with their HQ in Bilbao, Spain. The chapter includes a short vignette relating to each business to provide detail on the context and background within which each of these managers operate.

Managerial studies

In the literature there has often been confusion between managerial jobs, managerial behaviour and managerial work. Henri Fayol, who wrote about his own experience, was one of the earliest theorists and stated in 1916:

> To manage is to forecast and plan, to organize, to command (now motivate), to coordinate and to control.

Although these concepts are still valid today, they offered little to explain how managers behaved, so the last century saw the evolution of a series of studies dedicated to understanding managerial behaviour.

Sune Carlson in 1951 undertook the first piece of research in this area entitled *"Executive Behaviour: A Study of The Workload and Working Methods of Managing Directors"*. This study concentrated on understanding what tasks senior managers undertook, whilst at the same time attempting to understand the environment within which these tasks were conducted. The author studied the diaries of Chief Executive Officers over a four week period. The study consisted of seven senior executives operating in Sweden in the 1950s, with the author acknowledging that the Swedish community was rather small and the homogeneity between the CEOs relatively high. An important feature of the Swedish economy at the time was that it had a high degree of centralization, where the freedom of activity was curtailed by an increasing number of government regulations and restrictions imposed by trade associations, trade unions and employers' federations. As a consequence of this environment, the CEOs had to devote a considerable amount of time to public relations. The dimensions in the study looked at:

1   The place of work

2   The contacts the manager had with people and institutions

3   Communication

4   The activities undertaken

With reference to **place of work**, the study found that the CEOs spent around 32% of their time outside of the firm, leading to a lack of visibility in the firm as leaders and little in the way of delegation taking place. When looking at **contacts** and **communications**, the CEOs in the study rarely met with suppliers or clients and used little in the way of paper-based communications, but were more focused on networking and accessing information. There were however large differences in the behaviour of those in centralised versus decentralised companies. The **activities undertaken** indicated that the CEOs undertook a wide variety of tasks, often in an inefficient way and were often perceived as far removed from the main workforce.

The main conclusion from this research was that managerial work needed to be studied in its social context and the focus required to be on the **objectives, attitudes and goals** of those involved. Getting inside the manager's mind and understanding the social influences and those of the physical environment within which the manager is operating, are key to understanding behaviour.

This early study, although undertaken over 50 years ago, initiated the interest in studying managerial behaviour in order to identify common managerial activities, distinguish the differences between managerial jobs, offer guidance for managerial selection and training and make suggestions for improving effectiveness.

These early studies were referred to as the Work Activity School, where researchers investigated the content of managers' diaries in order to provide an insight into their activities. The findings of the diary studies suggest that managers spent the *majority of their time talking* and *listening*, in some cases up to 90% of their time and also indicated one common factor that managers *undertake a high number of small tasks in one day*, often being interrupted, rarely with more than half an hour alone.

12

Managerial competencies

An ability to multi-task, be a good listener, have excellent communication skills and an ability to organise are therefore key and are still valid for managers today.

There were a number of flaws with this approach, not least of which was an inability to compare what managers were doing with where, when and with whom they were working. Notwithstanding this, these studies provide valid contributions to our understanding of managerial behaviour.

Following on from these, the focus shifted to investigate *what* managers were doing, with three major US based studies looking into managerial behaviour and work. The first of these was by Leonard Sayles in 1964. He studied 75 lower and middle level managers in a large US manufacturing firm and the study was ethnological in nature, taking place over several years and including observations, interviews and feedback. Sayles described managerial work as **part of a social system** and emphasised the importance played by relationships which had a major impact on work efficiency. He highlighted the dynamics of social relationships:

> "Enormous personal energy is required to interact in as diverse and multiple roles as those encompassed by the typical executive position."
> (Sayles 1964, p. 260).

He identified lateral relationships as being particularly important as opposed to vertical relationships which had been a previous focus in the literature. Sayles' research identified managerial work as often mundane in nature and with high levels of frustration when managers were dealing with different business units' priorities. He suggested that managerial success was dependent on building and maintaining a predictable, reciprocal system of relationships across the firm. He argued that it was wrong to see planning and decision-making as separate activities, rather decision-making is a social process that is shaped by interactions with others. Stewart (1999) in her review of Sayles' work notes his focus on the amount of scope managers have to use their personality skills and energies to constantly re-stabilize the work processes and to introduce change, saying:

> "When the organisation is viewed as a complex series of interlocking patterns of human relationships, work-flow patterns and control patterns, the opportunity for the individual to innovate and shape his/her own environment becomes apparent." (Stewart, 1999, p. 106)

This quote from Sayles' work, although focusing on what managers do, demonstrates the overlap with managers' leadership skills, personality and the context within which the managerial work takes place. Although his study did not focus on the leadership element of a manager's role, he did make another important observation relating to the control a manager has and the importance of taking corrective action when work processes are malfunctioning. Stewart et al. (1994), in a study focused on comparing the behaviour of British and German middle managers, noted a large amount of their time was spent on *checking how work was going and taking corrective action.* (Stewart, Barsoux, Kieser, Ganter & Walgenbach, 1994)

The second major study was that of Mintzberg in 1973, where he observed over a week each, a total of five chief executives in different kinds of organisations. The most important aspect of this well cited study is his classification of 10 managerial roles into three main headings:

1 Informational
2 Interpersonal
3 Decisional.

The informational role of the manager is seen as his most important contribution to the knowledge in the area. In addition to which, his distinction of the interpersonal roles played by managers, as a *figurehead, leader* and *liaison* in the firm provide greater detail on the complexity of the senior managerial role. Although not classed as interpersonal, Mintzberg's research also defined the importance of *interpersonal relationships* and the manager as a *spokesperson* and a *negotiator*.

From an informational perspective Mintzberg portrays the manager as a "nerve centre for the monitoring and dissemination of information."

Mintzberg (1973) stressed the manager's preference for live action and the ability to be able to make a variety of decisions in a short time frame. Although sometimes criticised for the small sample size, Mintzberg's (1973) work has been replicated by many scholars, using his classification as a useful research framework.

The third study was that of John Kotter in 1982. This study was much wider in scope than Mintzberg's 1973 study and included 15 general managers in different firms, observed and interviewed over a period of time, as were their key contacts. The study also included the managers' characteristics and the context of the firms in which they worked, concluding that they worked in very contextually specific settings, which were acting as a barrier to them moving to a more senior management role in a different setting.

Kotter's key contribution to the knowledge on managerial behaviour related to two areas – *agendas* and *networks*. He suggested that managers developed an

12

agenda in the first six months to a year, linked to their goals and plans. In order to achieve their objectives they developed a network of contacts who could support them and invested heavily in this network. He also noted that agendas tended to be more strategic in focus and developed an approach to business which could be sustained over the longer term.

Like Sayles' earlier work (1964), Kotter (1982) also stressed the importance of relationships outside the straight line hierarchy and agreed with the Diary Studies that managers' roles were often fragmented, most of their time was spent with other people and tasks were disjointed.

In addition to these key early contributors to the literature Rosemary Stewart's work (1967, 1976, 1982, 1991, et al. 1994) took another focus, looking at the differences between managers' jobs and the implications for selection, training, careers and effectiveness. Her 1976 study although failing to develop an overall categorization of differences in managerial jobs, did identify categories of difference, namely:

1 Nature and difficulty of contacts required in the job
2 Whether the scope of the job was dependent upon the boss
3 Whether the job was exposed and mistakes were personally identified.

Stewart's key contribution in 1982 however developed a *demands, constraints* and *choices* model, which suggests that jobholders have flexibility in the way they undertake the role and can apply their management style and the focus they bring to the role. Demands being the essential work which needs to be undertaken, constraints the limiting factors and choices are the opportunities for jobholders to emphasize their own take on the role.

Throughout the discussion of the literature in the area of managerial studies, key elements are common with authors over the last 50 years demonstrating the complexity of managers' roles, especially those in senior management positions, whilst also increasingly recognising the importance of the context within which managers operate. Organisational culture and an individual firm's stage of development will have a direct impact on managers' flexibility to both undertake their jobs, the choices open to them and the approach which they adopt.

The next section in this chapter is dedicated to organisational culture and explores its impact on managers.

Culture and organizational impact

What do we mean when we talk about the 'culture' of an organisation? Do we simply mean the way people behave when doing business? To an extent, that's true. A client or potential collaborator may be impressed or put off by the way a company responds to their overtures. However, organisational culture is more than simply manners or style.

Standard management textbooks use different forms of words to define organisational culture, but these definitions can be summarised in the work of Andrew Brown (1998) who offers the following analysis:

> …the pattern of beliefs, values and learned ways of coping with experience that have developed during the course of an organisation's history and which tend to be manifested in its material arrangements and in the behaviours of its members

'Organisational culture' is defined in the *Dictionary of Business and Management* (1999) as:

> .. the common values and shared understandings present among members of an organisation.

'Organisational climate' refers to:

> .. a general term for the working environment within an organisation, referring to physical, social and psychological characteristics of that environment.

We use the word 'organisation' rather than 'company' or 'corporation' or any other word which indicates business, because organisational culture is not confined to the profit-making sector. All organisations may be said to have 'cultures', which are often described on their public facing websites, providing all stakeholders with an understanding of their values and the way they do business.

- A multi-national corporation, such as Iberdrola has a set of values which define the way it interacts with customers and stakeholders – these are clearly defined on their website: www.iberdrola.es/about-us/a-great-company/vision-values/

- A university has a set of values and beliefs which support the overall aims of intellectual excellence and research. Heriot-Watt University openly promotes the organisation's values to its many stakeholders: www.hw.ac.uk/about/careers/culture/our-values.htm

- A small family owned business' culture will often align with that of the family and its personal aspirations and the management style of the owner.

12

In this context, culture is often less readily identified and the relationship between family members can have a direct impact how decisions are made. Many small family run businesses demonstrate their values through their story or philosophy as is the case with Arran Aromatics. www.arranaromatics.com/our-story

■ A charity will have a culture which supports its work for a particular purpose. Medecins Sans Frontiers for example explains its Charter and approach: www.msf.org.uk/our-charter

These values, charters or cultures act as reference points for employees and all other stakeholders to better understand an organisation. Hilhorst and Schiemann (2002) when discussing the Medecins Sans Frontier case stated:

> Organisational principles are important for the performance and the well-being of volunteers: they serve as beacons, identity markers, and interpersonal 'glue'. It also becomes apparent that while in practice staff members renegotiate the formal principles of their organisation, they also adhere to patterns of organisational culture resulting in a number of ordering principles they deem typical of their organisation.

So, having established that organisations have their own cultures and climates we might ask "Why does this matter?"

We would suggest that it matters because the culture of an organisation has an impact on that organisation – it affects the type and quality of managerial decision making, the way in which communication takes place, how individuals are supported within the structure and the speed with which a business can respond to either a client's request, a competitor's campaign or a change in the external environment. An organisation's values, although intangible, form part of the firm's identity and brand image and are often promoted as part of their unique selling proposition to both customers and future employees alike.

In the first section of this chapter we looked at what managers are and what managers do. Now we will look at how the culture of the organisation influences *how* they do their jobs.

Charles Handy (1978), the acknowledged expert in the study of organisations, notes four different types of organisational culture. The model has been very influential and serves as a good illustration of the impact of organisational culture.

■ ## The power culture

Handy (1978) describes a web of power, with the owner or managing director, or other person of influence at the centre. The success of such an organisation depends on trust, empathy and ready communication. Managers within this type of culture are encouraged to perform tasks and make decisions independently, although always with an eye to the requirements of the centre.

This type of culture is common in small entrepreneurial, fast-moving organisations. It can readily be seen that success depends on the central person selecting managers who are comfortable with risk taking and issues of power and influence. The organisation will not prosper if a manager continually refers to the centre in order to receive permission or validation of his / her decisions.

■ ## The role culture

A 'role culture' organisation may be regarded as bureaucratic; this culture is often seen in large organisations with many functions and tasks, such as banks and the Civil Service. Handy (1978) describes this in terms of a Greek Temple. Each specialism (e.g. finance, marketing, logistics) forms a pillar, which is strong and independent. However, the specialist pillars link to each other through the roof, a broad band of senior managers.

To ensure the stability of this edifice, the role culture relies on procedures, rules, logic and rationality. There are, for example, strong reporting structures and controls. Within this culture therefore, managerial decisions will be influenced by rules, standards and best practice. There is little room for the free-wheeling independence of the entrepreneurial decision maker.

■ ## The task culture

Organisations with a task culture can be represented by a lattice. Power is based on expertise and knowledge, rather than charisma or high position.

The task culture organisation is team-oriented and project-based, with a fairly flat structure – no one person has ultimate power. Rather, power is invested where it is needed to get the job done. For example, a project may be headed by a design engineer, with a finance expert, a marketing expert and a production engineer reporting to him / her. When that project is finished, each person will move to another project, and may lead it or may be a team member. Power attaches to the skills needed at that moment, not to the nominal position held by each person.

Such a culture leads to a co-operative type of managerial decision making and is appropriate to an organisation which, for example, deals in products with

12

short life cycles and where innovation is needed. Media organisations, such as advertising or publicity companies, organisations working in innovative products or a very competitive market may offer a task culture. However, while a young manager may find this a great way to gain experience, a manager nearer the centre of the organisation may find it difficult to exercise overall control.

■ The person culture

This unusual cultural grouping is represented by a cluster. The organisation is a loose structure which serves only to support the individuals within it. For example, advocates or architects or dentists practice individually but share the cost of offices, printing and clerical assistance. Decision-making here is related to one's own personal objectives, with little impact on the organisation except where it affects shared services. This type of culture can be attractive to people who are interested in their own specialisms and feel no need to have a strong allegiance to an organisation.

What can we learn from this type of analysis? Perhaps the first thing is that, in order to be a good manager one must *understand the culture of one's organisation*. If your managerial preference is to seek input from senior colleagues, the fast moving independence of a web culture will not suit you. Similarly, if your main interest is in your own specialism, you are unlikely to be regarded as a good manager in the co-operative atmosphere of a lattice culture.

Secondly, *in order to be a good manager, you must understand your own style and preferences*. If your personal management style does not meet the culture of your current organisation, perhaps you can learn new techniques or methods of action which will help you function better in that organisation. Management styles are not genetically programmed! The successful manager seeks to learn. However, a wise manager hopes to find a position in a company which best matches his or her style.

In addition to Handy, Geert Hofstede's (1991) work focused on international cultures and how they shape organisations and the way they work. In today's environment of both global markets and global firms, *a successful manager is required to have a high level of intercultural awareness when dealing with both colleagues and customers from across the globe.*

■ Entrepreneurial culture

In discussing a firm's culture, one key area which needs to be included is that of entrepreneurial culture. The area of entrepreneurship is often perceived as pertaining to the small firm sector and there is little doubt that the vast majority

of the studies on entrepreneurship have focused on either the individual entrepreneur or the small firm as the unit of analysis. This does not mean however
that larger firms cannot engender an entrepreneurial culture in their approach
to management.

Kuratko (2002) describes an entrepreneur as:

"An innovator or developer who recognises and seizes opportunities,
converts those opportunities into workable/marketable ideas, adds
value through time, effort, money or skills, assumes the risk of the
competitive marketplace to implement these ideas and realises the
rewards from these efforts."

This highlights the importance of change as one of the key drivers in entrepreneurial activity.

One important aspect to consider is the size and stage of development of a
business. Small firms in the early stages of development are often characterised
by informal communication styles, unstructured decision making and ambiguity between roles with staff covering all functional areas of the business. The
managerial competencies required in this context are therefore very different
to the large established business, with *managers requiring high levels of intuition,
creative, adaptable not averse to risk and task oriented*. (Collinson & Shaw, 2002).

As the business grows the challenge for managers is to ensure that the
entrepreneurial approach to doing business is not lost, whilst the additional
complexities of a more structured managerial organisation are developed.

The case studies

This chapter has provided three very different company case studies which
demonstrate the variety of contexts within which managers work and advice
from senior manager from very different sectors. The overview of the knowledge and research associated with managerial behaviour and culture should
further your understanding of the complexities associated with being a successful manager and some pointers to the key skills required.

■ Arran Aromatics

Arran Aromatics is a small business based on the island of Arran off Scotland's
west coast. It started life in 1989 as a cottage-based firm, literally operating
from the kitchen table of the founders Janet and Iain Russell, a husband and
wife team. The business remains a family concern 25 years later, with Andrew

Russell, the son of the founders, as Director of Branding and co-founder Janet Russell still acting in an advisory capacity. The initial product range consisted of soaps and body creams, infused with original fragrances inspired by the landscape and scents of the island they loved.

The business grew quickly in the early years and soon moved to larger premises to support their growth into perfumery development. They also embarked on their first retail outlet based on Brodick Pier welcoming visitors to the island. In 1992 the Arran Apothecary range was launched based on traditional product designs from the Arran Heritage Museum. This range was followed in 1997 by the Arran at Home range offering candles and room scents based on traditional fragrances. The company quickly became a candle connoisseur and this product line is still key today.

As the company developed they also branched out into other areas, developing relationships with quality hotel chain Malmaison to supply their toiletries, as well as introducing a baby range in 2003. In 2015 the company have a total of 12 retail outlets across Scotland, an online store, a visitor centre based on the island of Arran offering tours of the facility and three manufacturing sites.

It has not all been plain sailing however for this small family owned business, which now employs a total of 120 people, predominantly based on the island of Arran. Over their 25 year history they have received substantial investment from Highlands & Islands Enterprise in the form of government subsidised training, manufacturing assistance and executive training.

The current Acting CEO and MD, Alan Wade, has been in post for 5 years and has seen the company through a period of consolidation which has resulted in a more focused approach to branding and a more strategic approach to development. Being an island-based business creates some issues for Arran Aromatics; firstly one advantage is that there is a strong service culture given the island's dependency on the tourist trade, but there is also a lack of technical expertise on the island to grow the business.

From a managerial perspective, Alan's greatest challenge has been in people management and in introducing into a small family run business more rigorous management control mechanisms. His key focus is on the people management aspects of his role. Given that the company has gone through high levels of growth and has ambitious plans to double its turnover in the next 5 years, a key focus has been ensuring that the communication of development plans is clear across the business.

My key focus throughout my career always in a small business sector, has been on building personal relationships and being focused on the team. I do not pretend to be an expert in all the functional elements of the business, that is not my role. I need to be able to take an overview perspective and bring the team along with me.

People management is the biggest challenge. My approach is to focus on helping people undertake their role and develop them where they need it. Open communication is essential in order that I can understand where we need to support the team.

Being a successful manager is about knowing your own strengths, being focused on the firm's objectives and being fully aware of the limitations. Don't try to be something you are not!

In a small firm management of the personal relationships is key. You need to be able to separate the personal relationship from the personal. People are often wary of change and growth, so to me a large part of my managerial role is dedicated to ensuring that firstly I am aware of the training needs of my staff, secondly they are keen to develop their expertise and lastly ensuring that performance is being monitored.

■ Iberdrola

Scottish Power Renewables is part of the Iberdrola Group and, combined with Iberdrola Renovables, is the world's No. 1 renewable energy developer. Scottish Power was acquired by the Iberdrola Group in 2007 and all functional areas within the group are managed centrally from Iberdrola HQ in Bilbao, Spain.

In addition to Scottish Power, the Iberdrola Group owns energy companies in Mexico, Brazil and the USA, with over 28,000 employees across the group. These international acquisitions have taken place over a period of years, Scottish Power being the first, with the most recent in the USA in 2015. This growth of the original Spanish business has therefore led to the company becoming a multi-cultural business, with different parts of the business being more integrated than others. As in all situations relating to mergers and acquisitions, there is a process of assimilation which takes place and a cultural shift in the way things are done and the approach to communication.

Iberdrola's focus in this process has been geared towards their Talent Management process. The company has a Global Leaders Programme, designed to identify future talent and support people to develop and enhance their skills. This programme is clearly aligned to the business' vision and values and is communicated at group, as opposed to country, levels.

The Management Development Unit works on projects to define a global talent assessment process, manage the training and development of executives on a worldwide level and review executives to ascertain their strengths and

12

detect areas to improve, both at a personal and global levels. The primary objectives of the development programmes are:

- Spread the corporate culture of Grupo IBERDROLA.

- Develop a leadership model based on company philosophy.

- The continuous improvement of the technical and market knowledge of each executive.

- Consolidation as an international point of exchange with respect to knowledge, expertise and good practices, in line with the new dimensions of the group.

Within this background Melanie Hill, Director of Organisational Capability, is responsible for talent development primarily within Scottish Power but at group level for accredited programmes. Given the group's key focus on developing talent from within and creating a group corporate culture, a key focus of her managerial role is in building networks across the group.

In a multi-cultural company such as the Iberdrola Group, Melanie states:

Communication is a key focus for me. It is not only about ensuring that the correct message is understood but more importantly delivered in the correct manner to ensure cultural differences are adhered to.

A key lesson for me has also been in the decision-making process. In the UK and US cultures the process is very open, linear and transparent. In Spanish culture however, decisions are taken through conversations with key individuals and progress is not often as obvious or measurable. It has taken a couple of years for colleagues within the UK environment to fully appreciate this difference. The key however to making it work is trust and I cannot stress enough the importance of building strong relationships with colleagues across the business.

My advice to any manager is to be yourself, know what you are good at but also know your own limitations and do not be afraid to take risks. You need to stand up for yourself and be confident in your knowledge, this can often be scary if challenging senior management.

Partner with people who will help in your areas of weakness and recognise their expertise.

Support your team and develop a team spirit which people are proud of. Looking at challenges at the team level helps to de-personalise an issue and moves away from a blame culture.

Managers need to be able to view a task from all angles and look at how it will impact across the business too.

Throughout my career I have had a series of generalist and specialist roles and this experience has definitely helped me to focus on what we are trying to achieve and look at it from an impact perspective as opposed to a personal level.

■ Scottish Fire & Rescue Service

The Scottish Fire and Rescue Service (SFRS) has its roots in 1824 and the foundation of the world's first municipal fire brigade in Edinburgh.

Through the years services developed, culminating in eight Scottish brigades. On 1 April 2013 these units combined collective skills and experience to establish the Scottish Fire and Rescue Service.

SFRS summarises its role as: 'Response and Resilience' and 'Prevention and Protection'.

Response includes firefighting of all kinds, attending road traffic collisions and specialist rescue, every type of incident has its own hazards, – unsafe buildings, a pileup of motor vehicles, chemical spillage, gas build-up – all requiring specialist skills

Resilience means planning and training for major emergencies such as terrorist attacks, major flooding or accidents that can lead to community crisis.

Prevention and Protection means working to prevent incidents from happening in the first place. By ensuring homes are safe, spreading the fire safety message and engaging with the community, SFRS protects lives and reduces the incidence of fire.

Approximately 8000 people, both uniformed and civilian, work together in SFRS.

Neil Galloway has nearly 30 years' service in SFRS. He is Station Manager for Paisley and Renfrew SFRS stations, responsible for all operations, from day to day staff management to directing fire and rescue operations.

Neil has risen through the ranks to his current position. Although there are now a variety of pathways, this is still the standard progression for firefighters. This gives a manager a deep knowledge of the organisation. Neil's advice is:

You don't need to be able to perform every task, but you should understand how they fit together. This is particularly important if you have been promoted internally – your colleagues may expect you to have many of the tasks you are asking them to do, so it's important that you understand the job and the ways in which it is done.

Building on the previous point, recognise and appreciate other people's skills and knowledge. Although they are junior to you, their expertise may exceed yours.

12

For example, Neil has many years of direct experience of firefighting and rescue but Glasgow Airport team is expert in dealing with aviation incidents and so he seeks their advice, (although as manger he may retain overall responsibility).

Teamworking is of particular importance in this example and Neil's advice is based on his long experience of SFRS, which has moved from a traditional to a more diverse management structure.

A team leader has day to day responsibilities for the team, which may require an inclusive style with discussion. However, in operational situations a more directive style is required. So, think about various management styles and be ready to shift styles when necessary.

Operational teams within SFRS are cohesive and the members know each other very well. If you are promoted to a higher position within your team, realise that your role has changed. Be ready to display detachment in some situations.

Key messages for a young manager?

Understand your organisation. In SFRS, safety is the overriding principle and managers need to keep this in mind when making decisions. What are the principles which support your organisation?

Learn to make decisions swiftly but with consideration – snap decisions aren't helpful, they have a detrimental effect on the team.

Understand that change happens all the time.

Trust is hard to earn, but easy to lose.

Listen

References

Brown, A., (1998) *Organisational Culture*, Prentice Hall

Carlson, S. (1951): *Executive Behaviour: A Study of The Workload and Working Methods of Managing Directors*, Stockholm, Sweden: Strombergs.

Collinson, E. & Shaw, E. (2001): Entrepreneurial marketing : A historical perspective on development and practice, *Management Decision*, **39**(9), 761-766

Fayol, H. (1916) cited in Gerald A. Cole (2003): *Management Theory & Practice*, p6

Handy, C. B. (1978). *Gods of Management: How they work, and why they will fail.* Souvenir Press.

Hilhorst, D & Schmiemann, N. (2002) Humanitarian principles and organisational culture: Everyday practice in Médecins Sans Frontières - Holland, *Development in Practice*, **12** (3-4), 490-500

Hofstede, G. (1991): *Cultures and Organisations : Software of the Mind,* McGraw Hill

Kotter, J. (1982): *The General Managers,* New York: The Free Press

Kuratko, D. (2002): Entrepreneurship, *International Encyclopedia of Business and Management,* 2nd Edition, Thomson Learning

Mintzberg, H (1973): *The Nature of Managerial Work,* London: Harper Collins

Sayles, L. R. (1964): *Managerial Behaviour: Administration in complex organizations.* New York, NY: McGraw-Hill.

Stewart, R. (1967, 1988): *Managers and their Jobs,* Maidenhead: McGraw-Hill

Stewart, R. (1976): *Contrasts in Management,* Maidenhead: McGraw-Hill

Stewart, R. (1982): *Choices for the Manager,* Maidenhead: McGraw-Hill

Stewart, R. (1991): Chairmen and their chief executives: an exploration of their relationship, *Journal of Management Studies,* **28**(5) 511-528

Stewart, R. (1999). *The Reality of Management.* Routledge.

Stewart, R., Barsoux, J-L., Kieser, A. Ganter, H. and Walgenbach, P. (1994): *Managing in Britain and Germany* Basingstoke: MacMillan

Witzel, M. (1999) : *Dictionary of Business and Management,* Edited by Morgen Witzel, International Thomson Business Press, pp.222

Websites

http://www.arranaromatics.com/our-story

http://www.hw.ac.uk/about/careers/culture/our-values.htm

http://www.hw.ac.uk/about/careers/culture/our-values.htm

http://www.msf.org.uk/our-charter

Index

Printed in the United States
By Bookmasters